IN THE AGE O

IN THE AGE OF MABO

History, Aborigines and Australia

Edited by Bain Attwood

ALLEN & UNWIN

First published in 1996.

Allen & Unwin Pty Ltd
9 Atchison Street, St Leonards, NSW 2065 Australia

National Library of Australia
Cataloguing-in-Publication entry:

In the age of Mabo: history, Aborigines and Australia.

Includes index.
ISBN 1 86373 841 X.

1. Aborigines, Australian—Land tenure. 2. Land tenure—
Law and legislation—Australia. 3. Aborigines,
Australian—Legal status, laws, etc. 4. Aborigines,
Australian—History. I. Attwood, Bain.

346.940432

Set in 10/11 pt Sabon by DOCUPRO, Sydney
Printed by KHL, Singapore

10 9 8 7 6 5 4 3 2 1

Contents

Introduction
The past as future:
Aborigines, Australia and the
(dis)course of History[1]

Bain Attwood

Twenty-five years ago English historian J.H. Plumb forecast the
death of the past. Whereas 'from the earliest days of recorded time'
human beings have 'used the past in a variety of ways' (and 'the
sense of the past [was] usually . . . linked in human consciousness
with a sense of the future'), in contemporary society, this was, he
argued, no longer the case: 'The strength of the past in all aspects
of life is far, far weaker than it was [even] a generation ago.' Plumb
principally attributed this decline to the nature of modernity which,
he believed, 'does not need the past. Its intellectual and emotional
orientation is towards change rather than conservation . . . The new
methods, new processes, new forms of living . . . have no sanction
in the past and no roots in it'. But he also blamed the discipline of
history itself for destroying 'the sanction that the past has in religion,
politics, education and morals nowadays'.[2]
   Applied to today's world, much of Plumb's gloomy prognosis
simply seems wrong.[3] In Australia, at least, there is 'a society with
a strong sense of the past', and this shows every sign of continuing
to deepen.[4] More particularly, when one considers matters pertaining
to the discursive relations between the original inhabitants of this
continent and other Australians, there is a growing conviction that
a sense of the past is integral to any sense of the future. One might
claim, moreover, that this situation is one which the historical
discourses of archaeology, anthropology and history have been
influential in creating.[5]

I

Historical discourses have long played a fundamental role in constructing the categories of 'Aborigines' and 'Australia(n)' and in

determining, however partially, the relationship between one and the other. History, in this context and in the beginning, was, in a sense, a European discourse; that is, it was particular to the Europeans but not to the indigenes.[6] One needs to appreciate, moreover, that, while time (and history) is an indispensable component of the European horizon of understanding, prior to the intense disruption provoked by British colonisation of this continent this might not have been so among its aborigines. Tony Swain has recently argued that aboriginal societies across Australia had a culture which accorded metaphysical primacy to place rather than to time: 'The essence of [Aboriginal] tradition is place, and . . . the Aboriginal interpretation of changes in their life-world has been cast in terms of space rather than history.' Europeans, he suggests, have tended to ignore the Aboriginal notion of being in the world inasmuch as we have insisted upon the perspective of time and history.[7] More to the point, I believe, History, as a discourse which deploys temporality as a marker of difference, has been the means by which Europeans have constructed Aborigines in terms of an absence or lack—they were either of another time or were even timeless, and so were not of our time, that is, modernity. For much of the last 200 years or so, this has been an ever present image of 'the Aborigine'.

Yet History was not only the colonisers' discourse; it was also a colonising one.[8] This is so inasmuch as History was necessarily prior to the exploration of the Pacific in the second half of the eighteenth century:[9] the primary motive for these particular voyages[10] lay in a scientific spirit which was intrinsically historical in its nature,[11] not only in the sense that such journeying was envisaged as a means 'to complete the history of man'[12] insofar as it would fill in the narrative of 'natural history', but, more importantly, because this movement in space was also seen in terms of travelling in time—more specifically, the ancient past—as well as of expanding the realm of natural (or secular) time, thus making History universal.[13]

The conceptualisation of this new world as the old was, more importantly, integral to the British colonisation of *terra australis*, that is, to the very founding of what was later to be Australia. History originated the terms of the continuing relationship between 'Aborigines', Europeans and the space of 'Australia' in the sense that the bearers of this imperial discourse believed that rights to place depended upon one's 'time'. To be specific, on the basis of the representations of Captain James Cook or, more particularly, Joseph Banks—for it was he who later recommended British colonisation—of *terra australis* and the aborigines during their voyage of exploration, the British Government determined in 1785 that

New Holland was a *terra nullius*, that is, no-man's land. Thus, following the established international convention of acquiring colonies, it was available for a unilateral claim of ownership on the basis of discovery and effective possession.[14]

Why is this so? Aboriginal hunter-gatherers were adjudged to have no property rights because of the way in which their place in time was construed by major seventeenth and eighteenth-century philosophical and legal authorities which, in turn, drew upon historical theories regarding human society.[15] In the opinion of Grotius, Pufendorf, Locke and others, hunter-gatherers (or 'savages' in their terms) had no concept of property because they were in the original state of nature.[16] This assessment was founded upon one or more 'historical' sources: the representations of antiquity found in classical history, and the representation of the Americas as 'the beginning [of] all the World'.[17] In their judgment these jurists and philosophers also relied, Nancy Williams notes, 'on what they characterised as a chain of authority that linked them with the past'.[18] A more fully developed philosophical and legal rationale for dispossession of indigenes was expressed in the eighteenth century by Scottish Enlightenment philosophers Adam Smith, Adam Ferguson and others, who developed a highly influential theory concerning the evolution of human society.[19] They contended that all human societies developed from a state of nature through four stages based on hunting and gathering, pastoralism, agriculture, and commerce. This theory was called, variously, 'The History of Civil Society', 'The Natural History of Man', and 'The Course of Empire'. Each of the four historical stages, these philosophers conjectured, were characterised by particular ideas and institutions concerning law, property and government. Similar to seventeenth-century writers, they conceived the first stage, that of hunters and gatherers, as having no concept of property and so their lands were deemed desert or waste, that is, *terra nullius*. The work of Smith, along with that of the Swiss jurist Vattel, profoundly influenced Sir William Blackstone's *Commentaries on the Laws of England*, which Rosemary Hunter in this collection (and other commentators) have described as the classic exposition of the English common law of colonial expansion.[20] As a consequence of the historical theory Blackstone and these other authorities expounded, then, aboriginal space was declared to be a *terra nullius*, and was thus appropriated by the British, on the basis that its owners were conceived as belonging to a particular historical time or to no time at all (and thus prehistorical).[21]

Once the British were in place in New South Wales, as Henry Reynolds notes in his chapter in this collection, some of the colonists who spent time with the aborigines were able to learn of their sense of ownership and so began to question the basis upon which the British held they were legally entitled to the land. Their concerns became particularly evident when white settlement expanded dramatically in the 1820s and 1830s. In the context of the resulting large-scale dispossession of the traditional owners, humanitarians, troubled by the impact of colonisation, adopted the words 'aborigines' and 'aboriginal'[22] in order to represent the indigenous people as the original possessors of the soil—the first people, indigenous to the place of 'Australia' and therefore prior to the time of the British and having a particular claim as such. The humanitarians, however, had only limited success in persuading the Imperial and Colonial Government to recognise native title, mainly because, however much their deployment of 'aborigine' and 'aboriginal' served to discursively connect or reconnect the indigenes to the place of 'Australia' as its first owners, they faced formidable opponents who represented the indigenes in other temporal terms in order to serve the contrary purpose.[23] Thus, many colonists only deemed the indigenes to be the aboriginal 'inhabitants, but not the proprietors of the land'[24] because they were first in universal time—ab origine (from the Latin), that is, from the beginning—and so possessed no property rights.

More commonly, though, colonists denied the indigenes these rights because they conceived of the aborigines in terms of another temporal deficiency: as 'savages' and 'wild men' living in a state of nature they did not use the land in a progressive manner, and so had no claim. Thus, one colonial newspaper editorialised:

> From the moment they arrived, until the present, they have not sought, and therefore not acquired as tribes a property in the soil—nor, as individuals, the ownership of things which grow or roam upon its surface. They have neither erected habitations upon it, nor pierced its bosom to make it minister to their support and comfort. Generation after generation, their thinly scattered tribes have wandered homeless over its fertile districts, unconscious or heedless of the treasures within them . . . We found the country in the state in which ages before the black people had found it—its resources undeveloped, unappropriated! In landing here, we exercised a right which we possessed in common with them. In locating ourselves on, and cultivating particular spots, we exercised one which they might previously have exercised, but which they did not.[25]

In time, this attribution of progress to European possession of the land and to Aboriginal dispossession came to constitute the predominant and the most enduring rationalisation for British colonisation[26] (and it is still very influential today, as I note in my chapter in this collection).

In the following decades of the nineteenth century and for much of this century, it was more or less forgotten that the British Government had ever seriously considered the question of native title, let alone entertained the possibility of formally acknowledging its existence or even recognising it by legislative or executive decree (see Henry Reynolds' chapter);[27] indeed, the contrary was increasingly asserted, most importantly by the courts where, as Rosemary Hunter discusses in her chapter, history in the form of precedent was later to ensure that the doctrine of *terra nullius* would be upheld.

If historical discourse played this role in British colonisation and thus in constructing the category of Aborigines, the writing of colonial history was soon to entrench these understandings. In the 1850s, for example, a historian of the newly named Tasmania (formerly Van Diemen's Land),[28] John West, who was more sympathetic to the plight of the indigenes than most colonists, could nonetheless sanction the British invasion in these terms:

> The original occupation of this country necessarily involved most of the consequences which followed: was that occupation, then, just? The right of wandering hordes to engross vast regions—for ever to retain exclusive property in the soil, and which would feed millions where hundreds are scattered—can never be maintained. The laws of increase seem to suggest the right of migration: neither nations nor individuals are bound to tarry on one spot, and die. The assumption of sovereignty over a savage people is justified by necessity—that law, which gives to strength the control of weakness. It prevails everywhere: it may be either malignant or benevolent, but it is irresistible.

This was, West averred, 'the path of history'. He claimed, furthermore, that 'no man [could] witness the triumph of colonisation, when cities rise in the desert, and the wilderness blossoms as the rose, without being gladdened by the change'.[29]

Later colonial historians echoed West's celebration of British colonisation. Alexander Sutherland, for example, reckoned it was not only 'a distinct step in human progress' but also an expression of 'natural laws'; his fellow Victorian, Henry Gyles Turner, concurred: 'The experiences of history were not to be reversed, and the wandering savage . . . was doomed to extinction by the progress of [British colonisation]'.[30] Indeed, the extinction of the indigenes was, as Reynolds has remarked, 'one of the proofs of progress, a benchmark to use while measuring the triumph of civilisation over savagery'.[31]

What also needs to be noted, however, is not only the obvious fact that colonial history was the story of the victorious colonisers (as national history was later to be too), but also (as Richard Broome in his contribution to this volume implies) the way in which the

logic of its narrative was systemic to the cultural hegemony of the
era. With the rising influence of evolutionary thought—often known
as Social Darwinism—the displacement and the 'dying out' of the
indigenes became a commonplace assumption, and was represented
as a natural course of events, 'a process that had been figured in
evolution'.[32]

By the very logic of this historical discourse, then, Aboriginal
survival—an Aboriginal future, in other words—was a contradiction
in terms: they were 'historical transients',[33] necessarily passing away,
and hence would soon no longer be (of the) present. As such,
Aborigines were perforce excluded from the teleology of history.
This social evolutionism was explicated in texts such as this school
primer, the opening passage of which read:

> When people talk about 'the history of Australia' they mean the his-
> tory of the white people who have lived in Australia. There is a
> good reason why we should not stretch the term to make it include
> the history of the dark-skinned wandering tribes who hurled boom-
> erangs and ate snakes in their native land for long ages before the
> arrival of the first intruders from Europe . . . for they have nothing
> that can be called a history. They have dim legends, and queer fairy
> tales, and deep-rooted customs which have come down from long,
> long ago; but they have no history, as we use the word. When the
> white man came among them, he found them living just as their
> fathers and grandfathers and remote ancestors had lived before
> them . . . Change and progress are the stuff of which history is
> made: these blacks knew no change and made no progress, as far
> as we can tell. Men of science [i.e., anthropologists] may peer at
> them and try to guess where they came from, how they got to Aus-
> tralia, how their strange customs began, and what those customs
> mean; but the historian is not concerned with them. He is con-
> cerned with Australia only as the dwelling-place of white men and
> women, settlers from overseas. It is his business to tell us how these
> white folk found the land, how they settled in it, how they
> explored it, and how they gradually made it the Australia we know
> to-day.[34]

In the context of the birth of the new nation, 'Australian history'
only began with Europeans, and so not only ignored the aboriginal
past but also erased the indigenes' prior presence. British colonisation was legitimated by naturalising a relationship between
Europeans—who by now were called Australians—and the land
Australia, thus denying any relationship between those who had
been the first to be called Australians and Australia.[35]

Aborigines were further consigned to the past but not to history
by dint of becoming the subject of anthropology rather than history.
Indeed, the Aborigines were valued by this new discipline *because*
they were construed as artefacts of the human past. Just as European

history constituted its object in a temporal sense—the modern, the present (and the future), the civilised—so too did European anthropology invent its object—the traditional, the past, the savage.[36] As Bruce Trigger has noted, 'the original differentiation between history and anthropology was a product of colonialism and ethnocentrism'.[37]

In the case of Australia, the later decades of the nineteenth century saw the autochthonous people become central to anthropological theory as it developed within the framework of social evolutionism. This occurred not only because they were regarded as one of the best examples in the world of early humankind—a paradigm of originality or primordiality which opened, it was believed, a window onto our beginnings—but also because local ethnographers responded to a pronounced imperial demand for colonial data. Hence, in 1927, Professor of Biology at the University of Melbourne, Walter Baldwin Spencer, one of the first Australian anthropologists, could dedicate one of his major works 'To Our Master, Sir James Frazer' and introduce it thus:

> Australia is the present home and refuge of creatures, often crude and quaint, that elsewhere have passed away and given place to higher forms. This applies equally to the aboriginal as to the platypus and the kangaroo. Just as the platypus, laying its eggs and feebly suckling its young, reveals a mammal in the making, so does the Aboriginal show us, at least in broad outline, what every man must have been like before he learned to read and write, domesticate animals, cultivate crops and use a metal tool. It has been possible to study in Australia human beings that still remain on the cultural level of men of the Stone Age.[38]

This construction of Australian aboriginal culture, as well as the 'denial of coevalness' upon which it was premised,[39] more or less characterised anthropological study well into the twentieth century, notwithstanding that structural-functionalism replaced social evolutionism as the dominant paradigm: whereas 'the earlier generation of [anthropologists] had relegated [Aborigines'] culture to prehistory . . . many of the next seemed to want to suspend it in [a] timeless vacuum'.[40] As Gillian Cowlishaw has noted, Australian anthropologists tended to define their object as 'traditional Aborigines', and pursued this quarry as though no change had occurred amongst Aboriginal communities.[41] In this denial of history anthropologists also excluded the principal agents of change—Europeans and other settlers (and thus relations between Aborigines and these newcomers)—from their field of view (or, inasmuch as they considered colonial relations and the processes of acculturation, they maintained a scholarly division between this and their primary object of study).

While the temporal illusion that Aborigines were not contemporary with 'Australians' was undoubtedly sustained by the spatial relations which existed between Aborigines and whites in twentieth-century Australia—the majority of 'Australians' lived in areas where few if any Aborigines were physically present—one can nevertheless argue that the historical discourses of history and anthropology were mainly responsible for creating this chimera. And together their narratives produced what the eminent Australian anthropologist W.E.H. Stanner was to call, in the 1968 ABC Boyer Lectures, 'the great Australian silence'.

This was not 'a total silence on all matters aboriginal', as some mistakenly assume, for there had been a veritable babble of Aboriginalist knowledge produced by Europeans since the beginning of the colonial encounter;[42] rather it was a narrative which was silent about 'ourselves and the aborigines':

> the story of the things we . . . unconsciously resolved not to discuss with them or treat with them about; the story, in short, of the unacknowledged relations between two racial groups within a single field of life . . . [the assumption that] the racial structure which is part of our anatomy of life has no connection with our civilisation past, present or future.

Stanner described this silence as 'a cult of forgetfulness' or 'disremembering' that had been 'practised on a national scale'. Rejecting the possibility that 'inattention on such a scale [could] be explained by absentmindedness', he claimed that it was 'a structural matter, a view from a window which has been carefully placed to exclude a whole quadrant of the landscape'. And, as well as there being a silence, there had also been a silencing: 'the great Australian silence', Stanner argued, 'reigns [over] the other side of a story', an Aboriginal history, the telling of which, he recognised, 'would have to be a world . . . away from the conventional histories of the coming and development of British civilisation'. As such, he chastised historians for 'having given the aborigines no place in our past except that of "a melancholy footnote"',[43] and called upon them to consider 'our unexamined history'.[44]

II

By the late 1960s, such historical work was already under way, as Stanner himself acknowledged: 'Something very remarkable has happened: the fact that the aborigines having been "out" of history for a century and a half are now coming back "into" history with a vengeance.' Indeed, he confidently predicted that the great

Australian silence would not 'survive the research that is now in course'.[45] Yet, it is quite clear that Stanner's lectures also inspired or compelled historians and other such scholars to make amends for their 'inattention' (and even today they remain an important reference point, as many of the essays in this collection testify). Among those influenced by Stanner's calling for 'another kind of history' was Henry Reynolds,[46] who was to become the leading historian in the field, after wisely disregarding the advice of senior historians of the day, such as the editor of the leading historical journal in Australia who told him 'there was nothing in it'.[47]

Over the last 25 years or more Reynolds and other historians have sought to address the great Australian silence, assuming the function of 'remembrancers' by reminding White Australia of what it would prefer to forget.[48] In time they created what I have called here the new Australian history (see the chapters by Richard Broome and myself in this collection). This has had, as Reynolds has remarked, 'important implications for our view of Australia past and present', because it has suggested that 'it is not just a matter of attaching Aboriginal history to the back left hand corner of the old homestead or of even glassing in the back verandah. The changes will ultimately have to be far more radical—a new floor perhaps, even new foundations'.[49]

During more or less the same period, archaeology was also providing a profound challenge to the notion of Australia by altering the chronology of its historical narrative as well as its originating moment, by positing these as both very ancient and Aboriginal, hence questioning the claim of the British to be its founders in 1788. Simultaneously, archaeological inquiry had the potential to provoke fundamental questions concerning the nature of history itself as it drew attention to the fact that the Aboriginal past, like the pre-colonial past of other indigenous peoples, had been relegated to *pre*-history and so excluded from the knowledge which was called history; it thus problematised the very distinction which had been integral to the production of history as a modern discourse—that of societies with writing and those without. Archaeological research further provoked a questioning of the politics of time underpinning this distinction by painting a picture of Aboriginal societies as adaptable, inventive and innovative, contrary to the anthropological figures of the timeless Aborigine, 'the unchanging people in the unchanging land', and 'stone age man'.[50]

Together with historians, leading archaeologists such as John Mulvaney, one of the founders of the modern discipline in Australia, have not only assumed the task of changing our sense of the past but also influencing the future. In this, it could be argued that they have been following in the footsteps of anthropology insofar as a

handful of its leading exponents, such as the Professor of Anthropology at the University of Sydney, A.P. Elkin, have, since the 1930s,
assumed the enlightened, moral task of combating racial prejudice
by representing Aborigines as the bearers of a worthy, noble culture,
and by recommending 'positive', ameliorative policies.[51] Over the
last two decades the scholarship of historians, archaeologists and
anthropologists has undoubtedly had a tremendous influence upon
Australia's intellectual and cultural milieu, so much so that one can
contend, as Richard Broome does, that major changes such as those
most recently heralded by the High Court's 1992 Mabo (or Murray
Islands) decision[52] are inconceivable without their historical
(meta)narratives;[53] or, one can argue, as Rosemary Hunter has, that
the new Australian history had become so compelling that the High
Court was forced to abandon its old legal narrative.[54]

What is less readily apparent are the factors which have enabled
these *disciplines* to be a force for change. Historical and archaeological scholarship have been dominated by a conventional
epistemology which assumes that the past belongs to another realm
of time which is separate from the present, and that consequently,
so long as scientific methods are adopted, it is possible for the
historian and the archaeologist to show the past as it really was
and to understand it on its own terms, and thus have independent,
historical truth.[55] In a culture that values 'objectivity', this stance
has undoubtedly helped in the acceptance of historical knowledge,
especially by the law, since it has similar procedures for establishing
'truth'.

However, at the same time as this epistemological approach has
borne fruit, it can also lead to some less satisfactory, even deleterious
outcomes. For example, positivism or objectivism, at least in theory,
requires historians and lawyers to privilege documentary rather than
oral evidence and facts rather than interpretation, meaning and
values, thus favouring, in this instance, Australian interests other
than Aboriginal ones, as Rosemary Hunter discusses. Although in
practice, Deborah Bird Rose notes, the legal system has proved in
some contexts to be more accommodating than this would suggest,
the positivist tradition nevertheless allows conservatives to accuse
Aboriginal historical narratives of being evidentially weak or false
and thus dismiss legal claims made by Aborigines as invalid. As
well, it enables conservative attacks upon the High Court's Mabo
decision and the like as a 'rewriting' or 'reinterpretation' of history.[56]

Objectivism can hamstring radical history in other ways as well.
For example, since it holds that history is the study of the past or
even implies that it is the past itself (a confusion encouraged by the
fact that 'history' commonly refers to both its object of inquiry and
the inquiry itself), the truths of history can readily be disregarded

or even scorned, as Andrew Markus and I note, by conservatives claiming that 'that's history'; in their view it refers to the past, not the present. Hence, while the recent historical scholarship has undoubtedly ensured that Aborigines and British colonisation have become present in our histories, thus ending the great Australian silence in that sense, the colonial past might nonetheless be said to remain absent from our historical consciousness. If there continues to be a silence in our history, then, this might be because the orthodox historical tradition fails to conceive of history as a hermeneutic and dialogic enterprise (or merely to represent those dimensions of the past which still exist in the present[57]), thus diminishing the sense of an ongoing relationship between past and present, and between Aboriginal and other Australian subjects.[58]

In fact, the potential these histories have for drawing connections between past and present (and future) is by no means entirely compromised, but this is so largely because most historians do not consistently practise their craft according to the disciplinary principles they otherwise espouse. Reynolds is typical inasmuch as he is well aware that the source of his histories lies in a present in which 'the past is still alive':

> I began this research because conventional Australian historiography seemed so inadequate to explain and illuminate the . . . experience of north Queensland. Nothing in my Tasmanian education had prepared me for the realities of race relations in what [Charles] Rowley called colonial Australia. It was not just the unaccustomed violence and hatred which often grew as lush as guinea grass but the smaller more subtle things—expressions, phrases, jokes, glances; even silences, which sprang up out of local historical experiences I knew little about.[59]

Thus, the conventional distinction between past and present collapses, and the connection between them becomes the ground upon which Reynolds makes his histories. This is like all history, it should be noted, since one always reaches the past 'by starting out from the present', and so history is 'necessarily written from a present perspective' and is 'always concerned with the meanings of historical reality for us, now'.[60] Correspondingly, Reynolds and other historians also seek to nurture among their readers an understanding that the past matters for the present; for example, in the introduction to 'the Townsville edition' of his celebrated *The Other Side of the Frontier*, Reynolds writes:

> This book . . . is . . . aimed primarily at white Australians in the hope that they will gain an appreciation of the Aboriginal part in the history of the continent during the last two hundred years . . . It is inescapably political, dealing as it must with issues that have aroused deep passions since 1788 and will continue to do so in the

foreseeable future. Many people may find it an uncomfortable
book. It will probably challenge myths and prejudices embraced by
both black and white communities.[61]

Reynolds' important work has served to articulate a historical
consciousness by linking past and present in the form of a liberal
or humanitarian tradition. In studies such as *Frontier* and, more
especially, *The Law of the Land*, it can be suggested that Reynolds
is seeking to recover other historical possibilities, in particular to
resuscitate a moral tradition (as well as political and legal precedents) in order to bestow continuity and hence legitimacy upon these
alternatives, and to counter conservative claims that they are revolutionary and aberrant.[62] Reynolds writes, for example, of 'the first
and second land rights movements'.[63]

While many might concede that history-making of this nature
has these redeeming features, there is an even more fundamental
reason why history is deemed to have only a limited capacity to
effect a truly post-colonial order. Although this new history has
taken Aborigines as its subject, some have objected that it has only
produced another *Australian* history rather than an *Aboriginal*
history.[64] This is to argue that historians (and archaeologists) have
both consciously and unconsciously assimilated Aborigines into their
own ways of understanding the world (for example, Aborigines as
progressive, *too*) rather than representing the Aboriginal past in
Aboriginal terms,[65] thus 'annex[ing] . . . the Aboriginal past to
Australian history'.[66]

On an even more fundamental level, one critic has argued that
'writing *history* about Aborigines is, necessarily, the imposition of
an alien framework on Aboriginal experience and Aboriginal
understanding'.[67] It is held, in other words, that history is an
inherently eurocentric discourse and as such can never properly
represent the Aboriginal past in Aboriginal terms. Yet, such critics
seem to be blind to the fact that Aborigines themselves have been
entering into the imperial colonial discourse of history with a
vengeance, decolonising it by transforming its content, form and
practice in ways which belie these misgivings about the nature of
history.[68]

III

The past two decades or more have seen an enormous growth of
interest among Aborigines in history, resulting in a discourse now
commonly known as 'Aboriginal history'.[69] This has been expressed
in a number of different forms: elderly people patiently recording
their life histories and stories passed down in the oral tradition;[70]

younger Aborigines painting (for example, Gordon Bennett[71]), writing, publishing, dancing, filming, acting and directing, photographing, and singing their people's stories;[72] clans eagerly joining with anthropologists and historians in order to press claims to 'traditional' land (see Deborah Bird Rose's chapter), or to seek redress for injury;[73] communities working alongside archaeologists to carefully excavate, preserve or solemnly rebury aboriginal remains;[74] young and old anxiously seeking lost relatives to repair broken families, restore kin relations and create genealogies;[75] Aboriginal spokespersons insistently proclaiming rights of ownership to the aboriginal past;[76] and Aboriginal intellectuals avidly ransacking academic and popular representations of 'the Aboriginal past' in order to invest Aboriginality with authoritative new (old) meanings in the present.[77]

Underlying the diversity of this historical endeavour are common assumptions: first, that the past is part of the present (future) of aboriginal peoples as 'Aborigines'; and second, that the past is a resource of crucial importance for constituting and nurturing Aboriginal identity. Thus, one elderly Aboriginal man who was removed from his kin when he was a child, has said: 'A lot of people say to me "You should forget these things now, things of the past". But to me it's not the thing of the past.' For this man and so many Aborigines, moreover, 'one important loss is their history', as Coral Edwards has noted—not 'history in the wide sense, but a sense of knowing who they are'. Thus, Aboriginal historians like James Miller have expressed the hope that 'other Kooris will trace their roots for it is in the past that we can find the strength to fight the battles of the future'. Writer Mudrooroo elaborates the logic of this: 'Aboriginal writers are not content with only writing about a past separate from their present being. The past is there only to explain the present and postulate ideals for the future. Still, the past is of the utmost importance in that it is there that true Aboriginality lies.'[78] As this suggests, much Aboriginal history-making is intensely personal and parochial; indeed, it is self-consciously so: 'Aboriginal historians are writing history for Aboriginal people . . . for our families and children . . . [Our] responsibility . . . to family, kin and community is keenly felt . . . Our versions of history . . . will be passed on to our children as our set of truths.'[79]

The content of Aboriginal historical narratives challenge conventional Australian history in much the same manner as the new Australian history does, only more so because of their special emphases—survival, continuity and difference. The most striking illustration of the first of these themes is apparent when one compares accounts of 'the killing times': although Aborigines do narrate stories which tell of colonists slaying Aborigines, they also relate how their forebears outwitted their adversaries by bushcraft, trickery or magic and thus denied the wish-fulfilment of that hegemonic narrative which decreed Aborigines were 'dying out'.[80] Continuity is attested to in the significance Aboriginal narrators attach to kin and place, implicitly belying the various ascriptions (such as 'half caste' and 'the destruction of Aboriginal society') of those Australian histories that stress discontinuity and amount to a denial of Aboriginality. In doing this Aboriginal histories proclaim, moreover, a sense of difference, defying the normative logic of the programmes of 'white Australia' and 'assimilation'.

Aboriginal histories also present a profound challenge to the discipline of history itself. This is evident in the narrative forms they assume, in particular those of oral history and myth.[81] Most Aboriginal historical narratives are oral testimonies and, as such, like any oral history, they constitute a different type of history.[82] History in the written, objectivist tradition ostensibly rests on certain assumptions: there is a radical disjunction between past and present, the past is complete, unchanging and unchangeable, and has an objective existence independent of the present. By contrast, history in the (Aboriginal) oral tradition assumes a conjunction between past and present, that the past is something which is fluid and shifting and so amendable to intervention, and has an inevitable subjectivity as people seek to establish meaning for the past in the context of their present. In the former there is an emphasis on the discontinuity and on the foreignness of things past, in the latter an emphasis on continuity and on the essential nature of things. This is so for both traditional Aboriginal accounts as well as modern ones, as Peter Sutton has noted.[83]

The differences between Aboriginal histories and the discipline of history is even more apparent when one considers myths as historical accounts, in particular the Captain Cook stories told across Australia (see Rosemary Hunter's chapter). Quite evidently these stories lack historical authenticity, since they are sharply at odds with the written historical record, and bear little resemblance to what is conventionally regarded as history. Like other Aboriginal oral testimonies, such as those considered by Howard and Frances Morphy, they can be regarded as providing images *of* the past rather than images *from* the past—'"recollections of times past" . . . that need bear no relation to what actually happened or was'.[84] As such, it might be concluded that they have no historical value. If we chose to extend our conception of history, however, such stories are undeniably historical inasmuch as they constitute the means by which Aborigines can understand their historical situation; that is, they help them make sense of the relationship between past and present. The Captain Cook stories are not, quite evidently, about

Captain Cook but concern the relationship between two peoples—
the British, who are represented as the invaders, and Aborigines,
who are represented as the indigenes—which Cook is considered to
have established because he assumes enormous symbolic importance
in Australian histories. But whereas in Australian myths Cook is
valorised as the discoverer of this country and the founder of British
settlement, in these Aboriginal myths he is the archetypal first white
man, an Australian Everyman who invades, colonises the land, and
imposes an immoral and unjust law on Aborigines.[85]

Aboriginal historical narratives not only help the colonised to
understand and endure their situation, as I have implied;[86] they also
constitute the means by which they might change the past in the
present by envisaging a future alternative to it. For, as John O'Neill
has reflected,

> Remembrance is the womb of freedom and must be cultivated long
> before men are able to name their slavery . . . Remembrance is the
> bodily infrastructure of political knowledge and action. It holds
> injustice to account and sustains the utopian hope that underlies the
> will to freedom and equality.[87]

Such histories are thus intrinsically political. As Erich Kolig has
noted of the Captain Cook sagas, while:

> myth often seems to condone and indeed foster the existing *status
> quo* . . . [it] can act as a catalyst for transcending the *status quo* by
> . . . [projecting] forth images of a better life . . . Myth has the
> power to transform existing reality into its image of it . . . [This is]
> knowledge that will direct [Aborigines] and through which they can
> once again become masters of their fate.[88]

Deborah Bird Rose has enunciated the logic of this: Aboriginal
narrators assume that the survival of Captain Cook's immoral law
depends on misrepresentation of, or the historical silence around,
the injustices of colonialism. Consequently, Aborigines believe that
remembrance is the key not only to survival but also to change—that
by telling their story other Australians will recognise the immorality
of their law and 'will turn away from destruction and turn back to
moral principles' and thus to a just and equitable future.[89]

The Captain Cook stories are, it should be noted, just one
example of Aborigines, once a people allegedly outside of history,
entering into the colonial discourse of history in order to change
the course of history. Since the late 1960s, if not much earlier,
Aboriginal political action has been inherently historical in its
nature, embedded in black histories they have narrated about white
Australia. This has especially been the case when Aborigines have
demanded rights for Aborigines *qua* aborigines or as the first

Australians, since these claims are obviously grounded in history, specifically in the prior aboriginal presence.

Aborigines' history-making has not only posed a challenge to the content and form of history but also to its practice, in particular raising the issue of who should narrate Aboriginal history and on what terms. As far as many Aborigines are concerned, 'Australian colonial history is proof of nothing more than the fact that history is always written by conquerors', used 'as a foundation for all of the self-sustaining myths that tend to justify the white man's dominance of Australia today'.[90] Consequently, Aborigines have not only reclaimed the right to tell their own histories but have also questioned the specific content of conventional Australian histories. Furthermore, they have been seeking to curb the dominance of Aboriginalist knowledge, which they regard as intellectual colonialism, by claiming the right of custodianship, even of ownership, of the Aboriginal past. Challenges such as this one have been issued frequently over the last decade or more:

> The Issue is control . . . We say it is our past, our culture and heritage, and forms part of our present life. As such it is ours to control and . . . to share on our terms. That is the Central Issue in this debate . . . We are not averse to working with others on preserving our heritage but we will fight to prevent our heritage being treated as an historic commodity. We are the custodians. You can either be our guests or our enemies. That decision can only rest with you.[91]

As Tim Murray notes in his chapter, such demands have had a considerable impact upon the practitioners of Aboriginal Studies. New relationships with Aboriginal communities have been forged so that, for example, many studies are collaborative in nature and have practical application: anthropologists are employed by Aboriginal land councils to research land rights claims, archaeologists conduct research at the request of Aboriginal communities, and historians have prepared submissions for official inquiries such as the Royal Commission into Aboriginal Deaths in Custody.[92] In museums, many curators have responded by informing Aborigines about their collections, providing access to these, and even 'returning' skeletal remains and artefacts to Aboriginal communities; and for their part, many archivists seek to protect Aboriginal interests by restricting the access of researchers whose projects have not been sanctioned by the relevant Aboriginal communities.[93] Even where tensions still exist, these can act as a spur for creative and dynamic work in the field of Aboriginal Studies. However, where Aborigines and scholars fear that the other threatens to destroy Aboriginality or historical study, such tensions can also be the source of enormous conflict, and result in outcomes deleterious to both.

IV

The importance of the new Australian history and Aboriginal history might be relatively limited were it not for the fact that presently many Australians believe that the past which is signified by Aborigines and/or Aboriginality holds the key to Australia's future.[94]

'The Aborigine' or Aboriginality has become central to the defining of Australian nationhood and identity to an unprecedented degree. Aboriginality has probably always been an element in the construction of Australian identity, but whereas its role was previously premised upon it being construed as a lack (vis-à-vis Australia's 'whiteness', modernity, progress, etc.), its significance now derives from it being imagined in positive terms, indeed upon it being idealised. While this appropriation of Aboriginality has antecedents in the pre- and post-World War II period (or even as early as the late nineteenth century),[95] it has only come to have a heightened importance in the last two decades, and especially so in the last several years. In order to understand why this is so, the process of identity construction and the present historical contexts in which this is occurring need to be considered.

Identities such as nationalities are both imagined and constructed; they are neither natural nor given categories, but are created by human imagination and actions.[96] Nationality is forged only by reference to an other, which it also constructs. 'Australians', for example, are constructed in the process of constructing the Aboriginal (or Asian, British, American etc.) other. More particularly, each category is imagined in terms of characteristics which are deemed to be the opposite of the other, and those (heterogeneous) characteristics of 'Australians' which are not recognised and accepted are displaced and projected onto the (Aboriginal) other, thus excluding, repressing and denying their presence within the Australians. In this process, there is obviously an interdependence of the two categories—'the Australian' only has meaning in relation to the (Aboriginal) other. This other, while secondary and subordinate, is nonetheless central, then, to the existence of the primary and superordinate category of Australians.

National and racial identities have seldom been imagined or created in the realm of everyday experience but have instead been the result of images which circulate in print and other media and come to be collectively held. This has been particularly so in the Australian context where the vast majority of Australian settlers have only 'known' Aborigines via a series of images which, as Jeremy Beckett has noted, 'construct Aboriginal people in their absence'.[97] Similarly, in the construction of Australian nationality the land has been a key symbol, represented in icons such as 'the bush', 'the outback' and 'the Centre', and myths such as 'the pioneer legend', even though or perhaps *because* it does not form part of the everyday reality of the majority of Australians.[98] In recent times, Annette Hamilton notes, these images have 'taken on a[n] . . . increasingly powerful character simply because they can, in an age of mechanical reproduction, be produced so quickly, so simply and so constantly'.[99]

In the late twentieth century, Australia, along with many other nation-states, is finding it increasingly difficult to produce a distinct nationality since this is being challenged by a range of cultural, political and economic forces which threaten to undermine the conventional sense of Australianness. These forces are both external and internal. Beyond Australia, the processes of globalisation give rise to a lessening of the power of national governments, a decline in the importance of local economic forces and a growing homogeneity of culture, all of which result in a diminution of the autonomy and distinctiveness of the nation-state. Within Australia itself, the politics of identity articulates new and old forms of cleavage among the populace, for example along the lines of sex, gender and ethnicity. These external and internal developments make it harder for the nation-state to produce a coherent and particularised national identity at the same time as they make it all the more necessary that the nation-state do so.[100]

In searching for markers of the cultural difference required to differentiate Australia from other nations, the nation-state can no longer utilise many of those which it has relied upon traditionally—whiteness or, more particularly, Britishness—because various factors (such as postwar immigration, decolonisation, and Australia's need for strategic and economic ties with Asian-Pacific nations) make this more or less impossible. In this situation, John Morton remarks in his chapter, many are increasingly drawing upon Aboriginality to define Australia as different and its people as indigenous to its region. Similarly, along with multiculturalism, Aboriginality functions as a means of representing a relatively homogenous Australia as culturally diverse and less European than it predominantly is.

The second context for the appropriation of Aboriginality is, as Andrew Lattas has argued, one in which a nationalist discourse conceives of Australian culture in terms of a serious lack or deficiency. In particular, settler Australians[101] are diagnosed as suffering from a crisis of identity. We do not truly know who we are because we are alienated from both the land and its original inhabitants. In other words, in this discourse, settler Australians are positioned as aliens in the Australian landscape; that is, we are strangers in a foreign land, without a sense of having originated here, removed from the realm of indigenous truths the land has to offer and so denied the means of knowing who we really are. Conversely, Aboriginal culture is constructed as comprising the vital elements which are deemed to be absent in settler Australian culture, and so our sense of alienation can only be healed by drawing upon Aboriginality.[102] Thus, the Governor-General Bill Hayden, opening the Great Australian Art Exhibition in 1989, said: 'I sometimes think that unless we obtain an understanding of the landscape and the truths as Aboriginal people know them we will always be aliens in Australia.'[103]

The appropriation of Aboriginality is also explicable in another, broader context,[104] that of disillusionment with modernity.[105] This has been especially evident in a number of counter-hegemonic discourses since the 1960s but it is no longer confined to these now. In this situation, settler Australians (and the First World generally) have increasingly construed Aboriginality as possessing positive dimensions (which contrast with the least desirable aspects of modernity), and are seeking 'to claim critical and valuable aspects of the [Aboriginal] Other as essentially part of [themselves]'.[106] In particular, Aboriginality is regarded as a source of power since it is held to be the bearer of spiritual or sacred truths, particularly concerning the land.

There is reason to believe that this image of Aboriginality owes much to anthropology. Ever since the late nineteenth or early twentieth century, when anthropology began to emerge as a discipline in Australia, it has emphasised the importance of the sacred in 'Aboriginal society'. In the work of metropolitan theorists such as Durkheim and local ethnographers like Spencer and F.J. Gillen, 'the idea of the sacred became indelibly associated with traditional Aboriginal society', and this 'predilection for the sacred' was just as evident in studies of later anthropologists such as T.G.H. Strehlow, Ronald Berndt and W.E.H. Stanner,[107] the latter claiming in 1965 that Aborigines were 'a very religious-minded people' and that their religion 'was probably one of the least material-minded, and most life-minded, of any of which we have knowledge'.[108] Until the 1960s anthropologists used the idea of the sacred in a diffuse manner, 'applying it to things and activities of many kinds', but increasingly they (most importantly, Stanner and Berndt) associated it with the land, either generally or particularly, thus imparting 'a certain solemnity to Aboriginal relations to the land'.[109]

While it may be objected that anthropologists were mostly writing for a specialised readership and hence could not be said to be influential, it can nonetheless be argued that their association of Aborigines with sacredness and the land came to command a much wider audience, 'once lawyers, politicians and the public began taking an interest in remodelling relations between Aborigines and the rest of the population'.[110] Conversely, one can also argue that changes in Australian intellectual and cultural life and a deepening concern for the *cultural* survival of Aborigines in the 1960s undoubtedly influenced the work of anthropologists such as Stanner and Berndt. Once this is recognised, one is able to contemplate the possibility that the anthropological idea of the sacred was metamorphosed into the idea of the sacred land or place ('site') largely, if not only, because of the central symbolic significance of land and a sense of place in settler Australian culture.[111] In other words, a culture fearful of its very lack in this regard constructs the Aboriginal other as possessing the very associations it desires.[112] And so, for example, whereas writers like Judith Wright once celebrated their own forebears' history for their union of land and lineage, they now locate that in the Aborigines their ancestors dispossessed.[113]

While a handful of anthropologists have undoubtedly directly influenced law and government policy with regard to Aboriginal land rights, as Deborah Bird Rose considers briefly in her chapter, their interpretive power as the authoritative Australian voice on Aboriginal culture has mostly been indirectly exercised, mediated in popular culture by exponents of New Age Religion, art gallery and museum directors, environmentalists, heritage managers, holiday promoters and other merchandisers, as testified by books such as Robert Lawlor's *Voices of the First Day: Awakening in the Aboriginal Dreamtime*, exhibitions like *Power of the Land: Masterpieces of Aboriginal Art*, sites such as the Gordon River, Uluru and Kakadu, and advertisements like Qantas' 'I still call Australia home'.

In these discursive appropriations of Aboriginality the commodified images are, in essence, historical in nature for it is assumed that Aboriginality has the quality of 'pastness'. Indeed, this is the principal reason why it is valued so highly, as I will shortly discuss. This temporal representation, it should be noted, is dependent upon a conception of Aboriginality in spatial terms; that is, Aborigines are constructed not only as temporally but also as spatially other— 'real Aborigines' are located in 'remote Australia', in particular 'the Centre' and 'the Territory'.[114]

In order to understand why 'the Aboriginal past' is valorised by a remarkably diverse range of discourses, it is helpful to note why the past more generally is regarded as valuable. David Lowenthal has suggested that the principal attractions of the past include the dimensions of antiquity and continuity.[115] Certainly, in the case of Australia, as Beckett has noted, 'the "antiquity" of Australian Aboriginal culture, if not its human bearers, has rarely been absent from constructions of Aboriginality, whether popular or official'.[116]

Antiquity is especially valued, Lowenthal contends, where it assumes a mystique by dint of its very ancientness or sheer inaccessibility. In new nations such as Australia, nationalists have traditionally sought to compensate for what they perceive to be a brief history by either celebrating the prehistoric natural heritage or by analogising human endeavour to that idealised by Greek legend or Biblical myth.[117] It is only quite recently that nationalists have sought to acquire an ancient past by celebrating Aboriginal culture. In this, archaeological research has played a key role by adding tens of thousands of years to human time in Australia, providing the nation with what the pre-eminent Australian archaeologist John Mulvaney has called 'a deep past'.[118] Those like Mulvaney have also played a vital role in linking this Aboriginal past to the land itself by seeking to incorporate them together into the 'national heritage' and thus 'the cultural life of the nation'. In major part, this new construction of the national heritage has focused upon the importance of 'conserving' Aboriginal heritage by 'preserving' particular places such as Kakadu, where it is deemed to exist.[119] This conventional spatio-temporal imagining of Aboriginality is also evident in popular archaeological texts authored by Josephine Flood, such as *The Riches of Ancient Australia*, in which she invites her readers on *A Journey into Prehistory*.[120] In turn, managers of the national estate have emphasised the significance of the Aboriginal past in seeking World Heritage Listing for particular places,[121] and it seems that Uluru National Park will become the first Australian site to receive this status primarily on that basis.[122] This construction of Aboriginality is furthered by a tourist industry which realises that 'the "natural" and the "old" have . . . appeal as viewable and easily recognisable commodities'.[123] Thus, for example, at the Anbangbang rock shelter in Kakadu National Park (as in all living history museums), visitors are invited to 'Revisit the Past' and view 'History at your feet'.[124] In these various ways, then, 'Aborigines' are both extolled as having an ancient past and 'deep and abiding links with the land',[125] and this is 'appropriated by Australian society into a generalised Australian [or world] heritage'.[126] And so, by dint of a continuing denial of coevalness, the Aboriginal past 'provides that sense of depth which is perceived to be lacking in the [modern] psyche'.[127]

The Aboriginal past assumes enormous value not only because of its ancientness but also for a quality that Lowenthal notes is often associated with this—primordiality. As exemplars of the original people of the world, Aborigines are not only utilised, once again, in the search for human beginnings, but also and perhaps more importantly in the quest for archaic knowledge, which is assumed to be the deepest and truest knowledge.[128] In this, New Age religionists, drawing on the work of Carl Jung and such sources,

construe Aboriginality and the land as the human collective unconscious. Thus, Lawlor, for example, can write:

> The Aborigines' rituals, beliefs and cosmology may represent the
> deepest collective memory of our race . . . I invite the reader on a
> journey to the most distant memory of our race . . . It is an invita-
> tion to enter, as in a dream, a lost memory of our race . . . A
> recollection of our origins—a remembrance of a sense of reality in
> its pure and primary form—is essential if we are to understand our
> present circumstance and imagine the possibilities of our collective
> destiny.[129]

In other words, Aborigines assume the place of our unconscious—
they have access to archaic religious and philosophical truths we
are no longer conscious of—and so can restore us to the sacred and
psychic order lost in modernity. As exemplars of primordiality,
however, Aborigines can also redeem us in another way. Just as the
originating historical discourse of dispossession maintained, Aborigines in this discourse are held to be in the original state of nature,
and so can tell us the ancient truths of Australia. Thus, they can
naturalise us—make us at home in this land.[130]

   Closely associated with this quality of primordiality is another
compelling dimension of the past which Aboriginality is assumed to
possess—that of primitivism. In contrast with a 'hard primitivism',
it reinvokes an earlier romantic image of 'noble savages' living in
harmony with nature,[131] holding the promise of 'a supposed inno-
cence and purity unspoilt by later generations'.[132] Consequently,
New Age religionists, hippies, and environmentalists have adopted
Aborigines as exemplars of their noble ideal.[133] Clothed in this 'soft'
primitivist guise, Aborigines are construed as *homo naturalis* and
thus as the means by which these settler Australians and others can
happily achieve the (re)integration of nature and culture they assume
is necessary if they are to be fully human.

   Aborigines are also believed to make good another perceived
temporal or historical lack of First World citizens by providing what
Lowenthal calls 'the sense of enduring succession'.[134] This imagined
Aboriginal continuity (or what can also be mistaken for permanence,
unchangingness, and timelessness)—the Aborigines' very lack of
history, in a sense—is enchanting for many people perturbed by
modernity. Swain, among others, has suggested that such Aboriginality is:

> a deeply cherished component of White Mythology: a domain into
> which we have projected our own 'terror of history' as [Mircea]
> Eliade would say . . . Faced with unprecedented change and
> 'progress' . . . European worldviews [have] needed to retain faith in
> the enduring, the primordial and primitive within humanity.[135]

In this context, Aborigines, as exemplars of 'pre-modern' peoples, become the bearers of these human values and practices. In the case of conservationists, for example, 'the litany of "a culture of 40 000 years old" stands for the notion of sustainable continuity against the destruction of 200 years of white settlement',[136] or, more generally, against historical change itself.[137] And for settler Australians suffering the modern condition of 'rootlessness', nationalists like David Malouf envisage that Aboriginality can assuage our 'anxiety about where and how we belong': 'the sort of past—the experience of having developed along with the land and its creatures—may be precisely what one needs (a sense of continuity, a line passing through from the remotest past into the remotest time to come) if one is to get a grip on the future.'[138]

Many settler Australians are not only drawn to appropriate the surplus value of that Aboriginal past which is ostensibly characterised by antiquity and continuity; they are also compelled to come to terms with it because it bears another quality of the past, that of precedence. As Lowenthal notes, precedence is generally valued because it demonstrates 'a heritage, a lineage, a claim that antedates others'.[139] In the colonial context, however, precedence assumes the form of the aboriginal prior possession of the continent, and as such can pose an acute ethical problem for settler societies like Australia. As already noted, for much of the last 200 years or more, the British act of dispossession has been elided in the Australian national consciousness, but since the mid 1960s this past has increasingly become a troubling presence, casting a shadow, some believe, over Australia's future.

This sense of dis-ease has been expressed by many Australian public intellectuals in recent decades, but perhaps none more importantly than one of W.E.H. Stanner's successors as the ABC Boyer lecturer, the historian and critic Bernard Smith,[140] who in 1980 raised this as a problem for the nation and offered an analysis and a solution for it.[141] For Smith, there are two matters 'of the greatest importance for the future of civilisation in Australia' or, more particularly, for 'the emergence and character of our own Australian culture': the fact 'that the country was acquired by the forcible dispossession of the indigenous inhabitants of Australia from their ancestral lands, a process that might be more fittingly described as invasion and conquest'; and the 'continuing presence of the Aboriginal people in Australia'. Together, they constitute 'the crucial challenge to our culture' because they pose 'a *central* problem for the integrity and authenticity of Australia today'. 'Our imminent future . . . will depend', Smith prophesied, 'not a little' upon whether this problem is addressed and resolved.[142]

The assumptions which inform Smith's assessment are peculiarly historical, and have two inter-related dimensions, one being ethical, the other psychological. For Smith, there is 'a close connection between culture, place and morality': in order for 'a culture to develop and survive [it] must put down firm ethical roots in the place from which it grows'. 'Ethical systems' are 'grounded in historical experience', Smith argues, and must provide 'sustaining beliefs [so] that when [societies] act, they act justly'. But in the case of Australia these foundations are shaky, because dispossession was the originating act of the nation, particularly in the sense that 'these acts of genocide and attempted genocide were being enacted most vigorously as that very time [the late nineteenth century] when our white Australian culture was being conceived and born, and . . . its very growth presupposed the termination of a black culture'. Our 'ethical foundations', then, fail to come to terms with 'a moral issue central to the nation's existence'—the dispossession of the Aborigines—and speak instead 'for a privileged section of the human race' rather than 'for the human condition'.[143]

Smith's analysis owes much to Christian theology. This is most evident when he compares the dispossession of Aborigines to the myth of the expulsion from the Garden of Eden, and represents the 'crimes perpetrated upon Australia's first inhabitants' as akin to the crucifixion of Jesus. This, he contends, is 'our shame' and our 'original sin'. As a consequence, 'Australian culture is suffering from a guilt problem'—it is 'haunted [by] . . . the spectre of Truganini'.[144]

In order for the nation to be able to act ethically, Smith believes, it must have a conscience—it needs to be conscious of what it has done, it needs to remember. But 'white Australians have tried to forget. Indeed at times it would seem as if all the culture of old Europe were being brought to bear upon our writers and artists in order to blot from their memories [the genocidal acts of dispossession]'. This is our secondary crime, Smith asserts, 'the continuing colonial crime, the locked cupboard of our history'; that is, we not only committed the original crime of dispossession but also another by 'forgetting' what we had done. As a consequence of this 'white blanket of forgetfulness', Aborigines have made 'little impact upon the Australian consciousness'.[145]

Smith's approach assumes a psychoanalytical dimension here. He writes of 'the crimes committed against Aboriginal society [which] have been suppressed and removed from our nation's memory'; of 'a nightmare to be thrust out of mind' for 'it continues to haunt our dreams'; and of 'the psycho-cultural mechanisms [of repression and projection] by means of which the new Australian society sought to put the Aborigines out of sight and out of mind'. For Smith, as for Freud and God, there is a cost to be paid for this repression of the unconscious, for this original sin: 'We of European descent, who continue to live in Australia, together with our children and grandchildren will lose', he warns, since 'the freedom of each is the condition of freedom of all'.[146]

Yet, for Smith (like Freud and God), 'a darker side cannot be covered up' for ever, because the repressed unconscious will eventually speak, and the nation can thus be helped to come to terms with its conscience. Indeed, Smith argues, this repressed unconscious is now speaking in the form of 'black voices', while he himself assumes the position of the 'concerned conscience' in the guise of both psychoanalyst and priest. As the former, his speaking serves to heighten awareness, rendering the unconscious conscious, and the past present. And when the nation has come to terms with its unconscious—the continuing Aboriginal presence—the priest can call for 'a process of atonement' (Smith had the bicentennial year of 1988 in mind as the culminating moment for this). Once settler Australians have confessed, Smith believes an 'effective interchange between the two cultures . . . between Aboriginal Australians and ourselves' can occur—'a kind of meeting . . . best . . . called a convergence'.[147] This amounts, in effect, to a healing integration of the unconscious and the conscious, the Aboriginal and the settler Australian[148]—to what has now been called 'Reconciliation'.

V

The conviction that the Australian future is contingent upon our coming to terms with the Aboriginal past has been very influential. Most importantly, it has been expressed at the highest political and legal levels, evidenced by the stance of successive Labor governments as well as by the High Court of Australia.

As Richard Broome notes here, the Keating government and the majority of the High Court judges in the Mabo judgment have accepted the new Australian history as an interpretation of Australia's colonial past. This is strikingly evident, for example, in Justices Deane and Gaudron's contention that a 'conflagration of oppression and conflict . . . spread across the continent to dispossess, degrade and devastate the Aboriginal peoples'; in Keating quoting (as have many journalists) this passage when he introduced the Native Title Bill into Federal Parliament; and in his portrayal of the terror of colonisation in the speech launching the International Year of the World's Indigenous People (see p. 70).[149] Simultaneously, Keating also emphasised that Aborigines have *survived* 'two centuries of dispossession and abuse'.[150]

Evident in this approach is both a realisation that the past has a presence and a strong conviction that it should not:

Much of the despair and degradation, conflict and disease, and many
of the problems which Aboriginal Australians face today are a consequence of this dispossession . . . The past lives on in inequality, racism
and injustice. In the prejudice and ignorance of non-Aboriginal Australians, and in the demoralisation and desperation, the fractured
identity, of so many Aborigines and Torres Strait Islanders.[151]

And, as such, this past also bears upon the future.[152] It is in this
light that Keating has chosen to construe the Mabo judgment as
'an historic decision'. As various statements illustrate, Mabo is
conceived as historic because it is imagined as a new historical
narrative[153] which can create the 'foundation' or 'basis' of 'a new
relationship between indigenous and non-Aboriginal Australians'
inasmuch as it provides 'a tremendous opportunity . . . to *transcend*
the history of dispossession' and become the history of the future,
instead of constituting the burden of the past.[154]

In adopting this position, the assumptions of both the Keating
government and the High Court Mabo majority are evidently akin
to those enunciated by Bernard Smith and others. For instance,
Robert Tickner proclaims that 'Mabo is probably the most important moral and ethical issue of our time'.[155] More specifically, these
figures speak in tones reminiscent of Smith's Christian and psychoanalytical language. Deane and Gaudron declare that 'the acts and
events by which . . . dispossession was carried into practical effect
constitute the darkest aspect of the history of this nation' and have
left 'a national legacy of unutterable shame'; for Keating, Mabo 'is
an issue that the country could not ignore . . . morally', and 'an
opportunity to heal a source of bitterness'—indeed, he claimed that
it 'may [even] have the potential to work a miracle'.[156] Deane and
Gaudron also insisted that 'an acknowledgment of . . . those past
injustices' is required, while Keating urged us to 'bring the dispossessed out of the shadows' and called for an 'act' or 'a process'
whereby we 'recognise and make amends for [the] past wrongs'
which 'we [have] failed to see'.[157] The cure, then, is deemed to lie
'in a deeper understanding by all Australians of the history, cultures,
past dispossession and continuing disadvantage of Aborigines and
Torres Strait Islanders . . . In short, we must come to terms with
our own history as a nation'.[158]

Keating has argued, moreover, that 'to deny these basic facts
[of dispossession] would be to deny part of ourselves as
Australians'—'to retreat from this challenge . . . would be to betray
not just the indigenous people of Australia, but ourselves, our
traditions, our future'—for 'the plight of Aboriginal Australians
affects us all . . . [We must] recognise that they are part of us, and
that we cannot give indigenous Australians up without giving up
. . . our own humanity'. Were we to do so, 'Australians would never

entirely live in peace or peace of heart', a belief the Prime Minister reiterated to a private audience in an informal speech on the eve of the 1993 general election: 'I'm more convinced than ever that we've got to make peace with the Aborigines to get the place right.'[159] In a similar fashion, Deane and Gaudron claimed that 'the nation as a whole must remain diminished unless and until there is an acknowledgment of, and retreat from, those past injustices'.[160]

So important is the (Aboriginal) past that it has apparently become a matter of truth for the Keating government. This is especially so with regard to Mabo. As the Prime Minister told the nation in a televised address: 'The Court's decision rejected a lie and acknowledged a truth. The lie was *terra nullius*—the convenient fiction that Australia had been a land of no-one. The truth was native title.' The judgment, he claimed moreover, provided the possibility for a new foundation 'because after 200 years, we will at last be building on the truth'. In a more general sense, addressing and resolving the Aboriginal past in the present becomes a litmus test for Australia's authenticity: 'There is no more basic test of how seriously we mean . . . that Australia is a first rate social democracy, that we are what we should be—truly the land of the fair go and the better chance.' If we do not pass this test of truth, we 'will be judged now and by history'.[161]

Similarly, the degree to which we move towards greater justice, equality, tolerance and harmony with Aborigines is a measure of our progress.[162] For Justice Brennan, 'it is imperative that in today's world that the common law should neither be nor seen to be frozen in an age of racial discrimination. The fiction [of *terra nullius*] was justified by a policy which has no place in the contemporary law of this country'.[163] For Keating, the Native Title Bill was an indication, he boasted, that 'we have reached an understanding of their experience—and our responsibility', while reconciliation can be 'a sign of our maturing as a nation', an indication that 'Australia has come of age'.[164] Thus, Australia's status as a modern, civilised and progressive nation depends on the degree to which it accepts and integrates Aborigines, whereas once its modernity was measured by its historical displacement of Aborigines and their 'absence'.

Just as the Keating government has been influenced by the new Australian history,[165] its policy also bears the imprint of the ways archaeology and anthropology have represented Aboriginality. Thus, Keating and others have celebrated Aboriginal culture in terms of 'the oldest culture in the world', of its '50 000 years', and as 'the oldest continuous civilisation on earth'. Simultaneously, Keating has emphasised 'the profound Aboriginal connection to the land', 'the age-old link between Aboriginal land and culture', and Aboriginal spirituality.[166]

As a consequence of these re-imagined qualities, Aborigines or Aboriginal culture is deemed by the government to possess what settler Australians do not have but which we nevertheless vitally need. This construction of ourselves as the lacking element is evident in references by Keating (among others) to settler Australians as 'non-Aboriginal Australians' and 'non-indigenous Australians'.[167] Consequently, the remedy is believed to lie, as John Morton argues here, in indigenising ourselves through Aboriginality: it is this which will provide us with a more authentic sense of being Australian. This has been repeatedly asserted by Keating:

> Indigenous culture has much to teach non-indigenous Australians. Indigenous heritage has much to offer our sense of national identity . . . Through [this], we can learn about who we are, and how we fit into the story of the continent . . . [It is] a wellspring of our national culture, and the more we make of it so the richer we will be . . .
>   The Aborigines and Torres Strait Islander heritage [is] an integral part of our national heritage. We have an immense responsibility to preserve the heritage of indigenous Australians, not because it is an interesting relic of the past, but because it is a living heritage . . . It informs our understanding of the land and our sense of belonging.[168]

Aboriginality is also conceived of by Keating as 'a defining element of our nationhood and culture' in the sense that 'it is an element of what sets us apart from all other nations'.[169] As John Morton notes, this reformulation of Australian identity occurs in the context of Keating seeking the means by which 'our culture, economy, identity, international direction and place in the world [can be] redefined and newly expressed'.[170]

At the same time as Keating valorises Aboriginality for the virtues which its 'antiquity' and 'continuity' symbolise, his government also recognises that another dimension of the past—that of precedence—contains a possible threat to the Australian nation in the form of Aboriginal sovereignty. Consequently, Keating has sought to neutralise this revolutionary potential by various means. First, he has repeatedly referred to Aborigines in terms of a common (Australian) humanity, as 'Aboriginal Australians' and 'indigenous Australians' and, less often, as 'the first Australians', and seldom as 'Aboriginal people' or 'Aborigines', let alone any of the terms Aborigines are now adopting which are, ostensibly, prior to and independent of 'Australian' naming (such as Koori, Murri, etc).[171] Second, where Keating has acknowledged the ancientness and continuity of Aboriginal culture he does not do so without linking it to that which he posits as prior—Australia; so, for example, although Aboriginal culture is referred to as the 'oldest continuous civilisation on earth', this is construed as 'the most remarkable fact about Australia'.[172] Furthermore, he makes it abundantly clear that inasmuch as native title exists it only does so insofar as Australia has or will recognise it—in other words, its existence does not stem from nor is legitimated by *Aboriginal* law and customs but rather from and by *Australian* law (in the form of the High Court and Parliament) and customs (such as 'our fair and democratic traditions'), and so the Aboriginal 'past' is contained by or subsumed within the Australian present for the foreseeable future: 'Native title land', Keating assured Parliament, 'is . . . kept fully within the reach of Australian law'.[173] In this way, the Prime Minister has explained, 'Aboriginal Australians [will be given] justice but . . . in a way that [not only] keeps the country cohesive' but actually moves us 'closer to a united Australia'.[174] It is in this light that the logic of Keating's insistence that Mabo and Reconciliation be linked together becomes clear—for those who seek to conserve the Australian nation in the wake of Mabo the latter is considered to be of vital importance.[175]

The valorisation of the Aboriginal past as Australia's future by the Keating government would be much less important and significant were it not supported by a broad cross-section of settler Australian opinion and had it not been articulated, albeit in a less developed form, for over two decades. In other words, there seems to be both a relatively strong degree of uniformity and longevity in the way many settler Australians conceptualise the Aboriginal past and the Australian future.[176]

The conviction that 'the Aboriginal past' represents the Australian future is all the greater because it is also articulated by many Aborigines, thereby authenticating in the eyes of settler Australians their own Aboriginalist discourse. To a large degree, Aborigines' construction of Aboriginality mirrors the settler Australian one I have outlined. Thus, although Aborigines, unlike other Australians, emphasise the precedence of aboriginal peoples, they too celebrate '40 000 years', 'countless generations' and 'the oldest culture in the world', and often figure the pre-colonial era in terms of a golden age or a pre-lapsarian Garden of Eden, drawing on noble images of ancientness, primordiality and primitiveness. In this, they reiterate a conjunction of spirituality and the land, representing this as elemental to their survival as Aborigines.[177] In this, place, or at least particular places,[178] acts as a focus for another dimension of the past that Aborigines emphasise—continuity—because, by attaching themselves to the land, it provides a means by which they can posit continuous links between themselves and the first inhabitants of the continent. The other means by which this continuity is articulated is through the principle of descent; thus, Aborigines can claim that they are the inheritors of the 'traditional culture'.[179] By these means,

Beckett notes, 'the past can be said to exist in the present . . . [and]
the present can be said to exist in the past, in the sense of being a
realisation of what was already there'.[180] Lastly, like settler Australians supportive of Mabo and Reconciliation, many Aboriginal
spokespersons have welcomed these developments as a sign of, or
as a means to achieve, recognition of their past, which can, in turn,
serve as a basis for a better future.[181]

VI

This construction of Aboriginality is not without problematic dimensions. The most important concerns its essentialism.[182] Although any
identity is, by nature, essentialist, and it is undeniable that this
particular one constitutes a powerful strategic tool for Aborigines,
this does not obscure that it has elements which nonetheless can
exact considerable political and cultural costs.[183] Beckett has aptly
described the dilemma Aborigines face as a result of being imagined
in terms of antiquity and continuity: 'Aboriginal people are caught
between the attribution of unchanging essences' and attempts 'to
bury them within [their "heritage"] as "a thing of the past"', on
the one hand, 'and the reproach of inauthenticity', on the other.[184]
As a consequence of this influential construction of Aboriginality,
the status of those who call themselves Aboriginal but live in settled
rather than 'remote Australia', bear the marks of miscegenation, and
practise no 'traditional culture'—that is, those who have been most
obviously affected by the course of history since 1788—is questioned
or dismissed. Consequently, as Deborah Bird Rose remarks, the
capacity of these people to secure important social, cultural and
economic gains is severely diminished.[185]
    In this context (which has been aptly described as one of
'repressive authenticity'[186]) many Aborigines have sought to adopt
the ideal of the 'traditional' Aboriginal past (or some other valorised
past such as 'heroic resistance') and incorporate it into their sense
of self and community as the essence of their Aboriginality. But a
sense of self ideally springs from a true dialectic between past and
present, simple ideals and complex reality, and is not constant but
contingent upon circumstances, fluid and changing, and it would
seem (as I have argued elsewhere[187]) that some Aborigines are
invoking a reified past which is so remote from their everyday
conditions of existence that it is unlikely to provide the basis for a
stable and vital identity. It is quite evident, moreover, that this
regime of authenticity not only encourages or forces many Aborigines to adopt a distorted sense of self, but also results in Aboriginal
communities representing their past in ways which are patently false

in historical terms. For example, under the *Native Title Act*, like other Aboriginal land rights legislation, Aboriginal communities are required to prove a prior and continuous association with the land they are claiming, and this necessitates the production of ethnographies and histories to support such a past even though these might be contradicted by empirical ethnographical and historical records which tell a story of discontinuity and dispossession.[188]

In turning to the past as a source for the future there is also the danger that, while such remembrance is liberating and empowering, Aborigines can delude themselves that the past can be recovered and repossessed 'as it really was'. In other words, they can be blinded to the fact that much of what happened in the past *has* determined the present and the future so that much of the dispossession cannot be righted. They lose sight of the fact that there is a past which is, in a sense, truly past.

There is also a risk that strategic essentialism might reproduce or sustain the dichotomies which underline much settler Australian discourse. As Edward Said has remarked of another form of identity politics, 'it is . . . likely to be as exclusivist, as limited, provincial, and discriminatory in its suppressions and repressions as the master discourses of colonialism'.[189] And as Tim Murray notes in his chapter, in a perverse reversal of colonial racism some Aborigines have come to believe that settler Australians have nothing of value to offer them, and so they deny themselves and future generations access to 'non-Aboriginal' knowledge which could be useful to them in various ways (just as it has been in the recent past[190]), and risk losing the support of settler Australians upon whom, Andrew Markus reminds us, they are politically dependent.

There are also flaws evident in the construction of a new Australian identity from the materials of the past. First, there is the risk in populist (rather than academic) histories that we merely replace one unsatisfactory past in which we uncritically celebrate the founders of Australia, with another in which we merely 'exorcise their disturbing legacy'.[191] There is the danger here that we will divest ourselves of a colonial past which draws upon a very rich and deep European or, more particularly, British history that *is* the source of invaluable cultural and political institutions and practices in the present, instead of accepting this historical legacy as part of the origins of our society, and coming to terms with it on an ongoing basis.[192] Furthermore, there is the risk that by creating ourselves as the lacking element *vis-à-vis* Aborigines, we will either create an invidious scenario in which we can never imagine ourselves as indigenous, or we will demand that Australians feel attachment to Aboriginality of such a degree that alienation will result. (Little will be gained, in other words, from our acquiring a new cultural cringe.)

In order for a strong and authentic Australian nationality to emerge, we undoubtedly need the convergence of cultures which Smith had in mind, but this requires that both settler Australian and Aboriginal cultures and histories be affirmed.

This raises the question of what role practitioners of historical disciplines should play in the making of a new historical conscious-ness and national identity. Many are probably inclined to argue that they should merely play the role of the sceptic. This would entail, for example, historians, archaeologists and anthropologists not only interrogating the content of conventional historical narratives but also Aboriginal histories, as well as contesting Aboriginal assertions of ownership of the past. On the first count, this critical stance could help guard against the acceptance of any presentist historical knowledge which is marked by silences, distortions and lies that are as pernicious as those which marked the great Australian silence. In this, quite obviously, historians have a role of defending history against an extreme relativism and subjectivism which denies that some historical accounts are empirically truer than others and rejects the possibility of historical truth of any kind. Historical scholars must steer a path between relativism and objectivism, practising a form of critical inquiry which yields approximate rather than abso-lute truths, in order to ensure that history, like the past, has a future. On the second count historians and other such scholars must refuse the claim of some Aborigines that there is only one story to be told and the demand that only they should narrate this or that we should tell it as they do. If we fail to do so, our chances of learning through history will be severely eroded, as will our own sense of self and culture, while the pluralism which lies at the heart of an authenti-cally democratic society and polity will be undermined.

Historians, though, can also play a creative role in the founding of a new history with which Australian citizens can positively identify, by writing (or continuing to write) histories of a particular kind. First, histories which would examine the moments when the ideals and values of both settler Australians and Aborigines have been upheld such that all peoples have benefited, and so genuine human progress can be said to be achieved. Second, histories such as those recommended by Tim Murray and myself,[193] which truly historicise the Aboriginal past and reveal not only continuities but also discontinuities, and which recognise that Aborigines and settler Australians are *contemporary* peoples with identities that are mutu-ally constituted rather than exclusionary and disassociative. Third, histories which would both draw attention to those occasions when mutually beneficial relations have existed between the two peoples, and highlight the necessary conditions for this. Such histories could play a vital role in realising a new future.

1 Aboriginal histories, Australian histories, and the law[1]

Rosemary Hunter

'Aboriginal history', 'Australian history' and Anglo-Australian law are three historical discourses with regimes of truth and histories of their own. Each has stories about law and the land, for different purposes and different audiences. In cases concerning land owner-ship and land rights, the discourses have intersected as Aboriginal people have demanded that the white law take notice of their stories. In turn, white law has demanded that those stories be told in a certain way: that they be refracted through the rules of evidence *and* through 'Australian history'. From early land ownership cases such as *Attorney-General v Brown* and *Cooper v Stuart*, to the major common law land rights cases, the Gove case and the Murray Islands (or Mabo) case, the status of Aboriginal claims has been determined by applications of evidential rules and interpretations of history. The earlier court decisions authorised (and were sustained by) a version of history which denied Aboriginal claims to the land. In the Gove case, for instance, the law told the Yolgnu plaintiffs that their history had no legal status. The Murray Islands case has authorised a new version of history, but at the same time the majority judgments have enlisted history to authorise law. The judges have suggested that the law's old view of history lacked credibility, making it necessary to bring law into line with the now-acknowledged 'facts' of history in order to restore the law's legitimacy. This suggests the existence of a complex, interdependent relationship between Aboriginal histories, Australian histories and 'the law'. In particular, law is not simply a form of power which confers validity on other stories; and as a discourse it is no more autonomous, self-sufficient or singular than any other.

1

Aboriginal histories

Ever since the European invasion, Aboriginal people have been producing histories,[2] for amateur ethnographers, missionaries, protectors, anthropologists and lawyers, as well as for themselves. Three kinds of histories will be discussed here: histories of creation; histories of invasion and dispossession; and histories of relationships to land.

Creation stories are the foundations of Aboriginal religious, moral and legal systems. They tell of travelling spirit ancestors who, in the course of their journeys, formed and marked out the earth and the sky and established the Law, mapping it onto the country. The ancestors fought with each other and struggled with other forces, and they became transformed into animals and birds, the land and the stars. Creation stories possess an eternal verity, an abiding truth through their location in a known place. As Chris Healy notes, 'the place of the history establishes its authority because place and its meaning are continuous'.[3] Proof of the story exists so long as the physical landmarks holding the spirits of the ancestors remain. Creation stories also bind together the land and the Law. In Pat Dodson's words, Law forms part of 'a complex intimacy between Aboriginal people and their country'.[4] The re-enactment and re-telling of Creation stories in ceremonies and narratives reinforces the Law. Because the Law is said to have been established by the ancestors rather than created by human agents, it is understood as a transcendent rather than a temporal phenomenon. Hence, it is not susceptible to alteration by humans to suit their needs at particular times, in contrast to the manipulability and corruptibility of English law, as explained below.

The white invasion of Australia brought about a radical disruption to the established order in Aboriginal societies. Histories of invasion and dispossession sought to make sense of what had happened and to situate new and devastating experiences within their moral economy.[5] A number of Aboriginal groups, for example, represent the white invasion of their land through Captain Cook stories, 'using that one figure to encompass a large set of people, processes and regulations'.[6] Thus, Captain Cook stories may exist even where the 'historical' Captain Cook did not go.[7] For instance, Percy Mumbulla from Ulladulla on the south coast of New South Wales tells of visitors who came ashore and gave gifts of clothing and hard biscuits. Then, as the visitors were pulling away to return to their ship, wild Aborigines came running from the scrub, tearing off the clothes and throwing the gifts back.[8] Cook's exchange was not a valid cultural exchange, and that is why his gifts were rejected. Significantly, this is not a Creation story since it is set in a temporal past and Cook is not making Law. Rather, he is outside the Law, a disruption to normal social life. That is also why he comes from the sea, as Healy explains: 'By definition a disruption cannot come from the land, because all the relationships of the universe are guaranteed in the land and through the Law. The land is the source of all order.'⁹

By contrast, Paddy Wainburranga's story from central Arnhem Land tells of a Captain Cook who operated within 'the Good Law'. This Captain Cook came to live at Sydney Harbour and introduced 'white man's things' such as axes and steel knives. He worked hard, minded his own business and resisted temptations. Eventually, however, he returned to his own land and was killed there by his own people. Then these new Captain Cooks—the sons of Captain Cook—came and started killing everyone and tried to take over the country.¹⁰ In this story, the first Captain Cook is within the Law. It is his sons who transgress the Law—signalled first in their killing of their father—and whose Fall brings historical death and destruction.

In another story, told by Hobbles Danayarri from Yarralin in the Victoria River District of the Northern Territory, the first, good white man who came to the Northern Territory was Ned Kelly. He brought the first horses and the first bullock, and was a friend to Aborigines. He was followed by Captain Cook, who was not so friendly:

> When him been start, that Captain Cook, still thinking about to get more land. From London and Big England, that's his country . . . And when that Captain Cook been come through down to Sydney Harbour . . . And lotta people, lotta women, lotta children, they're owning that city . . . And he don't askem, that man. Too frightened . . . He don't say, 'good day'. No. He say to him, ask him, 'this your country?' 'Yeah this my country' . . . And [he] puttem out those people, takem out them guns, and bullocks, and man. Captain Cook been shooting . . . all the people . . . That means Captain Cook getting ready for the country, going to try to take it away.¹¹

After repeating this performance all around the coast, Cook returns to 'start . . . building Sydney Harbour, that means he get all the books from London, Big England'.¹² The books contain Cook's corrupt, temporal law. This law takes its place alongside the guns as an instrument of domination. It is a corrupt law because it permits the taking of land and the killing or exploitation of its owners:

> Anybody sick, anybody sick in the guts or in the head, Captain Cook['s] orders: 'Don't give him medicine. Don't give him medicine. When they getting crook, old people, you kill them first. When

they on the job, that's right, you can have them on the job. But don't pay them. Let him work for free.[13]

And Cook's law, unlike Aboriginal Law established in the Dreaming, can be manipulated by men to suit their own purposes. As the narrator of the story points out: 'My Law only one. Your law keep changing.'[14]

These Captain Cook stories highlight the different meanings of the symbol 'Captain Cook' for Europeans and Aborigines.[15] For Europeans, Captain Cook has been the heroic 'discoverer' of the east coast of Australia and the precursor to its 'settlement'. For Aborigines, Cook is a code for dispossession and alienation. Captain Cook stories are also a vehicle for Aboriginal assertions of truths that Europeans have obscured or denied. One of these truths is that Aboriginal Law is older, more venerable and generally superior to the immoral Captain Cook law relied on by the European invaders.[16] Another, of course, is that the land belonged originally and still rightfully belongs to the Aborigines, and so its forcible acquisition by Europeans has no legitimacy.

Deborah Bird Rose notes further that Aboriginal histories of the pastoral industry in the Northern Territory keep alive the memories of appalling white brutality, and the centrality of Aboriginal labour to the establishment of the industry, in the face of white attempts to deny and destroy all traces of this past and to place themselves at the centre of economic development.[17] More generally, Aboriginal people in Australia have been concerned of late to record the languages and oral histories that have survived the last 200 years as an important source to set alongside the extensive and readily available European accounts of the past.

Australian histories

Traditional European historiography saw Australia before Cook as lacking history. 'Australian histories' in this genre began with Cook's 'discovery' of eastern Australia in 1770. Cook carried with him instructions from the Admiralty, advising him to take possession of any new territories he discovered in the name of the King, but where those territories were inhabited he was to take possession only 'with the consent of the natives'.[18] Cook did 'discover' the east coast of the Australian continent. His journal of the voyage shows that he did encounter natives, and that he did take possession for the British Crown, but not with the natives' consent—in fact without any reference to them at all in this regard.[19]

Two themes are discernible in subsequent Australian histories in relation to this event. First, there was seen to be a radical disjuncture between the pre-1788 Aboriginal past and the post-1788 'development' of white Australia: 'Australian history' began with Cook (or European explorers) and was the history of the European present, and thus Aborigines were deemed irrelevant.[20] In 1968, the anthropologist W.E.H. Stanner referred to this absence of Aboriginal people from mainstream Australian histories as 'something like a cult of forgetfulness practised on a national scale',[21] and this 'cult', as Richard Broome's essay shows, remained strong until the 1970s. Second, and as a consequence of this conception of Australian history, there was a denial of the prior existence of Aborigines and so few historians gave any consideration to whether Cook had acted lawfully in taking possession of the continent without the consent of the natives.[22]

By the 1980s, however, the dominant theme in Australian history had shifted from ignoring and justifying to including and challenging. The histories of the violent destruction of Aboriginal societies and of Aboriginal resistance were finally being written.[23] Henry Reynolds' work stands out in this respect. Notably in this context, *The Law of the Land* provides a sustained, carefully documented and compelling argument against the previous political and legal orthodoxies regarding the British acquisition of Australia. The fact that it is carefully documented is one of its most important features: it is the kind of history that the law can take notice of.

Heather Goodall has drawn attention to the links between Enlightenment history and law. Both are positivist disciplines employing parallel techniques for knowing what happened: the isolation of a particular problem or issue, the collection, interrogation and testing of evidence, the weighing and evaluation of competing claims, and the ultimate distillation of objective truth.[24] I will suggest below that this picture is oversimplified, since the processes of collection, interrogation, testing, weighing and evaluation involve interpretations which may be contested. At this point, however, Kenneth Maddock's essay on the Captain Cook stories may be cited as an example of the Enlightenment view of history. In this historiographical tradition documentary evidence is regarded as being more reliable, verifiable and weighty than oral evidence, and European historians are as suspicious of what people *say* as Aborigines have been of what Europeans write in books. Hence, Maddock tests a series of Captain Cook stories, including some of those outlined earlier in this chapter, against the *documented* history of the voyage of the *Endeavour* found in Cook's and Banks' records, and finds that there is no historical truth in the Captain Cook 'myths' he surveys.[25] He is absolutely right, of course, if 'historical truth' is understood as a particular discursive product. But this is not the kind of historical truth the stories were aiming at (as

Maddock himself notes). A question arises, then, as to what are the consequences if Aboriginal histories are not understandable within positivist paradigms: Does this necessarily mean legal non-recognition of Aboriginal claims?

Captain Cook's law

The dispossession of the indigenous owners of this country was achieved by force but justified by Captain Cook's law, which was a legal doctrine developed specifically by European jurists to facilitate colonialism. As mentioned earlier, the acquisition of Australia by the British Crown was achieved pursuant to international legal rules devised among the European powers to facilitate the division of the world between them, and the English rules and practices regarding the founding of colonies and the application of the common law therein.

The international law of the eighteenth century essentially validated the title of any sovereign who came to be in effective control of territory. It permitted the acquisition of new territory by conquest, or by forced or voluntary cession by treaty. Title to uninhabited territory, *terra nullius*, was open to all states under the doctrines of discovery and occupation. The treatment of indigenous peoples as objects rather than subjects of international law was justified by a view of those peoples as 'backward'[26] and thus not fit to be members of 'the family of nations'. This view was supported by interrelated religious and philosophical arguments. For example, Europeans had a duty to Christianise indigenous peoples or to bring them to the level of European civilisation; the indigenous population had no recognisable European-style political institutions or system of property law, nor did they cultivate and thus own the land.[27] The requirement of cultivation was prominent in the work of the Swiss jurist Vattel, whose advocacy of the application of the doctrine of occupation to uncultivated territories was influential in the categorisation of the Australian colonies as *terra nullius*.[28] Thus, the indigenous peoples of Australia were not accorded the limited recognition inherent in colonisation through conquest or cession, but were colonised on the basis of an expanded version of the rule permitting acquisition by occupation.

The international law was reflected in the English common law of colonial expansion, expounded in Sir William Blackstone's *Commentaries*. According to Blackstone, where territory was acquired by conquest or cession, the existing law of that territory remained in force until it was abrogated or altered by royal decree. Settled colonies, on the other hand, were colonies that were found to be 'desart and uncultivated', before they were peopled from the mother country. In a settled colony, English law was imported with the settlers, to fill the legal vacuum that would otherwise exist. So much of the common and statute law of England existing at the date of settlement, as was appropriate and adapted to the conditions of the new colony, was received in that colony.[29]

The classification of the Australian colonies as *terra nullius* in international law or as settled colonies in English law is well known. So, too, is Henry Reynolds' contention that once it became clear that the Australian colonies were not *terra nullius*, the British authorities were prepared to accept that the English law received there could and should recognise Aboriginal title to land. Yet the colonists failed to observe Imperial instructions by continuing to ignore the Aborigines, and legal developments followed suit. In an early property dispute between the Crown and a white settler, *Attorney-General v Brown*,[30] the New South Wales Supreme Court confirmed that pursuant to the doctrine of tenure—part of the common law received in New South Wales—all the waste and unoccupied lands of the colony belonged to the Crown 'for, at any rate, there is no *other* proprietor of such lands'.[31] In 1889, just over 100 years after the arrival of the First Fleet, a further colonial property dispute reached the Privy Council. The case was *Cooper v Stuart*,[32] and in the course of judgment Lord Watson claimed that when New South Wales was 'peacefully annexed to the British dominions' it had been 'practically unoccupied, without settled inhabitants or settled law'.[33] Clearly, this story would not stand up to Maddock's test of historical accuracy: by 1889 there *was* plenty of documentary evidence to contradict Lord Watson's assertions. But this judicial myth, unlike Maddock's Aboriginal 'myths', was sustained because judges are particularly powerful historians.

In English legal epistemology, the truth of a story is guaranteed by its saying in a particular location (a court) in the course of a particular ritual (a judgment). The story becomes, within the limits of its jurisdictional domain, the law. And if the judge who tells the story is a member of the Judicial Committee of the Privy Council, which sat at the top of the colonial hierarchy of courts, its jurisdictional domain is enormous and its truth is unassailable. Thus in 1971 in the Gove land rights case, Lord Watson's version of history prevailed over a plethora of historical 'facts', anthropological evidence and Aboriginal testimony to the contrary. The Northern Territory Supreme Court held itself bound by the Privy Council's decision in *Cooper v Stuart* that the Australian colonies were settled colonies—*terra nullius* in law, regardless of the facts.[34]

Whose truth? Which history?

The Gove case was an attempt by the Yolngu people of the Gove Peninsula in north-east Arnhem Land to prevent the destruction of their land by mining. As far as they were concerned, the arrival of white missionaries in the 1930s and wartime activities in the 1940s had done nothing to disturb their traditional relationships to their land. The arrival of the aluminium giant Nabalco was an unwelcome and unauthorised intrusion. In order to assert their right to control the land and to exclude the mining company, the Yolngu set out to explain their ownership, as Nancy Williams has noted:

> The leaders had taken to Darwin some of the ritual objects which their counsel characterised as 'title deeds' to their lands in order to show the judge. Their comments indicated that their perception of the proceedings at that point was based on the rituals of revelation in which clan leaders reveal the important knowledge symbolised by ritual objects. The judge and other white Australian 'important men' were expected, through acquiring the appropriate knowledge, to understand the grounds of the Yolngu claim. The Yolngu believed understanding them entailed acknowledging their existence as part of the natural order.[35]

But the way in which legal 'truth' is discovered in an Anglo-Australian court is radically different from Yolngu methods of determining the true story. The constraints of the legal forum and the strict regimes of truth applied presented enormous barriers to the validation of the Yolngu claim. For example, in a culture where knowledge is passed on orally rather than in written form, almost any information about tradition will contravene the English rule of evidence known as the hearsay rule. Hence most of the plaintiffs' evidence (for example, 'My father told me that this was Rirratjingu land') was sought to be excluded as hearsay, and it was necessary for their counsel to make detailed arguments on the question of admissibility.[36] Furthermore, as Dipesh Chakrabarty has noted, the law privileges positivist historical narratives. 'Can we . . . imagine ever winning a case', he asks, 'by flouting the rules of evidence . . . by employing, say, the narrative techniques of a Nambikwara myth?'[37] The Yolngu evidence was not, of course, presented in the form of positivist historical narrative, yet it was sifted through the rules of evidence, and only what remained could be considered.

In addition, the plaintiffs were compelled to present the substance of their case in a manner that the court could comprehend—to find an appropriate Anglo-Australian legal doctrine on which to base their argument. To this end, counsel for the Yolngu argued that if New South Wales was a settled colony, the common law that had been received in the colony included a doctrine of 'communal native title'. Such a doctrine had been recognised in American courts, and in other former British colonies.[38] It holds that where the Crown had gained sovereignty over a new colony, this did not necessarily include beneficial ownership of all the land in the colony. Rather, where there was pre-existing indigenous entitlement[39] to particular land, that entitlement continued to subsist under the Crown, unless and until it was extinguished by the Crown.[40]

However, the native title argument was rejected in the Gove case on the basis that there was no authority to support the existence of such a doctrine in the common law received in the Australian colonies.[41] The evidence for this was twofold. First, previous Australian legal authority, such as *Attorney-General v Brown*, ran directly counter to its existence, and overseas legal authorities provided no assistance. Justice Blackburn concluded that recognition of native title in other jurisdictions had not been achieved through the common law but by express executive action or legislative provisions, while in Australia there had been no such actions or provisions which expressly recognised native title.[42] Second, the events of Australian history gave no support to the existence of a doctrine of native title. Justice Blackburn stated:

> If the approach is made to the question of the existence of a doctrine of communal native title, on the assumption that it may have been the law notwithstanding that no court applied or declared it, then it is reasonable to ask a question which is rather a historian's than a lawyer's question—'Did people say or do anything which suggests that it was the law?' To the lawyer the answer cannot be decisive whatever it is, but it need not be insignificant.[43]

In distinguishing between lawyers' questions and historians' questions, and the relative weight of the answers to each, the judge was having it both ways. If his historical excursion had revealed a recognition of native title, he could have dismissed that conclusion as 'non-legal'. If, on the other hand, his foray into historical scholarship revealed no recognition of native title, that could be used to support his view of the law. Justice Blackburn concluded his detailed examination of the Australian historical material by noting that he was 'not here concerned to give a balanced historical account of the relations between the aboriginal [*sic*] and white races in Australia'.[44] All he did was interpret historical 'facts' in a way which confirmed the traditional legal story of *terra nullius*.

His Honour considered that the colonial policy of ignoring Aboriginal interests showed that communal native title did not exist in Anglo-Australian law. He noted that there had always been an official policy of concern for Aboriginal people in Australia, but that it took the form of protection and did not include recognition of native title. Indeed, he found that the protective attitude adopted was necessitated by the fact that Aboriginal interests in land had not been recognised. In particular, he construed the creation of reserves and the forcible removal of Aboriginal people thereto, regardless of the location of their ancestral lands, as the manifestation of an intention to dispose of all Australian land without regard to Aboriginal interests.[45] By contrast, Reynolds has pointed to a significant body of material which shows that the Imperial Government had intended the reserves to be a recognition of Aboriginal title rather than its negation.[46]

Justice Blackburn also considered the official reaction to John Batman's 'treaty' with several Aboriginal 'chiefs' for the acquisition of land around Melbourne and Geelong. Governor Bourke proclaimed Batman's treaty 'void and of no effect against the rights of the Crown'.[47] Justice Blackburn interpreted this as a denial of the existence of any Aboriginal title, hence the Aborigines had nothing which they could alienate to Batman or anyone else.[48] An alternative interpretation is that the proclamation was consistent with the common law recognition of native title, which was extinguishable only by the Crown. In accordance with the doctrine of tenure, white settlers could acquire land only from the Crown, not through direct transactions with the Aborigines.

The version of Australian history reproduced by the court in the Gove case enabled it, then, to step around the awkward but inescapable conclusion from the evidence that the Yolngu did have a highly sophisticated system of law,[49] a finding which would have knocked away part of the underpinning of *terra nullius*. But without a doctrine of communal native title, there was no legal linkage point between Yolngu Law and the white legal system, no theory by which the latter could recognise and give effect to the former. Thus, the law deployed and reaffirmed the standard version of Australian history to justify its continued deafness to Aboriginal histories of their relationships to land.

The Murray Islands case

In *Mabo v Queensland (No.2)*, the common law was again required to listen to indigenous history, although the Meriam people had quite a different history from the Yolgnu. No one could accuse them of not cultivating the soil, and they had even had documented disputes over land ownership. The plaintiffs, moreover, were not confronting a mining company and an economic imperative; rather, they stood against a discredited government with a bad human rights record which was seeking to assimilate Aboriginal land management into the general, commercially-oriented land management regime of the State. In addition, since the Gove case, there had been land rights legislation, the Australian Law Reform Commission's report on the recognition of Aboriginal customary law, moves towards Aboriginal self-management with the establishment of the Aboriginal and Torres Strait Islander Commission (ATSIC), and the Royal Commission into Aboriginal Deaths in Custody, which clearly linked the injustices of the present to those of the past.[50] Ultimately, then, the majority of the High Court was influenced not by the differences between the Meriam and the Yolngu, but by the historical sea change of the 1970s and 1980s in relation to Aboriginal rights.

Before they reached the High Court the Meriam plaintiffs faced the usual translation problems: telling their history within the constraints of the rules of evidence, and presenting their claim in the form of a legal argument against the doctrine of *terra nullius* and previous legal authorities. The evidence problem led to protracted hearings in the Queensland Supreme Court, from which a small residue of established 'facts' emerged to enable the case to proceed to the High Court for legal argument. The legal argument was again based on the assertion that the common law received in the Australian colonies included a doctrine of native title. Again, this required the court to interpret previous legal authorities, and to interpret Australian history. But whereas Justice Blackburn in the Gove case constructed legal and historical inquiries as separate issues, in the judgments in the Murray Islands case they are interconnected.

Justice Dawson dissented in the Murray Islands case on the basis that he was constrained by the traditional historical view, previously espoused by Justice Blackburn in the Gove case, that the Australian colonies were settled without regard to Aboriginal interests in land (see Henry Reynolds' chapter). He concluded his account of the absence of any recognition of Aboriginal title in colonial laws and policies by asserting the law's grounding within an immutable history:

> The policy which lay behind the legal regime was determined politically and, however insensitive the politics may now seem to have been, a change in view does not of itself mean a change in the law
> . . . [I]t would be wrong to attempt to revise history or to fail to recognise its legal impact, however unpalatable it may now seem.[51]

Justice Dawson appears to use 'history' as a means of consigning events firmly to the past, 'to separate present, justiciable controversies from those injustices that are merely "history"';[52] or in the former Liberal Party leader John Hewson's phrase, to 'draw a line in the sand' between the unremediable past and the present.[53] As shown in the discussion of the Gove case, however, Justice Dawson's interpretation of history was not the only one available. Although he claimed that the policies of the past presented him with a *fait accompli*, his position did involve a choice among the possible meanings that may be ascribed to the 'facts' of colonisation.

The debate in the Murray Islands case between Justice Dawson and the majority reproduced the academic debate between the 'old' and the 'new' Australian histories. The majority bestowed legal force upon the 'new' history, in some cases making direct reference to Reynolds' work.[54] This has drawn the criticism from the conservative historian Geoffrey Blainey, for example, that the majority's view of Australian history was 'unusual', and based on 'prejudice and misguided research'[55] or on the work of 'propagandist historians'.[56]

Why did the court change its historical tack? One rationale offered by all the majority judges was the need for the law to reflect contemporary notions of human rights rather than to perpetuate past injustices. Thus, for example, Justices Deane and Gaudron referred to 'the conflagration of oppression and conflict which . . . spread across the continent to dispossess, degrade and devastate the Aboriginal peoples and leave a national legacy of unutterable shame'.[57] They continued:

> Inevitably, one is compelled to acknowledge the role played, in the dispossession and oppression of the Aborigines, by the two propositions that the territory of New South Wales was, in 1788, terra nullius in the sense of unoccupied or uninhabited for legal purposes and that full legal and beneficial ownership of all the lands of the Colony vested in the Crown, unaffected by any claims of the Aboriginal inhabitants. Those propositions provided a legal basis for and justification of the dispossession . . .
> The acts and events by which that dispossession in legal theory was carried into practical effect constitute the darkest aspect of the history of this nation. The nation as a whole must remain diminished unless and until there is an acknowledgment of, and retreat from, those past injustices.[58]

The majority judges firmly repudiated the lie of *terra nullius*, as being discriminatory, unjust and unconscionable. For example, Justice Brennan: 'Judged by any civilised standard, such a law is unjust and its claim to be part of the common law to be applied in contemporary Australia must be questioned . . . [I]t is imperative in today's world that the common law should neither be nor be seen to be frozen in an age of racial discrimination.'[59] And Justice Toohey:

> [T]he consequence that, immediately on annexation, all indigenous
> inhabitants became trespassers on the land on which they and their
> ancestors had lived . . . was not a consequence the common law
> dictated; if it were thought to be, this Court should declare it to be
> an unacceptable consequence, being at odds with basic values of
> the common law.[60]

Here, then, the majority judges asserted that the legal system must
ultimately be based not on adherence to precedent but on justice.
The notion that the common law can be 'updated' in this way
is, however, problematic in traditional legal theory. That theory
holds that judges do not 'make' new law but rather 'find' or
'declare' the law that has existed all along. The theory is related
both to the historical existence of the common law as the embodiment of ancient customs and practices, and the constitutional
doctrine of the separation of powers, which requires that elected
representatives make rules and unelected judges merely apply established rules to particular cases. Justice Brennan, a relatively
conservative judge, confronted the problem of updating the common
law by claiming that the court may only 'adopt rules that accord
with contemporary notions of justice and human rights' if their
adoption would not 'fracture the skeleton of principle which gives
the body of our law its shape and internal consistency'.[61] He was
vague as to how skeletal principles might be identified,[62] but in his
view the notion that the British Crown gained complete ownership
of all land in the Australian colonies on its assumption of sovereignty was not such a principle.

Yet justice was not the only basis for Justice Brennan's decision.
In declining to follow *Cooper v Stuart*, for example, he argued that
'the facts as we know them today do not fit the "absence of law"
or "barbarian" theory underpinning the colonial reception of the
common law of England'.[63] He suggests, therefore, that there was
a need to bring the law into line with a widely acknowledged
historical 'reality', that is, that the law had become out of step with
history and must now be changed accordingly.

The judgment of Justices Deane and Gaudron shared the aim
of correcting the relationships between law and justice and law and
history, but their method of accommodating the new Australian
history into the law was quite different. Whereas Justice Brennan
saw the need to update the common law as of 1992, they rewrote
the law retrospectively, claiming that the common law *always*
recognised native title. Thus, they argued, 'in theory, the native
inhabitants were entitled to invoke the protection of the common
law in a local court . . . or, in some circumstances, in the courts
at Westminster', although their Honours acknowledged:

In practice there is an element of the absurd about the suggestion
that it would have even occurred to the native inhabitants of a
new British colony that they should bring proceedings in a British
court against the British Crown to vindicate their rights under a
common law of which they would be likely to know nothing.[64]

They also conceded that any such action would have failed because
of Crown immunity from suit. However, putting all this aside, they
stressed that:

The rights under [native] title were not illusory: they could, for
example, be asserted by way of defence in both criminal and civil
proceedings . . . More important, if the domestic law of a British
Colony recognised and protected the legitimate claims of the native
inhabitants to their traditional lands, that fact itself imposed some
restraint upon the actions of the Crown and its agents even if the
native inhabitants were essentially helpless if their title was wrong-
fully extinguished or their possession or use was forcibly
terminated.[65]

Thus, Deane and Gaudron claim that the law has been in step with
history all along, and that this must now be recognised.[66] There is
more than an element of the absurd, however, in this historical
fantasy. It seems to be just as counterfactual as the fiction of *terra
nullius*, but perhaps it is not surprising that an attempt to work
within the unconvincing theory that judges merely 'find' or 'declare'
the law should yield such an unconvincing result.

The majority's new interpretation of history was also accompanied by a new interpretation of previous legal authorities. In
particular, the majority considered that British colonial practice had
blurred the factual basis for the distinctions between conquered,
ceded and settled colonies. The most important thing was not how
a colony had been classified, but whether it had been inhabited. If
inhabited, the same legal principles regarding recognition of indigenous land titles applied: the Crown acquired sovereignty and
'radical title' to the land, but the indigenous people retained 'beneficial ownership' of the land unless and until their title was
extinguished by the Crown. Authorities from litigation over indigenous land rights in many parts of the world, which had been
dismissed by Justice Blackburn because they applied to conquered
or ceded colonies, were now referred to by the High Court because
they could apply equally to Australia, and help give content to the
doctrine of native title. The majority judges were free to pick and
choose between these various versions of the doctrine available, and
they did not all choose the same way. They disagreed, for example,
over whether unilateral extinguishment of native title by the Crown,
without consent, gave rise to a claim for compensation. Three said
it did and three said it did not. Those in favour argued that the

Crown's power to extinguish native title is subject to the same constitutional, statutory and/or common law requirements to provide 'just terms' as apply in relation to the termination of any subject's property rights by compulsory acquisition.[67] However, Justice Brennan asserted that only interests in land derived from the Crown are subject to such protections. Native title is not granted by the Crown, and hence is not so protected; rather, it is an incident of the Crown's acquisition of sovereignty that it may freely extinguish pre-existing titles, without any obligation to pay compensation.[68] Chief Justice Mason and Justice McHugh agreed with Justice Brennan's analysis, and the vote of Justice Dawson (whose view of the facts and law did not include compensation payments) tipped the scale against compensation.[69]

From their engagement with the new discourses of Aboriginal history and Anglo-Australian history, then, the judges produced a model of legal legitimation. This is so in several senses. First, the Australian legal system no longer turns its face away from the facts of history and from justice, in a way that might engender disrespect for the law; there is thus no longer a credibility gap between the legal 'truth' and the dominant view of history. Second, the law can no longer be blamed for what happened to Aborigines. In the words of Justice Brennan:

> To treat the dispossession of the Australian Aboriginals as the working out of the Crown's acquisition of ownership of all land on first settlement is contrary to history. Aboriginals were dispossessed of their land parcel by parcel, to make way for expanding colonial settlement . . . [I]t is appropriate to identify the events which resulted in the dispossession of the indigenous inhabitants of Australia, in order to dispel the misconception that it is the common law rather than the action of governments which made many of the indigenous people of this country trespassers on their own land.[70]

Attributing blame to white settlers and colonial governments thus allows the law to regain the moral high ground.

Aboriginal people, moreover, are assured that their ownership of the land, in terms of their own law, is capable of recognition by the white legal system. The judges agreed that the content of native title in any given case is determined by reference to the relevant traditional laws and customs.[71] The recognition of native title and the possibility of further native title claims has gone a considerable way to reversing Aboriginal disillusionment with and suspicion of the law. The white legal system no longer appears simply as an oppressive institution.

Simultaneously, most white Australians are reassured that their legal rights are safe by virtue of the fact that freehold title (the major form of residential land ownership) extinguishes any native title that might have existed there. Justice Toohey, for example, made a point of noting that 'nothing in this judgment should be taken to suggest that the titles of those to whom land has been alienated by the Crown may now be disturbed'.[72] Justices Deane and Gaudron also pointed out that native title may have been 'lost' 'by the abandonment of the connection with the land or by the extinction of the relevant tribe or group'[73] (for which read removals and massacres); while Justice Brennan suggested that native title, along with the traditional law and customs on which it was based, may simply have been 'washed away' by 'the tide of history'.[74] (These statements are clearly in a different tone from the earlier, frank acknowledgments of forcible dispossession and injustice. It is notable that the 'history' appropriated by the majority to legitimate the law appears in several guises, both hard-hitting and sentimental.) Finally, taxpayers' pockets are also safe, as no compensation is now due for the extinguishment of native title. The court made a grand confession of wrongdoing on behalf of white settlers and governments, but spared them the further pain of having to make reparation.

Thus it seems that in the Murray Islands case the High Court was primarily concerned with correcting legal history. While its attempt to forge a new relationship between Aboriginal histories, Australian history and the law undoubtedly did confer authority on new versions of the past, the Court's decision, by incorporating the 'true' history of colonisation into the law, was also an exercise in legitimation. Under the doctrine of the separation of powers, the problem of finding a substantive remedy for the effects of colonisation could be left to someone else.

2 Native title and historical tradition: past and present

Henry Reynolds

The High Court's decision in the case of *Mabo v Queensland (No.2)* has been hailed both in Australia and overseas as a milestone of legal reform. However, most of the discussion has focussed on the judgments of Brennan, Toohey, Dean and Gaudron which under-pinned the majority decision, while the main points of contention have related to the reasons why Mabo won rather than the reasons why Queensland lost. Little attention, then, has been given to the dissenting judgment of Justice Dawson, even though his views would be widely shared amongst that broad coalition of opponents of Mabo which includes prominent lawyers and academics, conser-vative State governments and the Federal Opposition. Dawson's arguments, I believe, need to be given serious consideration because they contain what would become key elements in any conservative counterattack on Mabo. To do so it will be necessary to consider the related questions of sovereignty, annexation, and extinguishment of property rights; possession; and historical recognition of native title.

Dawson began his argument with a consideration of the British assumption of sovereignty over Australia and in particular the claim asserted over the Murray Islands in 1879. 'The annexation of the Murray Islands', he observed,

> is not now questioned. It was an act of state by which the Crown in right of the Colony of Queensland exerted sovereignty over the islands. Whatever the justification for the acquisition of territory by this means (and the sentiments of the nineteenth century by no means coincide with current thought), there can be no doubt that it was, and remains, legally effective.[1]

He then quickly moved from the question of sovereignty to that of property. 'One thing is clear', he argued,

> and that is that, upon annexation, the ultimate title to the lands comprising the Murray Islands vested in the Crown. This was a necessary consequence of the exertion of sovereignty by the Crown. Thus it was that upon annexation of the Murray Islands the Crown became the absolute owner of the land and such rights as others might have in it must be derived from the Crown and amount to something less than full ownership.[2]

Dawson then moved to the key argument of the Queensland case—that any rights that the Islanders may have had were extinguished when sovereignty was claimed; in other words, the Crown acquired both sovereignty and property in a single judicial king-hit. Summing up the argument, he wrote:

> The defendant argues that if the traditional land rights claimed by the plaintiffs ever existed, they were extinguished from the moment of annexation. It contends that those rights could not have survived the assertion of sovereignty by the Crown unless they were recognised in some way. The defendant argues that not only were any traditional land rights over the Murray Islands not recognised, but they were extinguished by the exercise of a clear government policy which existed at the time of annexation and has continued since then.[3]

Having stated the Queensland case early in his judgment Dawson returned to the question in his concluding remarks in order to give it his stamp of approval. Any traditional land rights which the plaintiff may have had, he determined,

> were extinguished upon the assumption of sovereignty by the Crown over the Murray Islands. Accordingly, if traditional land rights (or at least rights akin to them) are to be afforded to the inhabitants of the Murray Islands, the responsibility, both legal and moral, lies with the legislature and not with the courts.[4]

Dawson wrote as the inheritor of a long legal tradition which held that in Australia the British Crown acquired sovereignty and the beneficial ownership of property as a result of the annexations of 1788, 1824, 1829 and 1879. The Chief Justice of New South Wales, Alfred Stephen, provided a classic statement in *Doe and Wilson v Terry* in 1849: Australian land had been 'unoccupied and waste' when the British arrived; consequently the 'title of the Crown as universal occupant' was a reality.[5] It was an interpretation which received the imprimatur of the Privy Council in *Cooper v Stuart* in 1889 when the Bench determined that in 1788 eastern Australia 'consisted of a tract of territory practically unoccupied, without settled inhabitants'. In fact there was 'no land law or tenure existing in the Colony at the time of its annexation to the Crown'.[6] The proposition was carried one step further by Justice Isaacs in the High Court in 1913 when he declared that the Crown became the beneficial owner of eastern Australia from the moment, on 12 October 1786, when Phillip received his commission from King George III. From that time 'the whole of the lands of Australia were already in law the property of the King of England'.[7]

These questions were raised again in the case of *Milirrpum v Nabalco Pty Ltd and the Commonwealth of Australia* in the Northern Territory Supreme Court in 1971. Justice Blackburn found that the Yirrkala people of the Gove Peninsula had no claim on their traditional lands in Australian law. Two impassable barriers stood in their way, one put in place by traditional society itself, the other by English law. Blackburn accepted that the Yirrkala had a form of customary law but declared that their relationship to the land was not a proprietary one—they had responsibility for their homelands but this was not 'an indication of a proprietary interest'. But of even greater weight was the decision of the Privy Council in *Cooper v Stuart* over eighty years before. It was, Blackburn declared, 'an authority binding on this court'.[8]

Dawson referred to this tradition but he developed it in important ways. He addressed the question of whether Australia had been a *terra nullius* before settlement, hedged his bets in several places, but concluded that it was safe to assume that 'the native inhabitants of the Murray Islands . . . held some sort of rights in land immediately before the annexation of those islands'.[9] Dawson in fact believed there was 'no need to resort to notions of terra nullius',[10] just as he held that the High Court was no longer bound by decisions of the Privy Council. This would appear to be a significant advance of the views of Stephen, Isaacs and Blackburn. On further consideration, though, it is a case of one step forward and several steps back. While *terra nullius* was the prevailing doctrine it could at least be argued that the Crown acquired that which had previously belonged to no-one. It was a question which had often been considered by eighteenth-century jurists. Vattel, for instance, observed that 'when a nation takes possession of a country which belongs to no-one, it is considered as acquiring sovereignty over it as well as ownership'.[11] But without 'notions of terra nullius' how does Dawson explain the fact that the Murray Islanders' 'rights in land' were transferred to the Crown and by implication the rights of all other indigenous Australians as a result of those other claims of sovereignty in 1788, 1824 and 1829?

Dawson's answer was that the only rights which could exist were those which were recognised by the Crown. If the Crown failed to notice the property rights of its new subjects they did not exist. They had no objective reality. If the Crown chose not to see

anything there was nothing there. Never was appropriation of
property made so easy. When New South Wales was settled the
Crown 'treated the land as its own to dispose of without regard to
such interests as the natives might have had prior to the assumption
of sovereignty. What was done was quite inconsistent with any
recognition, by acquiescence or otherwise, of native title'.[12] In effect,
the Crown could gain more by ignoring the rights of its subjects
than a foreign invader following a war of conquest, whose rights
over private property were thoroughly sifted by the international
jurists of the eighteenth and nineteenth centuries, such as Vattel
who observed that:

> The conqueror takes possession of the property of the State and
> leaves that of individuals untouched. The citizens suffer only indi-
> rectly by the war; conquest merely brings them a change of
> sovereign. But if the state is conquered, if the entire nation is subju-
> gated, what treatment must the conqueror accord it without
> overstepping the bounds of justice? What right has he over the con-
> quered territories? Some writers have dared assert the monstrous
> principle that the conqueror is the absolute master of his conquest,
> that he can dispose of it as his own property.[13]

It is perhaps unsurprising, then, that in one of the classics of
nineteenth-century international law Henry Wheaton argued that
the last time a conqueror took private property in Europe was in
the Norman conquest of Britain in 1066, but since then,

> among civilised nations of Christendom, conquest, even when con-
> firmed by treaty or peace, has been followed by no general or
> partial transmutation of landed property. The property belonging to
> the government or the vanquished nation passes to the victorious
> State, which also takes the place of the former sovereign . . . In
> other respects, private rights are unaffected by conquest.[14]

But the Murray Islands were not conquered, the Islanders
became British subjects from the time that sovereignty was claimed,
and the common law flowed into the new acquisition. How then
could the Crown dispossess its own subjects? The Crown was not
above the law. Prerogative power was no more extensive in Australia than in Britain and there the law had for centuries restrained
the power of the Crown to dispose of the subject's land. In fact, it
was 'not more solicitous of any thing' than to preserve the property
of the subject 'from the inundation of the prerogative'.[15] As Kent
McNeil observed in his recent book, *Common Law Aboriginal Title*:

> If the Crown wanted to acquire title to occupied lands along with
> sovereignty, it would have to seize those lands into its own hands
> by act of state before annexing the territory to its dominions. After

that, the indigenous people would be British subjects, and the Crown would be bound by British law.[16]

There is no evidence whatsoever to suggest the Crown actually confiscated the lands of the Murray Islanders before they became British subjects. Otherwise the Crown itself could only claim the land by British law. 'Act of State apart', McNeil argued,

> the Crown's claim could be based only on English law. Surely one cannot seriously argue that English law would apply to give title to the Crown, while at the same time denying the benefit of that law to the people who were actually on the land, using and occupying it as their ancestors had done for generations. Any suggestion that English law should be applied in such a selective and unequal manner deserves to be rejected as a transparent attempt to manipulate the law in favour of the colonisers.[17]

Dawson's judgment placed the Islanders in a unique and disadvantageous situation. They lacked the normal protection of the British subject faced with the 'inundation of the prerogative' because on annexation the Crown could choose not to notice their property rights. But they also lacked rights of people whose country was subject to defeat, invasion and a change of sovereign which had been recognised in international law since the eighteenth century. They were trapped in a legal no-man's land subject to a prerogative power more extreme than in any other conceivable situation—at the mercy of the Leviathan untrammelled by law or morality. The British Crown, contained in Britain itself by 700 years of legal and constitutional development, was able to break free when it moved into the colonies. Like a tropical cyclone it gathered strength as it passed over water and was able, when it reached the Torres Strait, to devastate the property rights of hapless Islanders who became on the instant trespassers on Crown Land.

But were not the Murray Islanders in possession of their land? This was indeed argued by the plaintiffs, and both commonsense and the historical record suggests they clearly were and had therefore the enormous legal strength accorded by European law to the presumed first possessor. Rights of possession received strong support in both the common and international law. John Selden, the father of English international law, argued in 1652: 'It hath been truly a custom of old, and which holds to this daie in the more eminent nations, that Vacancies are his who apprehends them first by occupation . . . This appears plain in the Imperial Law, nor do we know of any nation where it is not received.'[18] In his book, *The Law of Nations*, first published in 1788, G.F. von Martens observed: 'If possession be immemorial, if there exist no possession anterior to it, it is undoubtedly sufficient to set aside the pretensions of others . . . It is the consequence of the natural impossibility for any other to prove a right better founded than that of possession.'[19] Similar principles were espoused by Blackstone in his classic study of the common law, *Commentaries on the Laws of England*:

> But when once it was agreed that every thing capable of owner-ship, should have an owner, natural reason suggested, that he who could first declare his intention of appropriating any thing to his own use, and, in consequence of such intentions actually took it into possession, should thereby gain the absolute property of it, according to that rule of the law of nations recognised by the law of Rome: natural reason conceded to the occupant that which belonged to no-one.[20]

And a modern legal scholar, discussing the jurisprudential basis for native title, has noted:

> The notion that long occupation is deemed lawful, in the absence of proof to the contrary, is as ancient as the concepts of property itself; indeed the right to use that which one has created, possessed or occupied without wrongfully taking from another, is fundamen-tal to any legal system . . . In their early development almost all legal systems acknowledged continuous use and occupation as a sole source of title. Other methods of acquisition later evolved, but possessory title remained a founding principle; so much so, that it was regarded by Roman jurists as a rule of natural law which was immune from challenge. With the advent of feudalism which brought its own tortuous logic the royal grant came to supersede simple possession as the root of title in many jurisdictions, but the common law continued to regard possession itself as proof of own-ership.[21]

Dawson dealt with the question of possession near the end of his judgment:

> Alternatively, the plaintiffs argue that, whether or not they are able to establish that they have traditional land rights, they nevertheless have a title based on possession. This argument is heavily based on a theory advanced by Professor McNeil in his book *Common Law Aboriginal Title*, (1989). The starting point is that the plaintiffs' pre-decessors in title have been in occupation of the land since beyond living memory. Upon annexation, the common law was introduced into the Murray Islands as part of the law of Queensland. Under the common law, occupation is prima facie proof of possession and possession carries with it a possessory title, which is good as against those who cannot show a better title in themselves. Indeed, mere possession of land is prima facie evidence of a seisin in fee. Thus, say the plaintiffs, since they were allowed to remain in pos-session of their lands and since no one can assert a better title against them, they must be taken to hold their land by way of an estate in fee simple.

But, of course, any presumption that the plaintiffs have an estate in fee simple is rebuttable and any possessory title would not withstand the assertion by the Crown of its radical title. In other words, upon the assumption of sovereignty by the Crown, the plaintiffs or their predecessors could only retain such interests as the Crown chose to recognise by one means or another and, as I have endeavoured to explain, the Crown upon annexation asserted its right to the land to the exclusion of any rights of ownership on the part of the plaintiffs or their predecessors.[22]

So the rights of possession came to nothing. The only interests which could survive were those which the Crown chose to recognise. If they were not noticed, understood or known by Queensland ministers in 1879 they simply did not exist. There were no rules to curb their power. It was a matter of whim. Even if the Crown was ignorant of the facts, motivated by greed or racial antipathy, its actions could not be discounted.

Did the Islanders have rights of possession according to legal principles whose roots descend down to the origins of European law? Dawson said they did not, Brennan and Toohey disagreed. It was probably the critical point of the entire Mabo legal debate. Brennan wrote in terms that echoed the words of Vattel, von Martens and Blackstone: 'The ownership of land in the exclusive occupation of a people must be vested in that people: land is susceptible of ownership and there are no other owners.'[23]

Recognition by government is the critical factor in Dawson's judgment. He argues that the colonial authorities gave no recognition at all to native title rights and therefore they did not exist. Indeed it is apparent, he argued, 'that those in authority at the time did not consider that any recognisable form of native title existed'.[24] If there was any recognition, at any time between 1788 and 1879, his argument is seriously vitiated.

Dawson negotiated this difficulty by turning a blind eye to much of the relevant historical scholarship of the last decade. Like Blackburn before him he argued that 'the policy of the Imperial government during this period is clear; whilst the Aboriginal inhabitants were not to be ill treated, settlement was not to be impeded by any claim which those inhabitants might seek to exert over land'.[25] But whereas Blackburn's assessment was not surprising given the time that it was written—it broadly accorded with the historical scholarship available to him, and jurisprudence and historiography ran parallel—this is not the case with Dawson. He failed to use many of the most obvious sources and did not pursue the issues in question with the rigour which might have been expected. The historical record is critical to his argument but it was not examined with sufficient care.

First, Dawson failed to consider the recognition of indigenous rights implicit in the instructions given to navigators both before and after 1788. Second, he ignored the recognition accorded by senior colonial officials, among them Collins, King, Arthur, Bourke, Saxe-Bannister, Pedder, Gawler and Sturt. Third, he did not give sufficient attention to the growing concern about Aboriginal property rights in the Colonial Office from 1836 onwards, as evidenced by numerous references to native title rights in the memos and despatches of James Stephen, Sir George Grey, Lord Glenelg or Earl Grey and particularly in the Letters Patent issued to the South Australian Colonising Commission. Fourth, like many other legal and historical scholars, Dawson misinterpreted the reason for the Colonial Office's rejection of Batman's treaty with the Port Phillip Aborigines. Fifth, he misunderstood the legal basis for establishing Aboriginal reserves and the insistence by the Colonial Office that all pastoral leases in Australia contain a reservation preserving native title rights. I will now discuss each of these points in detail.

Instructions given to Cook included guidance as to what to do on discovering land hitherto unknown to Europeans:

> You are also with the consent of the Natives to take possession, in the name of the King of Great Britain, of convenient Situations in such Countries as you may discover, that have not already been discovered or visited by any other European Power . . . But if you find the Countries so discovered are uninhabited, you are to take possession of them for His Majesty.[26]

The significance of these instructions has been underestimated because they have been taken to represent Imperial thinking before the first settlement in 1788 but not later. Yet, similar guidance was given by the Secretary of State, the Duke of Portland, in 1800 to Lieutenant Grant who was about to embark on a voyage of exploration around the Australian coast. The instructions read: 'He will take possession in His Majesty's name with the consent of the Inhabitants, if any . . . and if uninhabited to set up some proper description as first discoverer and Possessor.'[27] There was, then, both before and after 1788, a clear distinction between inhabited and uninhabited lands. As von Martens had argued in 1788, someone had to be the first possessor of land. Either it was the indigenous people, or, if the land was empty, the Crown became both the sovereign and the owner of the property. It was, therefore, of critical importance that the British authorities believed, when the first fleet was planned, that Australia was largely uninhabited.[28] In those circumstances the Crown would gain both sovereignty and property on the point of annexation.

Given the erroneous perceptions which influenced planning for the settlement at Sydney, we should re-direct our attention to the settlement of the Derwent in Van Diemen's Land in 1803–1804. It gives us a much better picture of British policy because it was based on much greater experience of Australian circumstances. David Collins led the second and major expedition to the Derwent in 1804. He was already an old colonial hand as he had been a senior official at the settlement at Sydney from 1788 to 1796 and had learned much about Aboriginal society, of which he wrote in his book, *An Account of the English Colony in New South Wales*.[29] He realised that the Aborigines around Sydney Harbour lived in discrete and known territories and that 'each family had a particular place of residence from which it derived its distinguishing name'. The Aborigines were in possession of their land, and conflict arose because they 'entertained the idea of us having dispossessed them of their residences'.[30] The British also knew by 1804 that Van Diemen's Land was well populated as a result of the reports of the numerous expeditions which had visited the island from 1772 onwards. They knew Van Diemen's Land was not a *terra nullius* in the sense of being uninhabited.

When Collins arrived on the Derwent he issued a General Order dealing with the situation of the Aborigines. It declared that he had 'received it in command from His Majesty to place the native Inhabitants of whatever place he should settle at, in the King's Peace, and to afford their Persons and Property the Protection of the British laws'.[31] Collins' reference to 'property' is particularly significant, and the term 'possessions' was characteristically used in official documents issued at the time to describe moveable property. Informing Collins' policy was a clear understanding that the Aborigines were in actual possession of their land and had a sense of property. 'Strange as it may appear', he observed in 1791, 'they have also their real estates'. He explained that Bennelong assured him that an island in the harbour was 'his own property' and had been 'his father's before him'. Collins added: 'To this little spot he appeared much attached.' Bennelong said, moreover, that there were 'other people who possessed this kind of hereditary property, which they retained undisturbed'.[32]

Collins was the Deputy-Judge Advocate, the principal legal officer of the colony in Sydney. His writing clearly contradicts Dawson's belief that people in authority in early colonial Australia 'did not consider any recognisable form of native title existed'.[33] And Collins was not alone. Many officials recognised that the Aborigines were originally in possession of the land and that they had a form of land tenure: Governor King prepared a confidential memo for his successor Bligh in which he remarked that he had 'ever considered them [i.e. the Aborigines] the real Proprietors of the Soil'. In 1821, Governor Brisbane told a visiting missionary that the British were taking the land 'from the Aborigines of this country'. The Tasmanian Colonial Secretary referred to the Island blacks who had been 'removed from their native soil'; Governor Arthur wrote of the settlers as 'intruders on their native soil'; his successor, Franklin, argued that the settlers had taken possession of the land 'to which these poor creatures have a natural right'; and Governor Denison referred to the Aborigines as the 'former owners of the soil'. In Western Australia, Governor Hutt wrote of the Europeans taking 'possession of their countries'. On the other side of the continent, Governor Gipps issued an official statement referring to the Aborigines as 'the original possessors of the soil'; and his Colonial Secretary issued another alluding to them as 'the Aboriginal Possessors of the Soil'. In South Australia, Governor Gawler argued that the local Aborigines had 'very ancient rights of proprietary and hereditary possession'; and Charles Sturt, his Land Commissioner, referred to their 'natural indefeasible rights . . . vested in them as a birth right'.[34] It would be possible to add to this list the comparable views of Colonial Office officials, prominent British reformers, distinguished visitors to the colonies, prominent settlers, missionaries and clergymen.

There was growing concern in Britain about developments in Australia from the early 1830s. Many streams fed the swelling humanitarian movement: knowledge about the Black War in Van Diemen's Land conveyed by a large bundle of documents printed as a parliamentary paper in 1831; grave unease about the possibility of the extermination of Island Aborigines; and the re-direction of energies from slaves to native people after the abolition of slavery in 1833. The leading anti-slave crusader T.F. Buxton took up the cause of the indigenous people of the Empire, determined to see that they would be guaranteed 'some portion of their own land'.[35] He moved an address to the King in the House of Commons in July 1834, which was seconded by the Secretary of State for the Colonies and passed unanimously:

> that a humble Address be presented to His Majesty, humbly to rep-
> resent to his Majesty that His Majesty's faithful Commons in
> Parliament assembled, deeply impressed with the duty of acting
> upon the principles of justice and humanity in the intercourse and
> relations of this Country with the native inhabitants of its Colonial
> Settlements, of affording them protection in the enjoyment of their
> civil rights, and of imparting to them that degree of civilisation and
> that religion which Providence has blessed this nation.[36]

This Address was sent to all colonial governors, cloaked in the authority of both the Parliament and the Crown. It represented a watershed in colonial policy. The following year Buxton moved for the establishment of a Select Committee on the Native Inhabitants of the Empire, and in its final report in 1837 the committee strongly affirmed the importance of property rights. 'It might be presumed', the argument ran,

> that the native inhabitants of any land have an incontrovertible right to their own soil: a plain and sacred right, however, which seems not to have been understood. Europeans have entered their borders, uninvited, and when there, have not only acted as if they were undoubted lords of the soil, but have punished the natives as aggressors if they have evinced a disposition to live in their own country.[37]

Colonial Office policy for South Australia manifested this new attitude towards indigenous land rights. The first test for the new policy came with the negotiations between the Colonial Office and the South Australian Colonising Commission in 1835–1836. The Undersecretary (Permanent Head) James Stephen made his position clear when drafting the Letters Patent and determining the boundaries of the new colony. In an internal memo to Lord Glenelg he wrote about the difficulty of fixing the boundaries. 'How this can be done', he observed, 'in a Terra incognito I cannot imagine, nor how it can be done at all with any due regard to the rights of the present Proprietors of the Soil . . .'[38] Ten days later, Glenelg wrote to the Colonising Commissioner referring to the same problem. He noted that the 'Colony might extend very far into the interior of New Holland and might embrace in its range numerous Tribes of People whose Proprietary Title to the Soil we have not the slightest grounds for disputing'.[39] Taken together these two documents, written by the Minister and his Permanent Head, are of critical importance. They represent a milestone in British official policy towards Australia. Writing of lands over which sovereignty had been claimed since 1824 they clearly believed that an Aboriginal interest had survived and had to be taken seriously. A few years later, Stephen's view had been consolidated as a result of what had been learned of Aboriginal society after the first settlement was established in South Australia. In an internal Colonial Office memo, he wrote: 'It is an important and unsuspected fact that these tribes had proprietary rights in the soil—that is, in particular sections of it which were clearly defined and well understood before the occupation of their country.'[40]

The British Government took two steps to ensure that native title was respected. At a meeting on 2 January 1836, with Robert Torrens, representing the Colonising Commission, Lord Glenelg 'expressed a desire that the Commissioners should prepare a plan for securing the rights of the Aborigines which plan should include the appointment of a Colonial Officer to be called Protector of the Aborigines and arrangements for purchasing the lands of the Natives'.[41] It is true that the Commissioners did everything in their power to subvert the clear intention of the Colonial Office, but they never publicly challenged the principles involved. In the first official report of the Commission the following principles were outlined:

> In considering the subject . . . [of the Aborigines] the following objects should be aimed at: to guard them against personal outrage and violence; to protect them in the undisturbed enjoyment of their proprietary right to the soil, wherever such right may be found to exist; to make it an invariable and cardinal condition in all bargains and treaties made with the natives for the cession of lands possessed by them, in occupation or enjoyment, that permanent subsistence shall be supplied to them from some other source.[42]

The Letters Patent drafted for the new colony were even clearer on the principle of Aboriginal property rights. They included the clause:

> Provided always, that nothing in these our Letters Patent contained shall affect or be constrained to affect the rights of any Aboriginal natives of the said Province to the actual occupation or employment in their persons or in the persons of their descendants of any lands now actually occupied or enjoyed by such Natives.[43]

It was a clear definition of native title as understood in other parts of the Empire. The Aborigines had rights: property rights. They should continue to enjoy those rights of possession which could and should be inherited by their descendants like any other forms of property. It was significant that the same clause, without any substantial change of wording, was used in the Charter which established New Zealand as a separate colony in December 1840 and provided for Maori native title. We can assume that it was no accident that the same form of words was used; that it signalled the recognition of native title in both colonies. We know that the Colonial Office regarded the New Zealand version as a statement of fundamental principle. Lord John Russell, Secretary of State at the time, explained that in the Charter the imperial authorities had 'distinctly established the general principle that the territorial rights of the Natives, as owners of the soil, must be recognised and respected'.[44] It is reasonable to assume that if these general principles were established in 1840 and expressed in the clause cited above they would also have been in place four years earlier when incorporated in South Australia's Letters Patent.

Dawson, like Blackburn before him, misinterpreted the rejection by the Colonial Office of John Batman's treaty with the Port Phillip Aborigines, arguing that it illustrated the fact 'that the Crown considered itself to be the owner of the land, unencumbered by any form of native title'.[45] But the critical legal point in question was not whether the Aborigines had anything to negotiate with but the long-established principle that only the Crown could extinguish native title. Paradoxically, Blackburn provided an able summary of the relevant legal situation in a section of his judgment in the Gove land rights case entitled 'Principles Applied to the Acquisition of Colonial Territory'. The principles in question determined that:

> subjects of a sovereign have no power to acquire for themselves
> title to land from aboriginal natives; any such purported acquisition
> operates as an acquisition by the sovereign. This principle operates
> whether the actions of the subject amount to a conquest of the
> aboriginal natives, or the conclusion of a treaty with them, or
> merely a private bargain. The principle was often shortly described
> as the sovereign's right of pre-emption. Its existence and age are
> undoubted.[46]

It is a powerful rebuttal of the judge's own interpretation of the Batman business and the bevy of historians who have travelled in his footsteps. The government's rejection of the treaty was strictly in accord with the law of the period. But, as I have noted, it did not turn on the question of whether the Aborigines had any form of native title; it was not a question of the ability of the Port Phillip clans to *sell their land* but rather the inability of Batman to purchase when confronted with the Crown's exclusive right of pre-emption.[47]

Dawson was also convinced that the creation of reserves for Aborigines had no bearing on the question of land or 'involved the acceptance of any native rights over land'.[48] Once again the historical record does not support his interpretation. In Van Diemen's Land policy was premised on 'confining' the Aborigines to a smaller area, not dispossessing them,[49] and in South Australia the creation of reserves received its most sophisticated rationale in the writing of Governor Gawler and Land Commissioner Charles Sturt, the latter explaining in a letter of 1840 that:

> The aboriginal inhabitants of this province have an absolute right
> of selection prior to all Europeans who have settled in it during the
> last four years, of reasonable positions of the choicest land, for
> their especial use and benefit, out of the very extensive districts
> over which, from time immemorial, these aborigines have exercised
> distinct, defined and absolute rights of proprietary and hereditary
> possession.
>   The invasion of those ancient rights by surveys and land appro-
> priations of any kind, is justifiable only on the ground that we
> should, at the same time, reserve for the natives an ample suffi-
> ciency for their present and future use and comfort under the new
> state of things into which they are thrown—a state in which we
> hope they will be led to live in greater comfort on a smaller space

than they enjoyed before it occurred on their extensive original possessions . . .
    Such spots of course must be within the native district of the
tribe for whom they may be selected. If, in the proposition, you
have intended to recommend that the native tribes shall be
removed out of the haunts and districts, from time immemorial
their own, the Governor cannot for a moment countenance a
scheme which he is convinced would be practicable only by the
severest coercion, and extremely harsh towards men who, by their
general conduct, merit a very different treatment.[50]

Sturt and Gawler's attitude to reserves accords very closely with
the general principles discussed by M.F. Lindley in his classic 1926
study, *The Acquisition and Government of Backward Territory in
International Law*. Lindley explained that in colonial societies the
opinion:

was generally held that where tribes or communities were occupying an inordinately large extent of land merely for hunting, or even
for pasturing flocks and herds, there was no just reason why some
part of it should not be taken and put to more productive uses.
But it came to be recognised that sufficient land ought to be left to
the original occupants for their sustenance, and there arose the
policy of reserving definite areas for their exclusive use.[51]

Dawson and Blackburn both misunderstood the importance of
the decision of the Colonial Office to protect native title on all
Australian pastoral leases, a policy that evolved between 1846 and
1855. Concern about violence on the sprawling pastoral frontier
was apparent in Colonial Office despatches and memos throughout
the 1830s and 1840s. It was heightened in 1847 when a report
from George Augustus Robinson, Chief Protector of Aborigines in
the Port Phillip District, reached the Colonial Office. 'The claim of
Aborigines', he wrote,

to a reasonable share in the soil of their fatherland has not, I
regret to say, been recognised, in any of the discussions which for
so great a length of time, have agitated the public mind on the
question of rights of the Squatters, to the occupancy of the lands
of the Crown . . . The duty devolves on me to bring this Claim
under the notice of Her Majesty's Government for a reasonable
share in the soil of their fatherland.[52]

One of the Colonial Office officials who read the report stressed
the importance of the subject matter, underlining in pencil and
placing asterisks in the margin beside the twice-repeated phrase
about Aboriginal claims to a 'reasonable share in the soil of their
fatherland'. The intra-office memos were equally revealing. Herman
Merivale noted that Governor Fitzroy's attention 'must be drawn'
to the question. 'It would, of course', he wrote, 'be most unjust

that the Natives should be extruded in the manner described . . . from the soil of which till recently, they were the sole occupants'.[53] Secretary of State Earl Grey commented that the Governor 'must be instructed to take care that they are not driven off all that country which is divided into grazing [stations] and let under the recent regulations'.[54] Grey considered the matter one of the greatest importance. In a brief memo he explained that Aboriginal rights must be affirmed since it was a matter of life and death: action must be taken 'with a view to their preservation from being exterminated'.[55]

The resulting dispatch, sent to Sydney in February 1848, outlined a well-developed proposal which sought to meet the situation outlined in Robinson's report. Grey referred to the suggested creation of large reserves by way of compensation for the impairment of native title, arguing that, whereas such a scheme was appropriate elsewhere in the world, the nature of Australian geography and settlement patterns demanded a different answer. The dryness of the continent and the need for extensive grazing rights called for a peculiarly Australian solution. In fact,

> the very difficulty of thus locating the Aboriginal Tribes absolutely apart from the Settlers renders it more incumbent on Government to prevent them from being altogether excluded from the land under pastoral occupation. I think it essential that it should be generally understood that leases granted for this purpose give the grantees only an exclusive right of pasturage for their cattle, and of cultivating such land as they may require within the large limits thus assigned to them; but that leases are not intended to deprive the natives of their former right to hunt over these Districts, or to wander over them in search of subsistence, in the manner to which they have been heretofore accustomed, from the spontaneous produce of the soil.[56]

The Colonial Office had been forced to examine some of the same issues which exercised the mind of the High Court in the Mabo case. They considered whether pastoral occupation was 'wholly or partially inconsistent with a continuing right to enjoy native title', and concluded that it certainly was not. They were adamant that pastoral leases did not confer a 'right of exclusive possession'. The pastoralist's exclusive right of pasturage co-existed with the Aboriginal right of use and occupancy; they were 'mutual rights',[57] one was not superior to the other. On the other hand, the Colonial Office accepted that when the land was enclosed and cultivated the usage was inconsistent with a continuing Aboriginal interest although whether that interest revived if the land went out of cultivation is not clear. Earl Grey was even more emphatic on these points in another intra-office memo written in March 1849 in which he noted that it had to be assumed that the Imperial Government 'did not intend . . . to exclude the natives'[58] from land held under lease. What is more, he believed that the Australian *Waste Land Act* had provided the government 'no power'[59] to extinguish customary rights.

What, then, was to be done to protect the Aboriginal interest? Colonial Office officials were clear about what they wanted to achieve: 'the reservation in leases of Pastoral Land of the rights of the Natives'. It was not a case of creating new rights but the recognition of existing ones, the shaping of an instrument to ensure the 'continuance of their rights'.[60] They clearly interpreted a reservation in the precise legal sense of retaining or holding back some right, power or privilege. Equally, when they wrote of 'rights' they referred not to moral rights but to 'legal' rights. And the term 'right' was employed over and over again in official correspondence of the time.

How was the matter finally resolved? The New South Wales Law Officers, on receiving the initial instruction to provide for a 'continuance' of Aboriginal rights, argued that the matter could not be pursued without additional authority provided by an Order-in-Council. The Colonial Office accepted the advice and referred the correspondence to the Colonial Land and Emigration Office. The officials there were acutely aware of the political sensitivities so soon after the colonial agitation of 1844–1846, and suggested a form of words which disguised the specific purpose of the Order-in-Council, which was eventually signed by the Queen on 18 July 1849 to 'have the force and effect of law' in all the Australian colonies. It read in part:

> And whereas it is expedient that all such pastoral leases should contain such conditions, clauses of forfeiture, exceptions, and reservations, as may be necessary for securing the peaceable and effectual occupation of the land comprised in such leases, and for preventing the abuses and inconveniences incident thereto . . . [61]

The failure of the Order-in-Council to be more specific about Aboriginal rights has misled later commentators. But it was an issue which concerned the Colonial Office's Australian specialist Gordon Gairdner at the time. In a minute to Earl Grey on the draft Order-in-Council received from the Land and Emigration Commission, he scrawled: 'The entire extent of the access of the natives must surely be defined.'[62] With an eye to the politics of the situation Grey replied that the Order would 'be sufficient' as long as it was accompanied by an 'explanatory dispatch'.[63] So the true meaning of the measure was to be found less in the Order-in-Council, which was a public document published in the New South Wales

Government Gazette, and more in the dispatch, which was only for official eyes. In that correspondence, Grey re-emphasised the substance of his original dispatch of 11 February 1848 and reiterated that there could be 'little doubt that the intention of the Government was . . . to give only the exclusive right of pasturage in runs, not the exclusive occupation of the land, as against the natives using it for ordinary purposes'.[64] To underline his commitment to the issue, the Secretary of State told the Governor that if necessary he was to use discretionary powers under the Act to force squatters who had received leases prior to the publication of the Order-in-Council to accept the new conditions if they were 'disposed to insist on an unreasonable construction of their right of occupation'.[65]

Colonial Office policy and intentions were expressed much more clearly in correspondence with the Western Australian Government in 1850. Dispatches from the colony were received in May, enclosing three detailed alternative schemes for regulating the occupation of waste land. None of the schemes mentioned the Aborigines, an omission immediately noticed by Earl Grey. While reading the dispatch he minuted: 'one point I think has been overlooked.' He explained: 'If I am not mistaken a question arose in New South Wales as to the right of lease-holders to exclude the natives from their runs and it was found necessary to give some additional instructions upon that point. It is material that this will be attended to in the present case.'[66] At Grey's insistence, an extra sentence was added to the draft dispatch which was then returned to him for approval. The sentence read: 'You will observe that it is expressly provided by the [accompanying] Order-in-Council that no pastoral lease shall exclude natives from seeking their subsistence on the run in their accustomed manner.'[67] The Order-in-Council embodied the official direction in chapter V, clause 7, which read: 'Nothing contained in any pastoral lease shall prevent Aboriginal natives of this colony from entering upon the lands comprised therein, and seeking their subsistence therefrom in their accustomed manner.'[68] The clause was duly incorporated in the colonial pastoral regulations and gazetted on 17 December 1850. It was made quite clear to Governor Fitzgerald that he was to enforce the regulations, Grey noting that other clauses in the Order-in-Council gave him the 'fullest power to insert in all leases such conditions and clauses of forfeiture as may be necessary for the protection of the public interests in these or any other respect'.[69]

The reaction of Earl Grey to the Western Australian plans for pastoral occupation of the sprawling frontier territories provides us with the clearest possible picture of Imperial policy as interpreted at the highest level. We can trace with certainty the evolution of that policy from the ministerial minute scribbled on a dispatch in

May to the gazettal of the regulations in Perth at the end of the year.[70] We could not wish for a more complete endorsement of the policy of protecting Aboriginal occupancy rights on all land leased for pastoral purposes anywhere in the Australian colonies. Following the Mabo judgment we can see that the policy ensured that native title was not extinguished over the vast Australian range lands. It was, by far, the most important legacy of the Colonial Office's Aboriginal policy.

The serious problems apparent in the Dawson judgment, one must conclude, underline the strength of the others which found for Mabo and which linked Australian jurisprudence with the native title tradition of North America and with important aspects of international law. They bring together the customary law of the Meriam people with the doctrine of possession which can be traced back to the earliest traditions of European law. Dawson remarked that if the Murray Islanders were to be accorded some form of recognition for their traditional rights the moral and political responsibility should rest with politicians rather than judges, with legislators rather than courts. Many Australians are thankful that six of the High Court bench decided that the buck stopped with them and that our jurisprudence has been purged of its most notorious injustice, the doctrine of *terra nullius*.

3 Histories and rituals: land claims in the Territory[1]

Deborah Bird Rose

The *Aboriginal Land Rights (NT) Act 1976* produces an event in which a European judge (to date all male) decides whether or not a set of Aboriginal people are who they say they are. The Aboriginal people in question must produce for examination and cross-examination an identity that meets the requirements of an Act produced by Europeans. The onus is on Aboriginal people to 'prove' their identity according to an alien means of determining truth and falsehood . . . Surely neither justice nor reason can be said to prevail under a system that offers 'rights' only in the context of its own power to create a discourse of authenticity, to require conformity to that discourse, and to make final determinations on authenticity. It is difficult to conceive of a more cruel and elegant expression of cultural domination.[2]

A land claim hearing is an extraordinary procedure. History, Dreaming sites and actions, continued use of and care and concern for the country, and aspirations for the future all come together for a few days. Evidence is oral, the setting face to face, and Aboriginal people at last have the right to explain to a person whose understanding could make a genuine difference to their lives, just who they are, why they appear as claimants, what their relationship to the country is, and their hopes for the future. In a land claim, despite the peculiarities of the procedure, Aboriginal law speaks to European law through the duly constituted representatives of each, with the profound possibility of a result which does honour to both.[3]

I developed the first of these views while I was preparing materials for a land claim but had not yet seen the process through. A land claim hearing is understood as an event produced by the national Australian legal system and imposed upon Aboriginal people who

35

must submit to the coercion inherent in the law if they are to regain legal control of their homelands. This assessment finds little scope for national law to engage with Aboriginal law in spite of the ostensibly benevolent character of the legislation. There is an implication that Land Commissioners are bound by a method of forensic rationalism which is held to lead to truth but which, in practice, leads to colonial domination. The second reflection presents a view formulated from within the land claim process. I do not resile from my view that the *Aboriginal Land Rights (Northern Territory) Act 1976* (hereafter referred to as the Act) is an instrument of colonial domination, but I am now required to state that contemporary colonial domination is far more complex than I had then imagined, offering zones of empowerment and synergistic accommodation within the structure of restriction and coercion, as well as seeking more fully to incorporate Aboriginal people within structures of government. Nowhere are the contradictory, complicit, and mutually embedded double binds of relations between indigenous people and the colonising power more evident than in a land claim. This assessment represents my thinking after seeing Aboriginal people acquire a zone of control where they encompass forensic rationalism within rituals that inform and transform all the participants, and that produce owners of country in terms of both Aboriginal and government law and culture.

There is an extensive literature on anthropological and legal issues stimulated by land claims under the Act,[4] much of it offering competing views on how anthropological models of land tenure and social organisation must or might be understood. There are also some publications which offer Aboriginal people a voice on these issues.[5] There is also a vast amount of public debate, much of it critical and some of it remarkably uninformed, about the injustices (as perceived by widely disparate groups of people) of the Act. But there is a surprising paucity of written words (aside from anti-land rights propaganda) devoted to the fact that since the Act was put into practice, large portions of the Northern Territory (about 36 per cent of the land and 85 per cent of the coast to date) have come under Aboriginal Freehold Title; that large numbers of Aboriginal people have been found to be 'traditional owners' within the terms of the Act; and that this has not happened as an accident of history but as a result of Commonwealth legislation.

The first land claim in which I acted as senior anthropologist for the claimants was the Jasper Gorge/Kidman Springs Land Claim, heard in 1988. Since that time I have worked on numerous other land claims as senior anthropologist for the claimants, as a short term consultant to land councils on various matters, and as the Aboriginal Land Commissioner's consulting anthropologist. This chapter is formulated from within that experience. My focus is on claims which have been well presented and have elicited recommendations which have returned land to Aboriginal people. While not wishing to deny that there have been some unsatisfactory outcomes (and thus people have legitimate grievances which must be addressed), my purpose here is to examine a less public face of land claims: the many subtle ways in which Aboriginal people socialise the process and make of it a hybrid event in which their purposes can be accomplished. One lesson to be drawn is that far from being victims of coercion, many Aboriginal people have practised their own arts of social interaction to seize a measure of control over the process, and through their own actions have won legal recognition of their ownership of land. This is a testimony not only to their own skills, but also to the determinations of Land Commissioners which have enabled Aboriginal evidence to be heard fairly.

This chapter is divided into two parts. In the first I discuss the major limitations of the Act and the zones of Aboriginalisation that have developed under the Act. The second part is devoted to an analysis of histories and rituals within the presentation of Aboriginal evidence in land claims.

I

The Act suffers from a number of features which prevent it accomplishing the kind of justice that accords with the spirit in which it was passed.[6] It is also the case that different Aboriginal Land Commissioners have interpreted the Act differently, and some judicial decisions have enlarged the scope of the Act while others have had the effect of diminishing it. As I will discuss below, there has been a general trend toward enlarging the scope, but it is also the case that some decisions which could have been drawn upon to enhance that trend have not become standard practice.

Claimable land

Only unalienated Crown land can be claimed; if the claim is successful, the land is transferred to Aboriginal Freehold Title and is legally held by a Land Trust on behalf of the 'traditional owners'. In addition, all the land that was defined as reserve land prior to the passage of the Act became Aboriginal Freehold Title with its enactment.

Some groups of Aboriginal people are in legal possession of the whole or substantial parts of the country with which they assert a

relationship of ownership or belonging. Other groups are in possession of portions of land so small as utterly to trivialise their
aspirations. A few people are in possession of nothing at all under
Aboriginal Freehold Title. Territory initiatives which have been
designed, apparently, to overcome this shortcoming, generally (not
always) offer blocks of land to disadvantaged people which are so
small and so peripheral to any possibility of economic enterprise,
that they continue to mock both Aboriginal people and the spirit
of the Act.

The effect of the legislation is that some groups have been
massively advantaged economically, culturally, psychologically, and
in terms of their long range prospects for cultural and social
survival. Most of the Aboriginal people who have a high national
profile as people whose culture, language, arts, and politics are
thriving are the owners of large tracts of land (Warlpiri peoples and
Arnhem Land peoples are two examples). In the Territory an
Aboriginal elite is developing as a result of the Act. Yet, as I discuss
in greater detail below, many Aboriginal people who have understood the intention of the Act to be to reinstate a rule of justice
by returning at least some of the conquered lands to their original
owners, and in some sense to recompense Aboriginal people for the
ways in which their stolen lands and unpaid labour contributed to
the wealth and power of the Territory and the Australian nation,
have had to confront the fact that what is available to them to
claim under the Act is only a minute and economically non-viable
portion of their homelands. Consequently they have experienced a
great sense of disillusion and loss.

Gender

Male dominance in the Australian legal system, and the greater
numbers of male anthropologists involved in land claims, especially
in the early years, have generated hearings in which Aboriginal
women have been marginalised. Justice Toohey sought, by reference
to Section 51 of the Act which allows 'The Commissioner [to] do
all things necessary or convenient to be done for or in connection
with the performance of his functions',[7] to lessen this. For instance,
in hearing the Daly River (Malak Malak) Land Claim he considered
how he might receive a submission prepared by anthropologist
Diane Bell in conjunction with the women claimants in the light of
Bell's wish to restrict it such that the only man to read it would
be the Aboriginal Land Commissioner:

> it should be clearly understood that if I receive the material it will
> not necessarily be denied to other parties. As it happens, all coun-

sel participating are male but there are a number of female legal practitioners in Darwin and elsewhere whose services could be enlisted for the purpose of reading the report, just as there are female anthropologists who could be engaged for the same purpose. This may present some practical difficulties . . . But they are not insuperable.[8]

This decision, however, has not been accepted as a matter of course either by legal practitioners or by Aboriginal women. It arose again in the recent Palm Valley Land Claim during which the Aboriginal Land Commissioner Justice Gray made a similar decision,[9] but the problem remains for Aboriginal women that the Land Commissioner is a man. In the Jasper Gorge/Kidman Springs Land Claim, for example, the women claimants first decided that they would make an exception for the Land Commissioner and other men and show them some of their secret-sacred ritual. The event was agreed upon for late in the day so that the women would have most of the day to make their preparations; the men took the Land Commissioner and all the others on a series of site visits which were more conveniently made without women. As soon as the men had left I went to ask the women how they wanted to organise the day. There was a problem, they told me. They had decided they could not do it. One of the women explained: 'From Dreaming right up till now no man been look that thing. We can't lose that Law.' Not only did they not lose the Law; they speeded it up so that by the time the Land Commissioner returned the business was over and done with. There was nothing further to discuss.[10]

Far more disappointing than the limitations of the legal system, which under Justice Gray are being overcome, is the reluctance of land councils to do their best to ensure that women claimants get equal opportunities to articulate their status as land owners. There has often been a tunnel vision approach which asserts that as long as people get their land it does not matter who gives evidence. As I discuss these matters elsewhere,[11] I confine my comments here to noting the fact that insofar as the land claim record (written materials prepared in advance, the public hearing itself, references to performance in the context of secret-sacred knowledge, and the final report by the Aboriginal Land Commissioner) documents a people's relationships to land at the time of the inquiry, the record is extremely narrow and gives a most biased and discriminatory representation of Aboriginal women as land owners and as managers of country, knowledge, sacred domains and social relations.

'Traditional owners'

The Act's definition of 'traditional owner' is remarkably brief. It
defines Aboriginal traditional owners (section 3[1]) as 'a local
descent group of Aboriginals who have common spiritual affiliations
to a site on the land, being affiliations that place the group under
a primary spiritual responsibility for that site and for the land, and
who are entitled by Aboriginal tradition to forage over that land'.
In the early 1980s Justice Toohey made a number of significant
decisions concerning this which have continued to inform claims
and to be debated in claims.[12]

The findings of the Aboriginal Land Commissioner define, for
a moment in time, just which people are the 'traditional owners'
of country under the Act. Different Land Commissioners have
formed their views according to different principles. In some land
claims, people who identified themselves as 'owners' of country,
and were so identified by others, were not found by the Land
Commissioner to be members of the land owning group. This has
been the case especially for people whose relationship to country
is through a female genealogical link.[13] There have been varying
interpretations of what is meant by 'descent' under the Act: for
purposes of the Act, can women transmit rights of ownership, or
can only men transmit such rights? It is now accepted that Justice
Toohey was correct in his report on the Utopia Land Claim when
he stated emphatically that 'the Land Rights Act is not an exercise
in anthropology':

> Whatever the situation in anthropology . . . I do not think I should
> approach the matter with some preconceived model in mind to
> which the evidence must accommodate itself. Rather it is a matter
> of listening to the witnesses and asking, in the light of that evi-
> dence, who may fairly be said to constitute the local descent group
> for the land claimed. The answer in this case may not be the
> answer in the next.[14]

Findings which exclude people whose ownership is traced
through a woman need not be binding on the claimants, since it is
always open to Aboriginal people to carry on their land owning
practices in the same way as they did before the Land Commissioner
made his recommendations. In the short term, however, many
people have been deeply hurt and angered at having the Land
Commissioner exclude them from the land owning group in spite
of their own evidence and that of all their peers. The next decade
will clarify the extent to which Land Commissioners' decisions
become potent factors in the ongoing politics of land. At this time
there appears to be an intensification of land disputes, and it seems

inevitable that the Land Commissioners' findings of traditional ownership will increasingly play a role in conflict. The possibility exists for intensification of development of elites, and for increasingly bitter disputes in which Land Commissioners' findings are used by elites as instruments of oppression.

Land owning groups

The Act requires the existence of a land owning group. Although the Act nowhere specifies that the claimants must possess knowledge of and continuity in country, the criteria of ownership are framed in such a way as to require knowledge and physical presence. Thus, for example, 'common spiritual affiliation to a site on the land' requires both knowledge of sites and demonstrations of common spiritual affiliation. As practice has developed, common spiritual affiliation is often interpreted as beliefs about the spiritual/sacred quality of some sites and as religious practices in respect of the sites. Similarly, primary spiritual responsibility is usually interpreted to mean that there is at least a core set of people who carry out religious practice in respect of country.

Land Commissioners have not found it necessary that each member of the group be required to demonstrate active exercise of primary spiritual responsibility. Indeed, it is well recognised that some of these responsibilities are restricted by age and gender, and so will predictably not be exercised by all members of the group. In addition, as a general rule, elderly people who are no longer active, and young people who have yet to acquire responsibilities more extensive than the responsibility to learn, are not debarred from the status of traditional owners. So, too, for Aboriginal people who were removed from their families at an early age. While many such people may not exercise primary spiritual responsibility, it is open for the Land Commissioner to find that they are traditional owners within the meaning of the Act, and in a number of land claims such findings have been made. In my experience, however, this is the exception rather than the rule, as people who have been removed from their families find it especially difficult to show that they are members of the land owning group. Thus, one must conclude that the Act has been designed primarily for people who have been able to sustain continuity with their country, and a rigid or restrictive interpretation of the Act will not favour people whose history has separated them from their country or from the knowledge of their country.

Justice Toohey's findings in his Report on the Finniss River Land Claim with respect to the Kungarakany claimants offer alternatives to such a rigid interpretation, and deserve to have had a greater impact than has been the case. The Kungarakany claimants were a group of essentially urban Aboriginal people two generations removed from intimate association with the country of which they claimed to be traditional owners within the terms of the Act. One of the issues that was raised was their Aboriginality, and whether they could even begin to qualify as traditional owners. Justice Toohey stated:

> As I said in the Uluru Report, the definition of the Act is 'genetic rather than social' (para. 115). The dictionary definitions are framed in such a way that people having mixed racial origins are not excluded from a race with which they are genetically linked. Despite submissions made to the contrary . . . there is nothing in the Act to compel the view that a person who is descended from both Aboriginal and non-Aboriginal ancestors cannot be considered an Aboriginal. References to Aboriginal tradition and sacred sites and the elements of traditional Aboriginal ownership do not operate to narrow the scope of the definition. They are directed at the beliefs, roles and responsibilities of Aboriginal people, not at who is an Aboriginal.[15]

Thus, in this claim, Justice Toohey phrased the question as one of adherence to Aboriginal tradition. Consequently, he found many of the Kungarakany people to be traditional owners within the terms of the Act:

> I am satisfied that among the claimants who gave evidence there was a general desire to maintain Aboriginal traditions, at least to the extent that it is possible within the lifestyles they now lead. It was reflected in various ways—an interest in language, the use of Aboriginal names, the recording of stories, some ceremonial life and . . . an active participation in Aboriginal organisations.[16]

Land claim practice

A set of unofficial practices has developed around the hearing of an Aboriginal claim to land which emerges from Land Commissioners' efforts to provide conditions which enable a fair presentation of Aboriginal people's evidence, and from Aboriginal people's own demands that their voices be geographically and socially situated. In the course of successive hearings a vocabulary has developed to refer to these new practices.[17] Aboriginal people's evidence, for example, is referred to as 'traditional evidence' whether it refers to the past, present or future, to matters religious, or to issues such as people's hopes for a store, clinic or bore.

Traditional evidence is customarily heard from a base 'in the bush' on or near the land being claimed. The purposes are several: to enable the Land Commissioner properly to see the country in question; to enable the witnesses to speak with the particular authority derived from being in one's own country; to enable the evidence to be assessed in its context. The hearing also involves numerous 'site visits' where evidence is given concerning the site, some of the knowledge associated with the site, statements of which claimants are responsible for the site, discussion of practices of land management and foraging, discussion of practices of care (primary spiritual responsibility for the site), and life history information connecting claimants and their ancestors to the site. Typical life history evidence of activities at a site include whatever people have done there: camping, foraging, mustering, mining, herding goats, attending to windmills, gathering for ceremony.

Site visits are contrasted with 'sit-down evidence' during which more formal evidence is elicited dealing with genealogies, history, kinship, current living conditions, future plans, and all the other matters deemed most efficiently discussed in that context. Evidence is always taken from individuals who are surrounded by other members of their group; members of a land owning group sit together, listen to each other's evidence, and pass the microphone back and forth amongst themselves as they answer questions in detail, add to each other's details, and confirm each other's statements.

Most land claims in the Northern Territory have been opposed by the Northern Territory Government. Hence, Aboriginal claimants can expect to be cross-examined to a more or less aggressive degree depending on the degree of opposition, although generally the government's lawyers have endeavoured to treat claimants with respect since there is little point in attempting to destroy the witnesses' credibility through cross-examination. In any case, such ploys are completely out of character with the purpose of the hearing which is to enable the Land Commissioner to conduct an inquiry. Claimants are cross-examined in all the contexts in which they give evidence, including restricted sessions. Their responses to cross-examination are complex, differ among individuals, and change during the course of the hearing. In one claim I was involved in, a senior woman, known to her peers as a woman of extraordinary knowledge and excellent teaching abilities, became so distressed that she retreated into murmuring the story of her main Dreaming in answer to every question put to her in cross-examination; in another claim a knowledgeable senior woman became so incensed that she refused to give further evidence. Senior men, in my experience, patiently bear aggressive cross-examination for a while, but patience can turn to anger and finally to disgust, and some have retorted by asking questions of their interlocutor. More significantly, most Aboriginal witnesses are completely credible, and aggressive cross-examination usually serves to reinforce this impression. During the course of most hearings, claimants gain confidence: that their knowledge is being understood and valued; that cross-examination does not detract from their case; that the strength they experience as knowledgeable owners of country is being communicated both to the Land Commissioner and to the opposition.

Finally, land claim hearings are not marked by a rigid adherence to rules of evidence. Many lawyers new to land claims go through a period of culture shock as they adapt to practices such as: witnesses listen to each other's evidence; witnesses are not asked to take an oath; there is a great reliance on Aboriginal oral traditions which might otherwise be regarded as 'hearsay'.

In sum, Land Commissioners conduct an inquiry under a set of practices which is quite unlike anything their fellow judges experience, and the structure of the hearing has been significantly Aboriginalised in ways that enable Land Commissioners to hear Aboriginal people's evidence fairly.

II

Ross Howie, legal counsel for the claimants in the Tempe Down Land Claim heard in November 1994, stated in opening: 'All land claims are a conversation with history.'[18] From the point of view of the anthropologist, two main types of histories are especially pertinent in these claims: regional social history, and personal histories of the claimants and their ancestors, as these can be understood through both written documents and Aboriginal oral traditions.

Every claim book (report of the senior anthropologist on behalf of the claimants) either contains a submission on regional social history or is accompanied by a separate history submission. Such submissions uncompromisingly insist that people be heard and understood on their own terms. The impetus comes from Justice Toohey's decision that claimants' evidence must be heard in terms of their own organisation of knowledge, rather than in light of anthropologists' models. Anthropologically, the Act was heavily influenced by A.R. Radcliffe-Brown and W.E.H. Stanner's views that the basic land owning unit throughout Aboriginal Australia was the local patrilineal clan,[19] but as claim after claim has shown this model of land ownership offers a very poor fit with claimants' views of their mode of land tenure (although there have been, and undoubtedly will continue to be, some claims in which this mode of land tenure is central); and successive Land Commissioners and the full Federal Court (in *Northern Land Council v Olney*) have demolished the tyranny of anthropological models of Aboriginal land tenure.

In fairly abstract terms, the historical submission starts with the supposition that whatever models people may have in their heads about Aboriginal people's traditional modes of land ownership, that model will neither be able fully to account for these people nor be relevant as a measure of them, and that only their historical experience—of their own culture, of colonisation, of the culturally and historically embedded practices of memory and survival—will enable an understanding of their modes of land ownership. The overall objective of the history submission, then, is to communicate to the Aboriginal Land Commissioner and all the interested parties the historical conditions which account for the particularities of these people's relationships to country.

Thus, history submissions offer an opportunity to examine analytically many of the particularities of the claimants' own statements. For example, in one claim I am familiar with, claimants recognise and acknowledge groups of the order of the anthropological model of clans, but at the same time contend that their land owning group is not the clan but rather a larger group defined by languages. Most pertinently, a historical analysis of population loss, group mergers, and patterns whereby people were sedentarised within colonising institutions can be pivotal in explaining, in a logic that makes sense in court, just why the mode of tenure presented by the claimants is necessary and appropriate to the conditions of their lives as they are now. Other particularities are likely to include: residence patterns, which account for the clustering of knowledge in certain areas; policies for the removal of children, which account for the different life experience among claimants; work experience, which accounts for the different geographies of knowledge among individual claimants and, frequently, between women and men.

In addition to this function, each historical submission has the quality of being a master narrative of cultural survival. The author of a history submission aims to show that it is entirely credible that these people know who they are, where they belong, why they belong where they do, and how they express that belonging. Given that so many groups have endured severe and protracted attempts by government and others to erase precisely this knowledge from living memory and practice, the history submission is vital.

Individual life histories are often briefly summarised in the history submission, but are drawn out more fully in evidence. The purposes of life histories include: explaining how the person gained their knowledge of country (their work, residence and marriages, and the social characteristics of the communities within which they were nurtured); clarifying the limitations to the person's knowledge (drawing on the same facts as above); describing occasions on which the person was taught and, for older people, occasions on which the person is now teaching others about the country; explaining parents' life histories at least to the extent that they document relevant conception and birth sites, and lay the basis for the person's acquisition, or lack of acquisition, of knowledge; using the life history as a narrative structure for demonstrations of knowledge— for example, a woman who travelled throughout the claim area with her parents on dingo scalping expeditions, uses the structure of these trips to discuss place names, Dreaming sites and tracks, water holes and soaks, sites of bush tucker, as well as her parents' right to forage, and more.

Western knowledge has a tradition of distinguishing between history and myth, but many Aboriginal cultures weave the two in such a way that in many contexts there is no essential distinction. Historical evidence inevitably touches on the mythic,[20] often in ways that require the Land Commissioner to attend closely to that which is entirely unfamiliar. An example is the conception of a man named Edward Johnson, a senior claimant in a number of claims to land around the western fringe of the Simpson Desert. He stated (and this was supported by his peers) that his conception at a particular Dreaming site meant that he was an 'owner' for that area. In the terms of the Act, one would say that his conception gave him a common spiritual affiliation with other members of the group associated with the sites on that Dreaming track, and gave him primary spiritual responsibilities for sites and land in the area of that track. Mr Johnson told his story in evidence, and a condensed version of the evidence gives an indication of the complexities of cross-cultural communication in a hearing:

> Edward Johnson: That belong to Yewerre [a site] that eagle . . . [and they were around here] hunting around for meat and things . . . They fly from Yewerre to Artetykale [a site] and he seen it, bloke laying down . . . Yes. Might be me, I think. Yes, it started screaming through the—screaming you know . . . And then another bloke [eagle] come right in there and he come down, hooked that one [me] . . . And lift him up and drop it again, and then another bloke on a ride on air he come down . . . He pick up, you know . . . He drop it there . . . And they drop it [me] at Aweyinteme [a site] . . . White fellow call them Red Bank . . . Lot of red ochre in that bank, you know . . . Do you [know] what is—red ochre means? That blood, you know, from that young fellow . . . [21]

The claimants' lawyer Ross Howie asked Mr Johnson: 'Why is it you, Edward?' and Mr Johnson replied: 'Well, just in story line,

they told me, oh, you have got to be in the story . . . My brother
told me that.'[22]

In sum, from an anthropological and legal viewpoint, histories—personal and regional, oral and written, sacred and
secular—are essential to the presentation of evidence. As submissions and as claimants' evidence, histories provide the context for
the central assertion that the claimants are traditional owners of
the land within the terms of the Act. Local histories are set against
the metaphysical frame of sacred origins, and encapsulated within
a master narrative of survival.

Oral culture

A land claim brings oral traditions face to face with traditions of
the book, and there is always a possibility that the written word
will take precedence over the testimony of the living people who
are, of course, experts in their own culture. The Land Commissioner
must weigh the evidence of the past in relation to the present, the
written in relation to the spoken. In some land claims written
documents from the past are so sparse that the question barely
arises. In other cases, such as that of Arrernte people of Central
Australia, massively documented by two generations of Strehlows,
the issue is bound to arise. Jim Wafer, senior anthropologist for the
claimants in the North-West Simpson Desert Land Claim, states:
'In our work on this land claim we have had to remind ourselves
constantly that the bearers of Arrernte culture are not the books
written by earlier generations of anthropologists, but living Arrernte
themselves.'[23]

Within the land claim context Wafer's analysis of Arrernte oral
culture is most insightful, since he notes the risks to the claim if
the claimants' culture is expected to display the kind of organisation
characteristic of European law, philosophy or theology:

> Aboriginal traditions in general have not been systematised by the
> kinds of processes that written records make possible, through the
> juxtaposition and comparison of different versions of the tradition.
> There is no canonical version of Arrernte traditions, comparable to
> the canonical books of western theology. The creation of a canon
> requires written records, so that different versions of the traditions
> can be compared, a single version elevated to the status of ortho-
> doxy, and other variants declared secondary or heterodox.
>   A major characteristic of oral cultures is that different parts of
> their traditions are preserved in the memories of different people,
> with the inevitable overlaps and gaps. It is not usually the case that
> any one individual has an overview of the whole of the tradition.
> In the case of overlap, it is quite common for different individuals

to know different versions of the same part of the tradition, because of the way variations occur as the traditions are transmitted over time and across geographical distance.[24]

How, then, do people ever manage culturally or socially to cohere? The answer is through their conjoined practices, the most socially significant of which for Arrernte people is ceremony:

> For Aboriginal people in general, the proof of the consistency of their tradition, and of their consensus with regard to it, does not lie in their adherence to some type of theoretical synthesis of the tradition, comparable to a creed, but in their ability to perform the appropriate ceremonies . . . the tradition is validated in a series of concrete situations, rather than by reference to an ideal model preserved in writing . . . This makes it very context-specific.[25]

A land claim hearing is one such concrete situation: a moment when ownership is enacted, validated by a community of peers, and proved to others.

Some Aboriginal narratives

From the point of view of the claimants some narratives of the past prevail which are quite different from those of the anthropologists. Life histories are important evidence for the claimants, particularly to the extent that they constitute the genealogy of their knowledge, locating rights to knowledge in social relationships which are founded in land, and locating the authority of knowledge in the preceding generations. Most of the claimants, most of the time, do not validate their knowledge by testing it against other frames of reference, and certainly not by validating it with reference to the written word. Rather, they validate their knowledge by demonstrating that its authority derives from previous generations: they know, and they have the authority of knowledge, because they were told. Authorised knowledge, in short, has a human genealogy and is orally transmitted.

There is another highly significant dimension to history (regional and local) for many claimants. In contrast to the anthropologist's master narrative of cultural survival, many Aboriginal claimants frame their accounts of the past within a master narrative of colonising injustice. Hobbles Danayarri, a master storyteller and political/historical analyst, for example, told lengthy narratives of Captain Cook which describe and analyse the range of injustices perpetrated by the colonisers against those whom they conquered. He concluded his narratives with the pastoral strikes of the Victoria River District and the achievement of land rights. One of his most powerful oratorical deployments was his report of a conversation between Tommy Vincent Linjiyarri (leader of the strikes) and Lord Vestey (then owner of Wave Hill Station). Tommy Vincent is offered everything but land, and he rejects all the offers: 'Tommy Vincent told Lord Vestey: "You can keep your gold. We just want our land back".'[26] Many Aboriginal people have understood the Act in precisely these terms: as an acknowledgment of injustice and as an attempt at recompense,[27] and their presentation of their 'historical' narratives has been in the spirit of establishing the injustice so as to define the parameters of justice owing to them.

That the anthropological and the Aboriginal narratives draw upon the same facts is important; the two narratives are different but not contradictory. The former is oriented toward questions of proof under the Act; the latter is oriented toward questions of justice in the relations between indigenous people and the colonising state. It is certainly one of the many ironies of the Act that the Land Commissioner is not authorised to accord to the second of these narratives a degree of weight at all comparable to the first.

Land claim ritual

Ritual action is action that effects a transformation. Aboriginal land ownership is validated through ceremony: it is ritually produced, and through ritual a relationship between person and country is produced, sustained, nurtured, and regenerated; it is caused to come into existence and to have its existence verified. The proof is in the practice.

It is possible that some of the people involved with land claim hearings regard them as performances; the claimants show and tell, the judge decides, the minister hands over the title. Mystery is meant to be banished from the court, and rationality to rule. The power to transform the status of the land is power the judge exercises as an agent of the Australian nation. Many Aboriginal people understand the event quite differently. For them a land claim hearing is a ritual, and many Aboriginal people are masters of the arts of ritual. In the best land claims, the claimants seize the hearing, develop their own structure of action which runs in tandem with the formal hearing, and transform the hearing itself into a ritual over which, from their position as apparent supplicants, they preside. Their ownership of country is performed; the performance is a ritual act which generates the 'proof' of ownership and ultimately opens the Australian legal system to enable Aboriginal Freehold Title to be handed over to them.

Hearings open with sit-down evidence of a formal nature:

tendering of documents, introductory remarks, and basic orientation
to the claim, usually followed by introductions of the first group
of people to give evidence. The physical plan demonstrates some
of the structure of the event: judge and his associates and assistants
in the centre, land council personnel on the right-hand wing,
Northern Territory Government and other opposing groups in the
left-hand wing, claimants on the fourth side of the square facing
the judge. Once the formalities are concluded, presentation of
evidence takes on a rhythm: the cadence of question, answer, and
clarification of evidence in chief, the periodic bursts of cross-examination and re-examination. As the hearing proceeds, if it proceeds
well, the claimants gain confidence in a number of propositions:
that the Land Commissioner really is there to listen to what they
have to say; that cross-examination can be exhilarating as well as
painful; that their knowledge does indeed hold up under an alien
and often ill-informed scrutiny.

Knowing that this event can be transformative, they seek to
take control so as to transform many things. Their legal status in
respect of the land claimed and their relationships among themselves
will be transformed, as will their relationships with non-claimants,
their ability to gain bureaucratic and economic control over some
portions of their lives, and many of their relationships with the
Australian nation.

Thus, for example, on the last day of the Jasper Gorge/Kidman
Springs Land Claim hearing the claimants announced that they
intended to put on a 'show' for the Land Commissioner that would
involve music, dance, and body art. Their purpose, as stated by the
women, was that they wanted to show the Land Commissioner that
women and men act together in the management of knowledge.
This final 'show' was a ritual inversion of the hearing, and the
reversals were so marked and humorous that the intent could not
be missed. It was organised for night time, it was held outside of
the bough shade where the hearing had been held, and the spatial
organisation was determined totally by the claimants. The judge
and all other non-Aboriginal participants (lawyers, anthropologists,
field assistants, etc.) were told that we would be summoned when
the claimants were ready for us, and that we could sit and wait in
the meantime.

When called, we were told to stop at the bough shade to pick
up our chairs and then come forward half way and sit at a particular
place. After waiting half way we were told to bring our chairs
forward and to arrange ourselves in a row facing the area that had
been designated as a dancing ground. The claimants used the
headlights of their vehicles as spotlights for the dancers, and with
imaginative use of space, lighting and personnel created a 'show'

that was by turns impressive, sweet and humorous. The children provided humour inadvertently (in part), and some of the men took up the clowning role with exuberance. The women danced; it was their first opportunity to show the judge that they had a law to back them up.

To conclude the 'show' a senior regional law woman grouped the women together in a huddle to make the sounds that speak to the country, and with her hands and arms she gestured with downward motions. Then she turned to the 'audience' and said (from memory): 'We opened the country up for you, and now we are closing it down again.'

III

A land claim hearing is, I have suggested, a hybrid event that allows for multiple systems of knowledge and meaning to engage with each other without being annihilated. Within the structures of colonial domination this must be reckoned an achievement.

In my 1987 review of Gumbert's work I stated that Aboriginal people were required to produce an identity that meets the requirements of the Act. This both is and is not what happens. The practice is that Aboriginal people offer evidence of the parameters (temporal, spatial, spiritual) of their relationships to land under claim and they offer the proofs (knowledge and practice) of their stated relationships to the land under claim. Lawyers and anthropologists seek ways to access the evidence in terms of the Act, and in this regard the Act has proved to be flexible and responsive to the histories, cultures, and aspirations of many Aboriginal claimants.

The two systems of law—Aboriginal and national Australian—are incommensurate, and it is undoubtedly the case that participants leave the hearing with radically different views of what happened.[28] Different views of the meaning of the past in relation to the present (different histories, one can say), are an example. I think that many claimants leave the hearing feeling a sense of achievement about what they have communicated through the telling of their life histories; they are likely to believe that they have demonstrated the injustices perpetrated against them and thus explained why the Land Commissioner should return land to them. Many believe that they have validated their ownership of knowledge by describing in detail its genealogy.

The Land Commissioner, however, as I have noted, does not make a decision on the basis of past injustices, and while he may well be moved by the stories the terms of the Act require that much of the historical information be situated within a narrative of survival rather than one of justice. Equally, the culture of forensic rationalism requires that evidence be tested and validated against a set of references other than itself (circular arguments are not good evidence according to linear logic). Consequently, the judge is likely to understand the genealogy of knowledge as a narrative of survival rather than as a narrative of validated authority.

The judge has gained a set of understandings which will enable him to make a legally defensible decision, and has done so under conditions which are wildly divergent from standard courtroom practice, but which nonetheless meet the requirements of the Australian judicial system. The claimants, by contrast, have been engaged as objects of scrutiny in a foreign, structurally coercive, and highly stylised event. They have grasped its structure and style, and they have infused the event with their own sense of story, proof, drama, and ritual. Many claimants leave the hearing asserting that they have 'won the court', expressing their sense of having gained control of the event as well as anticipating gaining Aboriginal Freehold Title.

Almost two decades of land rights in the Northern Territory are now producing a paradox. Given the overall coercion inherent in the fact that claimants have to prove their ownership to an agent of the Australian nation, the Act was framed in fairly open terms. It did not specify in detail the type of anthropological models to which the Aboriginal people might be required to conform, and did not insist upon people demonstrating secret knowledge. It did not in any way require genetic uniformity among individuals, or uniformity of beliefs and practices from one group to another. Phrased more positively, and abstractly, the Act embeds Aboriginal ownership of land in a system of kinship; it states that owners have a spiritual relationship with their country; and it states that this spiritual relationship confers both rights (principally to forage) and responsibilities (unspecified, except that they are spiritual).

In the course of the many hearings, it has become clear that Aboriginal people in those regions of the Territory which are claimable, have many similarities of history, modes of land tenure, systems of knowledge and proof. The possibility is that in the post-Mabo era these land claims may become a canon of authenticity for proof of land tenure systems which could oppress and dispossess other Aboriginal people, not entirely because of the Act itself, but rather because of the cultural specificity of the claimants within its zone of applicability. Paradoxically, the Aboriginalisation of the process has transformed the abstractions of the Act into expectations of culturally distinct practices, and it is this very Aboriginalisation which may become a further instrument of colonial domination. In sum, the virtue of the Act is its accessibility to Aboriginalisation. This virtue has the potential to become a form of terror, however, if Aboriginal people in other parts of Australia are required to reproduce this particular Aboriginality and, unable or unwilling to do so, fail to achieve legal recognition as native title holders.

4 Historians, Aborigines and Australia: writing the national past

Richard Broome

In February 1951, Bill Bull, a 62-year-old Kurnai man from East Gippsland, was sentenced to six months gaol for begging alms while playing the gum leaf on Princes Bridge in Melbourne.[1] He had a string of 60 convictions dating back to 1920, including 25 for begging and others for obscene language, drunkenness and offensive behaviour. In a letter to the Melbourne *Sun*, 'Australian' of Murrumbeena congratulated Bull on conducting his own appeal and testified: 'He was arrested a few minutes after I gave him 3d. He did not ask me for it, nor did I see him ask others.'[2] Judge Streeton reduced his sentence to the rising of the court which happened immediately after, Bull having already spent seven weeks in Pentridge Gaol as he had been unable to post bail. The *Sun* editorialised the case, itself an unusual event, and asked: 'In this year of celebration [the jubilee of Federation], what have we done to help the original Australians? Have we already forgotten our pledge in the Declaration of Human Rights? . . . We have a solemn duty', the editor declared, 'to educate and advance the Aborigines; otherwise we stand guilty of callous and tragic neglect'.[3] Bill Bull was convicted twice in 1953, again under section 72 of the *Police Offences Act*. The second time was the day after he left Pentridge following a six-month stint. A prominent lawyer, Frank Galbally, was approached to conduct his defence, which caused Bull to weep in his cell over the first legal aid offered him in 30 years before the courts.[4] Bill Bull died the following year at the Fitzroy lock-up and faced a pauper's grave, a fate Sergeant S. Joyce of the Station hoped he would avoid: 'It would be a bad finish for the poor old soul. He was a real old gentleman. There was nothing wrong with him—he was just a wanderer. Most times we brought him in just for his own sake.'⁵

These glimpses of Bill Bull's long encounter with the law are elements in the larger story of the injustices experienced by Aboriginal Australians. However, these fragments also reveal a growing awareness of such injustices by other Australians. Many forces, external and internal, shaped this growing awareness. The *Sun's* editor referred to international humanitarian obligations which were part of changing world opinion towards indigenous people in the context of postwar decolonisation. Justice Leeton, Frank Galbally, and even Sergeant Joyce in his own way, revealed themselves as part of that thin strand of humanitarianism evident within our society from its earliest beginnings, and this was strengthened as postwar Australia was remade by a revolutionary polyethnic immigration programme, the availability of large-scale higher education, the experience of overseas travel by the young, and a growing affluence that encouraged a greater cosmopolitan tolerance among many Australians.⁶ Aboriginal political activity also helped to reshape Australian thinking about Aboriginal people.

Such forces for change demand careful elucidation, but my aims here are more modest inasmuch as I will be exploring the contribution of Australian historians to the reshaping of popular attitudes to Aborigines and to the creation of a climate of opinion in which the High Court found *terra nullius* untenable. I will focus on twentieth-century representations of Aboriginal people in general histories and encyclopaedias, as well as the major anthropological and later specialist writings in Aboriginal history that informed these popular works, since these works reached and probably influenced far more Australians through junior schooling, home and local libraries, than academic history has done.⁷

Since Willem Jansz in 1606 called Aboriginal people on the west coast of Cape York 'Heathens, which are man-eaters', and Jan Carstensz described the Carpentaria River people in 1623 as 'the most wretched and poorest creatures that I have ever seen in my age or time',⁸ Europeans have been constructing images about Aboriginal people in Australia for their own purposes. This can be seen in representations by Captain James Cook and Joseph Banks in 1770⁹ and those of later observers, whose images were used in debates about the nature of humanity and its relations with the natural world.¹⁰ Ignorance, indifference, arrogance and racial ideology shaped these European views of culture contacts on the Australian frontier. In the following century these views were reproduced by historians. Most writers of Australia's history were concerned with justifying domination by representing the British settlement of Australia as eminently peaceful, intent on drawing a veil over violence so as not to sully Australia's reputation or injure the sensibilities of post-frontier readers.[11]

Histories of Australia written from the 1900s to the 1930s were as derogatory of Aboriginal people as the earlier writings and probably more dismissive. One example is Ernest Scott, Professor of History at the University of Melbourne and founder, in 1927, of the first Australian history course. In his *A Short History of Australia* (1916), which was reprinted 22 times over seven editions until 1964,[12] Scott focussed on the European 'finding' and 'exploration' of Australia, land settlement, the growth of democratic government, Federation, and Australia at war. Aboriginal people first appeared as the 'black and painted savages' who knew nothing about the gold and silver that Van Diemen sought in Australia, because 'they were too low down in the scale of civilisation even for barter'. Scott paraphrased William Dampier's 1699 views of the Shark Bay people unabashed: 'the natives were utterly repellent. They were black, ugly, fly-blown, blinking creatures, the most unpleasant human beings he had ever encountered.' Scott further claimed that Aborigines 'had no domestic arts or domestic animals . . . Even the bow was beyond their invention'. He paid scant attention to initial cultural encounters but stated that Aborigines were not aggressive—they were made so by the brutality of white settlers and their convict servants. Scott pulled no punches in writing briefly but powerfully of punitive expeditions sanctioned by Governor Brisbane and poisonings by settlers. Yet, while Aborigines were victims of a 'grim and hateful' process, Scott deemed it to be 'inevitable' for 'they were not a people easily absorbed, or adapted to civilised life'. Thus their presence in his 462-page history did not extend beyond the frontier.[13]

F.L.W. Wood, lecturer in history at the University of Sydney and later a Professor of History in New Zealand, published *A Concise History of Australia* in 1935 which had seven impressions in eight years and continued to be issued until 1950. In this account, Aborigines received scant attention, except as troublesome characters to explorers from Cook to Kennedy. They were fleeting cardboard figures on the backdrop of European exploration and appeared as aggressors save for three exceptions. Wood claimed that in the mid-1930s 'those of the south have died out since the white man's invasion'—corrected to 'practically disappeared' a paragraph later—and those in the north numbered only 60 000. They fell to disease, strong drink and 'could not defend their hunting grounds and sacred places, for black men with spears could make no headway against the white man's guns'. With no sense of an Aboriginal resistance, except to lone explorers, Wood depicted the

Aborigines as pathetic, falling to the scythe of white settlement. They appeared briefly on a dozen pages of his 365-page history, but not in the index.[14]

Keith Hancock's celebrated juvenilia *Australia*, published in 1930, said even less about Aborigines. They appeared in the book once—as victims of colonisation. Aboriginal people, wrote Hancock, shut off from 'cooperative intelligence' for centuries,

> never imagined that first decisive step from the economy of the chase which would have made them masters of the soil. Instead, they fitted themselves to the soil, modelling a complex civilisation of intelligent artificiality, which yet was pathetically helpless when assailed by the acquisitive society of Europe.[15]

There was some admiration here, and a critique of his own culture, yet no attempt to understand culture contact beyond the greatest generality.

Encyclopaedias of the late nineteenth century included Aboriginal people, although initially there was no interest in their contact history with whites, or in their present condition. In 1895 the ten-volume second edition of *Chambers's Encyclopaedia* contained a 1750-word article on 'Aborigines' by J. O'Halloran, Secretary of the Colonial Institute, which characterised 'the human natives of Australia' in social evolutionist[16] terms as 'isolated and peculiar', like Australia's botany and zoology. Although he saw Aborigines as human, his description of them was derogatory: Their calves were 'feeble', their brow 'receding', their nose 'squat', their mouth 'big and uncouth', their ears 'pricked forward' and their intellect, despite admirable skills in tracking, weapon-making, language and crude art, 'operated wholly within the range of the rudest bodily senses'; they were nomads who had 'no architecture, almost no weaving, no pottery and may almost be said to have no religion'; their 'sensations have hardly if at all, reached the length of sentiments, far less sentimentalities'; their morality and laws were 'entirely reduced to the notion of property'; their life 'alternates between satiety and semi-starvation'. O'Halloran believed Aboriginal people in the 1890s were at half their pre-contact estimate of 150 000 because, 'like almost all other savages, [they] are rapidly vanishing before the advance of civilisation', falling to 'diseases and vices they acquired from Europeans'. Violence was not part of the equation of decline, O'Halloran wrote, but elsewhere he stated that Aborigines had murdered whites in reprisal for 'prior atrocities committed by the convicts or other reckless Europeans'.[17]

The eleventh edition of the 29-volume *Encyclopaedia Britannica*, issued in 1910, contained a 5000-word article by Arnold Channing of Oxford University, written in the mode of social evolutionism and drawing upon works by the anthropologists Walter Baldwin Spencer and Frank Gillen, Alfred Howitt, Lorimer Fison, Henry Ling Roth and Katherine Langloh Parker.[18] Almost half the text was devoted to the origins of the Aborigines, arguing for a Dravidian migration from the Indian subcontinent of ancient proportions judging by the 'low state of culture of the Australians'. The derogatory physical description of the Aboriginal people mirrored that of *Chambers's Encyclopaedia*, but with the added claim that 'the skull is abnormally thick and the cerebral capacity small'. The entry contained a hard-edged section on 'character', alleging that:

> in disposition the Australians are a bright, laughter-loving folk, but they are treacherous, untruthful and hold human life cheaply. They have no great physical courage. They are mentally in the condition of children. None of them has an idea of what the West calls morality, except the simple one of right or wrong arising out of property.

In their treatment of women—an important nineteenth-century index of 'civilisation'—they ranked, according to Channing, 'lower than even the Fuegians'. Their life was one of 'prehistoric simplicity', having no cultivation, no permanent housing, no domesticated animals save dogs, and no higher political organisation of chiefs or kings. However, it was conceded that they had complex social organisation, marriage rules, initiation rites and vague notions of an after-life.

In 1927, the two-volume *Australian Encyclopaedia* was published, the first such local product. It contained a 22 000-word article on 'Aborigines' and others on Aboriginal words and music. Baldwin Spencer, whose opening section was couched in the language of social evolutionism, claimed Aborigines were 'the most archaic people extant and, in many respects, reveal the conditions under which the early ancestors of the race existed'.[19] He believed Aborigines had not been stimulated by competition with other races and ferocious animals to agricultural production and other intellectual developments. His introduction was followed by twelve specialised sections on Aboriginal origins, physical characteristics, social organisation, beliefs, customs, and weapons, most of which he wrote himself, with several by William Ramsey Smith, Head of the Department of Public Health in South Australia. Arguing against conventional wisdom, Smith stated that 'the Australian race is not degraded, physically, mentally or morally'. He described them in positive language as often tall and muscular, and with admiration concluded: 'one can hardly be said to have seen human grace of carriage who has not seen an aboriginal walk.' Smith claimed they 'are polite, proper in their behaviour, modest, unassuming, gay, fond of jokes and laughter, and skilful mimics'. They were also 'cheerful', 'honest', of 'high' morality and often 'show great courage'.[20] In the final section, 'Destiny', Smith referred to their deaths from disease, white violence, ill treatment and neglect, and alleged that indifference and neglect 'apart from some State pittance and a modicum of State supervision' still existed in the 1920s. Then, with an unusual sense of scientific fallibility, Smith concluded:

> To one who knows how the blackfellow even in a single lifetime reacts to new influences—moral, intellectual and mechanical—the facts seem to upset all theories of cranial capacities, cerebral functioning and mental operations. They raise the question, indeed, whether ordinary anthropological investigations and tests supply the kind and amount of evidence with which we credit them for elucidating the evolution of races and the relations of peoples.[21]

It is unlikely that such wisdom carried more weight than Baldwin Spencer's opening judgment that Aborigines were 'the most archaic people extant'.

School texts also conveyed powerful images of Aborigines, as much in the form of silences as what was actually said. The volume of the *Oxford Geographies* adapted for Australasian schools during and before the 1920s claimed Aborigines were few and diminishing in number, their origins were obscure and 'in their natural state they are a very primitive type'. Ignoring a whole world of Aboriginal land use, it added: 'One of the few points of importance connected with them in Australian geography is that many place-names are taken from their language.'[22] The Victorian school readers for grades one to eight, issued between 1928 and 1930 by the Victorian Department of Education, similarly included little material on Aborigines and portrayed them as treacherous savages or fading victims of the 'laws' of Social Darwinism.[23]

The *Sanitarium Children's Abbreviated Encyclopaedia*, a stapled, double-columned booklet of 100 000 words issued in 1946, was at the cheapest end of the compendium market. Probably more young eyes read and saw its enduring nineteenth-century images than any other text at the time on Aborigines, for this booklet was the Australian publishing sensation of the century. Over 600 000 copies were sold within a few weeks of publication in 1946, suggesting that one in five households possessed a copy.[24] The booklet could be enhanced by the addition of 60 coloured swap cards collected from Sanitarium breakfast foods: Weet Bix, Granose or Cerix, and health products. Its entry on 'Aborigines' ran to a sixth of a page out of 72 pages, about the same size as the following entry on 'acacia'. But unlike 'acacia' which had a swap card, it was accompanied by a black and white line drawing of two Aboriginal men making implements. The entry, echoing Baldwin Spencer's social evolutionary words, began: 'The Australian Aborigines are the oldest people extant and no members of the human family reveal more exactly the conditions under which primitive people existed before the dawn of civilisation.' Because they were unchallenged by dangerous animals, it continued, the Aborigines' only concern was to eat and live. They made 'neither mental nor physical attempt to produce in a material way' and 'lived on anything edible'. It added: 'even at the present time Aborigines in their native state wear no clothes, build no dwellings nor till the soil.'

The entry on 'Aborigines' in the second, 1951 edition of the *Sanitarium Children's Abbreviated Encyclopaedia* was longer than that on 'acacia', accompanied by a colour swap card showing Daisy Bates, author of *The Passing of the Aborigines* (1938) caring for Aborigines, and written in the categories of social rather than physical anthropology. It told young readers that Aborigines were divided into 680 tribes, themselves subdivided into clans and sections, each with their own laws, religion, songs, ceremonies and ways of collecting food. It described their tool kit and stated that 'Aborigines are skilful artists and craftsmen'. But after noting their population decline, without explanation, it concluded that 'these people are a dying race' despite the efforts of missionaries and others such as Daisy Bates. An article ostensibly on Aborigines had become a eulogy for white humanitarianism.

Yet, the change between the two editions was quite remarkable despite the failings of the later one. This partly reflected the publication in the late 1940s of another work in the Sanitarium Children's Library Series: *Aboriginal Tribes and Customs*. This 14-page book of 50 coloured swap cards was prepared by Frederick D. McCarthy, Curator of Anthropology at the Australian Museum, Sydney. It contained 200 words on each of 50 topics including: 'The Council of Elders', 'The Aboriginal Women', 'The Aboriginal Artists', as well as more predictable entries on material culture, food collecting and weaponry. There was even one entry on 'String Figures and Aboriginal Games' with a line drawing of a man marking a fur ball, like the Victorian Aboriginal game 'marngrook'.[25] Here was a people with a rich culture, a family life, leisure time, skills and land with boundaries shown on a map on the back page. It was masculinist, for the women received scant attention, and were said to have 'a hard and rather monotonous life' although they did have their own 'secret stories and dances'. And it was also essentialist inasmuch as no depiction of Aborigines other than the 'traditional' one was provided. But it was an advance on the former passive, 'have-not' view of the first *Sanitarium Children's Abbreviated Encyclopaedia*.

The Sanitarium Children's Library Series, except for the first volume, rested on changes in anthropology that emerged in the 1930s. In the generation or two before World War I ethnography in Australia had been the preserve of amateurs, but their work fuelled the writings of such eminent theorists as Andrew Lang, J.G. Frazer, Emile Durkheim, Sigmund Freud and Bronislaw Malinowski. However, with the decline of social evolutionary approaches to ethnography from the 1920s, Australia, which had been seen as the best field for observing humanity in a state of 'savagery and primitiveness', lost its primacy.[26] Despite the funding of Australia's first Chair of Anthropology at the University of Sydney in 1923 by the Rockefeller Foundation, fieldwork among Aborigines languished in the 1920s and 1930s. World War II saw funds dry up completely, and this drought lasted until the creation of the Australian Institute of Aboriginal Studies in 1961.[27]

Despite the paucity of funds, some classic studies were published from the 1930s to 1950s by W. Lloyd Warner, A.P. Elkin, T.G.H. Strehlow, D.H. Thomson and R.M. and C.H. Berndt. Elkin's work was the most influential of these at a popular level, and after succeeding A.R. Radcliffe-Brown to the Chair of Anthropology at Sydney University in 1933 he consolidated and expanded the discipline through his administrative skills and government contacts.[28] Elkin's *The Australian Aborigines: How to Understand Them* (1938) went through five editions, seven reprints and three European translations by 1974, as he expanded and updated it. This was a remarkable book for its time, ascribing a dignity and intellectual depth to Aboriginal culture when most Australians in the 1930s still considered Aborigines to be 'primitive savages' doomed to oblivion. For instance, Elkin's chapter on 'Aboriginal Philosophy, Rites and Beliefs' stated:

> the Aboriginal philosopher finds plenty of material on which to exercise his thought, his analytical powers, and his urge for systematic and logical construction. I shall take his place and endeavour to present a view of life and the world which is inherent in the conduct, beliefs and rites of the Aborigines of Australia.[29]

Aborigines were not only philosophers, for Elkin carefully outlined Aboriginal religion, totemism, social structure, family life, initiation and the secret life. In an expanded edition in 1954 he added chapters on art and ritual, music and dancing, sorcery and magic, and in 1970 a separate chapter on the relationship to the land.

It is easy to overlook the contemporary impact of the book in the light of Elkin's recently perceived failings which are evident in the passage cited above. Elkin had few doubts about his ability to 'take his place'—to know Aborigines and their culture—and he made vast general statements about 'the Aborigines of Australia'. In particular he conceived of Aboriginal culture as static and incapable of change, and so he believed it broke under the stress of culture contact, that the surviving people of mixed descent had no culture, and that their only salvation from a cultural void was assimilation.[30] Certainly Elkin's was the most influential voice in the formation of the new assimilation policy that held sway from the 1940s to the mid-1960s. He outlined his views in a number of pamphlets and a book, *Citizenship for the Aborigines* (1944). While this policy was an advance on those of the past in that it reflected democratic and humanist values, and promised Aborigines social, political and material equality, it was founded on residual social evolutionary assumptions: a belief in white superiority and the fitness of European culture alone for the modern world. Aborigines were to become like whites because that was best for them. Elkin, in god-like fashion, modelled culture contact in 1951 in a famous and oft-quoted article, claiming it led inexorably to assimilation and citizenship as long as whites assisted Aborigines to 'intelligently appreciate' European culture.[31]

The work of Elkin, his protégés and others, found a wide audience in the Sanitarium Series and through other such popular representations. For instance, in 1949 the UNESCO General Conference urged an exchange of exhibitions to foster cross-cultural understanding, and an Australian exhibition prepared over three years at the Australian Museum, Sydney, toured Australia, New Zealand and North America. Its accompanying brochure, *Australian Aboriginal Culture* (1953), containing 23 by now predictable social anthropological subjects, was reprinted twice, and sold 100 000 copies before new editions were prepared in 1973 and again in 1983 and 1989.

The transfer of specialist knowledge to a popular audience was most elaborate in the nine-volume second edition of the *Australian Encyclopaedia* (1958), which contained 104 two-columned pages on Aborigines, and other ancillary articles. Frederick McCarthy wrote most of the sections on material culture and Ronald and Catherine Berndt authored those on cultural anthropology. The last twenty pages included sections on contact history by Norman Tindale including one on frontier violence to 1930. Tindale's account was hopeful but shaped by the view 'that the future of half-caste Aborigines will be best served by their ultimate absorption into the general community'.[32] This stance reflected prevailing views, and in the late 1950s a flood of assimilationist literature with a pseudo-anthropological basis emanated from the Department of

Territories for use by the National Aborigines Day Observance Committee. Their intention can be gauged by the titles: *Our Aborigines* (1957); *Assimilation of Our Aborigines* (1958); *Fringe Dwellers* (1959); *One People* (1961) and *The Aborigines and You* (1963). In the 1960s research into Aboriginal matters boomed, especially after the establishment of the Australian Institute of Aboriginal Studies. Archaeological research in the 1960s pushed back the Aboriginal presence in Australia from 10 000 to 40 000 years, showed that ancient Aboriginal people were flexible in the face of massive environmental, climatic and sea-level changes, and revealed them to be technological innovators and practitioners of the earliest known art, cremation and symbolic use of ochre.[33] John Mulvaney in his *The Prehistory of Australia* (1969) opened with a challenge: 'the discoverers, explorers, and colonists of the three million square miles which are Australia, were its Aborigines . . . Their persons, social institutions and material equipment were cited as survivals from the dawn of mankind, exemplars of brutish savagery. The facts are otherwise.'[34] In the same decade, the publication of F.D. McCarthy and M. McArthur's 'The Food Quest and the Time Factor in Aboriginal Economic Life', part of the findings of the 1948 American–Australian Scientific Expedition to Arnhem Land, and an influential collection edited by R. Lee and J. De Vore, *Man the Hunter* (1968), led to arguments by Marshall Sahlins and others that Aborigines in pre-contact times had been 'affluent', dramatically inverting the view of Aborigines and other hunters and gatherers as miserable savages first posed by Jansz, Carstensz and Dampier.[35]

Anthropology (and archaeology) began to shake off the mantle of assimilationism by the 1970s and encourage more tolerant understanding of Aboriginal people. For instance, the section on Aborigines in the fourth edition of the *Australian Encyclopaedia* (1983) had been fully revised (under Mulvaney's editorship) 'to make it clear that European exploration and settlement took place in an already inhabited land'.[36] Its 63-page entry included a ten-page historical section written by Charles Rowley who was to initiate serious research in Aboriginal history. The Aborigines were not stereotyped in this edition but were presented through a diversity of images.

The generalist writing of historians in the 1950s and 1960s gradually reflected the advance in archaeological and anthropological knowledge. In 1952, Max Crawford, Professor of History at the University of Melbourne and a man who emphasised a moral conception of history, published *Australia*, the first general history this century to give Aborigines their own chapter. Based on the writings of Elkin, Strehlow, Thomson and earlier works by Spencer and Gillen, Crawford gave a sensitive account of traditional Aboriginal culture, emphasising the power of religion, lore and tradition. But despite being a student of change in human affairs, he dutifully followed Elkin and Strehlow, seeing Aboriginal culture as static: 'Established tradition gave certainty and security, but robbed the natives of invention and initiative.'[37] Crawford also argued that the first settlers missed the strengths of Aboriginal culture because Aboriginal social organisation and cohesion were outwardly invisible. And he emphasised the strength of attachment to land in a fine piece of writing: 'So may be realised his love of home. He knew the land and the species that grew and lived on it; he knew, in greater or less degree, its legendary history and its spiritual inhabitants; and, in the sense that he and his fellows were identical with their ancestors, it was their own creation.'[38] The Aborigines, however, did not enter into the rest of Crawford's history, except in three paragraphs on frontier violence, which he believed was caused by mutual misunderstandings and white brutality. Crawford still echoed late nineteenth-century social evolutionary thinking, writing: 'it is clear that two cultures were meeting which could not both survive.'[39] Nonetheless, he called for further research on frontier relations.

A.G.L. Shaw, at the University of Sydney, learnt Crawford's lesson by reading Elkin as well. In his opening to *The Story of Australia* (1955) he covered some of the same prehistory as Crawford, albeit with less sensitivity and detail, compressed as his account was into three pages. Shaw was steeped in primary sources and had read E.J.B. Foxcroft's *Australian Native Policy* (1941) and Paul Hasluck's *Black Australians* (1942), two of a handful of histories published in the first half of the twentieth century which dealt with relations between Aborigines and Europeans. However, Shaw wrote only a few lines on colonial culture contact, although he did include an enlightened page on the Aboriginal condition in the 1930s.

Gordon Greenwood, Professor of History and Political Science at the University of Queensland, did not learn the same lesson from Crawford. *Australia: A Social and Political History* (1955), which he edited and which was sponsored by the 1951 Jubilee Celebrations Committee, contained no index reference to Aborigines and only half-a-dozen oblique references in the whole book. F.K. Crowley's first chapter on the foundation years mentioned Aboriginal people twice and then as being no serious impediment to settlement. Instead, he judged that 'the most characteristic feature of the Australian Colonies during the foundation years was undoubtedly the punishment of convicts',[40] and the chapter on pastoralism managed to squeeze Aborigines out of the obligatory catalogue of dangers facing the squatters. The remaining chapters were equally silent on Aborigines as if a conscious decision to exclude them had been made. Greenwood's *Australia* was reprinted until 1977 and read by cohorts of students studying Australian history in schools and universities in the 1960s. Douglas Pike's *Australia: The Quiet Continent* (1962) did little better. Following an earlier historiography, Aborigines appear as foils to explorers, either as trouble or as faithful unnamed helpers. Pike's subtitle harked back to nineteenth-century images as well, for 'here was no cradle of civilisation . . . no local battles or revolutions disturbed this peaceful isolation'.[41] Like other popular works of the period, it was a view with no clear eye to black–white encounters in this country.[42]

The legacy of Crawford flowered in Manning Clark who moved from a lectureship at the University of Melbourne, to a professorship at the Canberra University College (later the Australian National University) in 1949. His two volumes of *Select Documents in Australian History* (1950 and 1955) made only fleeting references to Aborigines, notably encounters with First Fleeters, John Batman and the Myall Creek murderers. The opening volume of his *A History of Australia* (1962) contained numerous references to Aborigines who, in the Clark mode, were often allowed to speak for themselves but who were also posed as inflexible conservatives who passively suffered the fatal impact:

> the failure of the aborigines to emerge from a state of barbarism deprived them of the material resources with which to resist an invader, and left them without the physical strength to protect their culture. Other peoples have recovered from the destruction of their culture, but that of the aborigines was to wither in contact with other races; for the aborigine was also endowed with a tenacious, if not unique inability to detect meaning in any way of life other than his own, and by one of those ironies of human affairs it was this very inability to live outside the framework of his own culture that prevented any subsequent invaders from using the aborigine for their own purposes.[43]

Clark's *A Short History of Australia* (1963), which was devoid of these unfortunate and erroneous generalisations about conservatism and staticness, saved students from the silences of Greenwood by commencing the great task of writing Aborigines into Australian history. Whereas his mentor Crawford had recognised Aboriginal culture and prehistory, Clark peppered his short history with brief, but pertinent, glimpses of Aborigines and their relations with whites. This stemmed from his interest in drama, humanist values, and in presenting voices of the past. In Clark's account, Phillip's arrival into Sydney Cove was jeered by Aborigines who made 'angry gestures with sticks and stones', and they also fought settlers for the 'theft' of their land. Clark traced government policy from Macquarie's Native Institution at Parramatta, through Governor Arthur's 'black line' in Van Diemen's Land, to the failed Port Phillip Protectorate, a humanitarian–pastoralist struggle over policy which Clark dramatised through the Myall Creek massacre and trials. Just as importantly, he presented some Aboriginal voices and actions: One Aboriginal man at Macquarie's Parramatta feast 'burst out laughing, leapt in the air, and made other wild gesticulations'; Wylie, ever the one-dimensional faithful companion of Eyre, is shown 'greeted with "wordless weeping pleasure" by his own people'; and as Dame Nellie Melba sang 'God Save the Queen' at the opening of Parliament in 1927 an Aboriginal man demanded to see the 'whole plurry show' but was led away.[44] These were only snippets and were utilised for the sake of dramatic effect and as a foil to European stories, but it was like a breath of fresh air.

The postwar changes emerging in historical representations of Aborigines can also be well illustrated by the case of Russel Ward. Ward's literary training, and socialist and Marxist leanings, resulted in the writing of an extraordinary history about the origins and development of the Australian self-image, *The Australian Legend* (1958). His interest in social history from below led him to make some remarkable observations about Aborigines, spelt with a capital 'A', unlike the usage adopted in contemporaneous works by Crawford, Shaw and Clark. Furthermore, while Ward was attacked later by Mervyn Hartwig for denying the presence of racial intolerance and racial ideology in pre-1850 Australia,[45] he did not shy away from acknowledging any killings or the spread of venereal disease by whites. He also argued that Aborigines, or at least Aboriginal men, exercised some control over whites in sexual transactions. And, in a little noted passage—'If, as has been argued, the bushman's esprit de corps sprang largely from his adaptation to, and mastery of, the outback environment, then the Aborigine was his master and mentor'[46]—Ward raised the novel idea of Aboriginal influences on whites, thereby reversing the usual conception of cultural change.

Several years later, Ward wrote his first general history, *Australia: A Short History* (1965), for the American undergraduate market. He revised it in 1982 as *Australia Since the Coming of Man*, adding three themes 'barely mentioned in the *Short History*, or in other general histories of Australia—the doings of Aborigines, of explorers and of the female half of the Australian people; and it examines the relationship of each group with the dominant, white, male establishment'. Ward continued his radical manifesto, writing: 'I am for the weak not the strong, the poor not the rich, the

exploited many not the select few.'[47] Ward opened his treatment of
Aborigines with a long discussion of the latest archaeological
thinking on the origins, migration, cultural diffusion and technological changes of ancient Aboriginal people. He portrayed a
dynamic culture stretching back, he claimed, probably 100 000
years, and characterised this society as a 'primitive communism', a
classless, egalitarian society, except for gender relations—an image
that was not to him anti-modern, but (following W.E.H. Stanner)
simply another human path. However, the Aboriginal penchant for
co-operation and conciliation, and their inferior weapons ill-
equipped them to deal with the European invaders. Thereafter, he
posed Aborigines as victims of 'vicious racism' on the frontier, dupes
of Batman, and people deprived of welfare rights by the early
Commonwealth. Yet Ward also presented them as activists in the
tent embassy of 1972 and in land rights campaigns. They also
featured in many photographs in this heavily-illustrated history. And
just as Ward opened his history with Aborigines, he closed it with
an account of how the Western Australian Liberal Party deprived
Aborigines of votes in the 1977 state election, but ultimately lost
the seat in a subsequent poll to an Aboriginal candidate Ernie
Bridge.

   Ward's writing of Aborigines into Australian history is more
evident in his recent book, *Finding Australia: The History of
Australia to 1821* (1987). Aborigines occupy the first 74 of this
413-page book and appear on more than 40 other pages; in all
they claim a quarter of the book. His first chapter extends his 1982
discussion of the archaeological record in sophisticated ways, based
on extensive reading in the literature. His second chapter focuses
on technological change, language, customs and social organisation
just prior to first contact. The remainder of the book contains
significant discussion of cultural encounters both brutal and
humane. Aborigines appear as victims but also as active subjects.
They incorporate white castaways, and return others, resist
Christianising efforts and experiment with new economies on government farms. Ward again ends with a culture encounter: a visit
by Governor Lachlan and Mrs Macquarie on their last day in the
colony to Boongaree and his people at the George's Head farm
which Macquarie had granted them. Australia's finest governor
chose to spend three of his last precious hours with his 'Sable
friends' as he called them. Ward had captured a fine cross-cultural
moment.[48]

   The journey from Ernest Scott's brief concern for a dying race
to Russel Ward's more detailed account of Aboriginal pioneers and
negotiators is conceptually a long one. In what ways, I now wish
to consider, have specialist historians shaped this journey and, more

specifically, the context of the Mabo decision?[49] There was only a trickle of specific historical work about Aborigines in the 1940s and 1950s, most notably Hasluck and Foxcroft's works noted above, Clive Turnbull's *Black War* (1948) and the survey by John Mulvaney of European views of Aborigines since 1606.[50] To be fair, academic history was only getting into stride in the 1960s after its small beginnings in the 1940s; the first academic appointment in Australian history was not made until 1948 with European and British history remaining the core of university studies until the 1960s.[51] Moreover, the Australian Institute of Aboriginal Studies which began to fund research in 1961 did not take an interest in contact history until the early 1970s. However, in 1963 the Social Sciences Research Council funded the 'Aborigines in Australia Project' headed by Charles Rowley, and it published more than a dozen works, some of them historical in nature. The most important of these was Rowley's seminal and mammoth trilogy, *Aboriginal Policy and Practice* (1970–1971), largely a historical work,[52] which established the field of Aboriginal history.

Rowley argued that colonial administrators failed Aborigines by attempting to civilise and Christianise them through special laws and institutions, and by their inability to protect them from rapacious settlers. Indeed, official punitive expeditions at times assisted settler violence. Rowley condemned the past silences about Aborigines, and called for a historical interest in Aborigines that would inform policy makers about Australia's past race relations and recognise Aboriginal resistance.

Rowley's work inspired younger historians, including Raymond Evans, Henry Reynolds, Michael Christie, Noel Loos and Lyndall Ryan, to address the themes of white violence and Aboriginal actions.[53] Evans' account of the Queensland frontier initially revealed the savagery and terror there, driven by racial stereotypes and frontier opportunity. Christie argued for a deliberate attempt by pastoralists to exterminate the Aborigines of Port Phillip, and also a strong Aboriginal resistance and a significant political opposition during institutionalisation. Loos documented a vigorous Aboriginal resistance on the North Queensland frontier. Ryan similarly researched the strong Aboriginal resistance to pastoralism in Tasmania, and, meeting the Cape Barren Island people, also documented their survival in order to counter the myth of Tasmanian Aboriginal extinction. And Reynolds argued for a variety of Aboriginal strategies—resistance, accommodation and appropriation—in the face of the European presence. All these historians made contact with Aboriginal people which informed and politicised their histories as Rowley had hoped.

In 1980 I wrote a concise synthesis of this recent research which has since been reprinted annually and is now in a second edition.[54] At the same time, Reynolds wrote *The Other Side of the Frontier*,[55] a classic work which revealed how traditional ideas of reciprocity, sorcery, exchange, and so forth, shaped the active and varied responses of Aboriginal people to Europeans on the frontier. This work dispelled the passive image of Aboriginal people and brought them to the centre of frontier history. While Reynolds characterised the frontier as violent, his book also contained seeds of a new paradigm—that of accommodation—which was signalled by Bob Reece in 1987[56] and elaborated by Ann McGrath and Marie Fels in works on the Territory's cattle frontier and the Port Phillip Native Police,[57] as well as by Reynolds in his later study, *With the White People* (1990). The other notable book of the 1980s was Noel Butlin's *Our Original Aggression* (1983), a work of theorising the likely Aboriginal pre-contact population levels. It encouraged the authors of the first volume of the bicentenary history, *Australians: An Historical Library*[58] to suggest a pre-contact figure of 750 000, double the traditional estimate (while Butlin in a posthumous work *Economics and the Dreamtime* (1993) has argued for an estimated pre-1788 Aboriginal population of 1.25 million people).[59]

Landmark histories of the last decade all bear the imprint of the new perspectives in Aboriginal history, often because the practitioners of this new sub-discipline also wrote for these mammoth works. For instance, there is a marked imprint in the multi-volume *Australians: An Historical Library*, especially as Reynolds, Tim Rowse, Andrew Markus, McGrath and others were contributors. The first of the five 'slice' volumes, *Australians to 1788*, is devoted almost entirely to Aboriginal prehistory. The other four 'slices' contained approximately ten to thirty per cent of Aboriginal material depending on the volume. One of its bicentennial rivals, the four-volume *A People's History of Australia Since 1788* (1988), devoted between 10 and 20 per cent of its space to Aboriginal people. Similarly, Aborigines and Aboriginal people are well represented in recent state sesquicentenary histories: *Aborigines of the West* (1979), the three-volume *Victorians* (1984), and the three-volume *Flinders History of South Australia* (1987). Aboriginal history penetrated local and regional history in the 1980s,[60] and even the Australian War Memorial's bicentenary history of Australia.[61] By the 1980s it was difficult to read any significant work of Australian social and political history without encountering Aboriginal people, and increasingly they were actors in history, not passive victims.

Most of these histories used Aboriginal history to reflect in part on Australian society and culture. For instance, in my preface to

Aboriginal Australians I linked my history directly with our self-knowledge as Australians:

> If we as Australians are to face the future confidently, we must be
> fully aware of the forces that have shaped the Australian experi-
> ence. We must know ourselves. The study of Aboriginal history is
> an important part of that self-knowledge . . .
>   Race relations in Australia have often been a raw history of
> European dominance over Aborigines due to superior numbers,
> resources and firepower. Both peoples have been changed and dis-
> torted by this struggle for power. The Aborigines have been
> denigrated and oppressed, while the Europeans have generally
> assumed the dehumanised role of oppressors, and have had a false
> sense of their own superiority. All Australians must see their history
> for what it was, and is, before any mature Australian outlook can
> develop.[62]

Earlier, Bernard Smith in his 1980 Boyer Lectures had identified the presence of guilt within Australian society, as the 'locked cupboard' of our colonial past was opened and Australians were 'caught out as it were red-handed playing the genocide game', and called for 'atonement' for these crimes.[63] Other historians have expressed these sentiments in impassioned histories. For example, in *Caledonia Australis: Scottish Highlanders on the Frontier of Australia* (1984) Don Watson, an admirer of Manning Clark, traced the rise of the Scots at the expense of the Aborigines of Gippsland, claiming that, 'far from being inevitable, the destruction of Kurnai society was gratuitous and grotesque'.[64]

It was significant that on being elected Prime Minister in December 1991 Paul Keating appointed Watson as his speech writer. His sense of vision on Aboriginal affairs has undoubtedly been enhanced by Watson's presence. This is best reflected in Keating's December 1992 speech at Redfern to herald the International Year for Indigenous People, in which he stated that Australia's treatment of Aboriginal people would be the litmus test of Australian democracy and of our self-knowledge. Australians must recognise Aboriginal Australians as part of themselves: 'We cannot give indigenous Australians up without giving up many of our most deeply held values, much of our own identity—and our own humanity.' In this unprecedented official speech by an Australian Prime Minister, and one that owes much to the work of historians I have outlined, Keating continued in this powerful vein:

> We took the traditional lands and smashed the traditional way of
> life. We brought the diseases. The alcohol. We committed the mur-
> ders. We took the children from their mothers. We practised
> discrimination and exclusion. It was our ignorance and our preju-
> dice. And our failure to imagine these things being done to us.

With some noble exceptions, we failed to make the most basic
human response and enter into their hearts and minds.

Rather than feed the unconstructive emotion of guilt, Keating
believed we must now 'open our hearts': 'Mabo is an historic
decision—we can make it an historic turning point, the basis of a
new relationship between indigenous and non-Aboriginal Australians.'[65]

Keating, Watson and other Australian historians are by no
means alone in their expression of these sentiments, for in nationalist discourse generally in recent years Aborigines have been
appropriated by others concerned with national self-knowledge and
guilt. Andrew Lattas has drawn attention to the redemptive function
some nationalists have imposed on Aborigines: the Christ-like suffering of Aborigines 'is meant to restore settler Australians to a lost
sacred moral order'. It is also believed that Aborigines and their
religion can teach 'white settler Australians to view the land as their
mother'. Indeed, as Lattas argues, 'Aborigines are used to confer
and establish a unique identity for Australian culture and for the
Australian nation'.[66]

In the High Court Mabo ruling it is undeniable that Justices
Deane and Gaudron reflect in their judgment the new historical
knowledge about Aborigines as well as the themes of guilt, recognition and self-knowledge. They stated that 'if this were an ordinary
case' the Court could not be justified in re-opening fundamental
assumptions about the property law of Australia over the past 200
years; however, the circumstances of the case were unique, they
argued, for the dispossession of Aboriginal land 'constitutes the
darkest aspect of the history of this nation' and the subsequent
'conflagration of oppression and conflict' left 'a national legacy of
unutterable shame'. 'The nation as a whole', they concluded, 'must
remain diminished unless and until there is an acknowledgment of,
and retreat from, those past injustices'.[67]

Justices Toohey and Brennan have also had more than a
nodding acquaintance with the new Aboriginal histories. As the
Northern Territory's Aboriginal Land Commissioner from 1977 to
1982, Toohey spent days on end sympathetically listening to Aboriginal historical testimony about their land rights, while one might
conjecture that Brennan, who wrote the lead judgment, was familiar
with recent historical arguments through the work of his son, Fr
Frank Brennan, author of Sharing the Country (1992) and several
other works on land rights.

Until the 1950s histories, encyclopaedias and other popular works,
informed by social evolutionary ideas, represented Aborigines as a
primitive and passive people. From the 1950s new social, political

and intellectual forces, some of which were evident in the case of Bill Bull, urged historians to imagine Aborigines in new ways that increasingly brought Aborigines to the centre of Australian history as active subjects. General histories of Australia and other historical works reflected these new perspectives that were refined in the new sub-discipline of Aboriginal history and in turn shaped new ways of thinking about Aboriginal people in schools, universities, the media and all parts of Australian society. While land rights had been unimaginable in the 1950s, they were increasingly the subject of legislation in the 1970s. The courts were not immune to these new imaginings which penetrated to the very heart of the common law. The six affirming judges of the High Court in the Mabo case all graduated between 1950 and 1965, a time when there was a sea-change in white Australians' conceptions of Aboriginal Australians. Their unidentified associates in the case are younger. As the judges grew up in the law, historians, as I have shown, built up a corpus of knowledge about Aboriginal history, challenged the silences, and discredited *terra nullius*, such that in 1992, in the face of the historical testimony of the Murray Islanders themselves, the judges believed they could no longer uphold the fictions of the past.

5 Creating a post-Mabo archaeology of Australia[1]

Tim Murray

In September 1994, the inaugural meeting of the European Association of Archaeologists was held in Ljubljana in the Republic of Slovenia. For students of things post-modern, the location of the conference and the fact that its primary focus was on exploring the ways in which archaeological research has abetted the creation of European identity, it all had a pleasing symmetry. But underlying all the talk about archaeology and European identity, which actually began late in 1992 at the Theoretical Archaeology Group meetings in Southampton, was a serious discussion of how European societies could defend themselves against the resurgence of micro-nationalism, fascism and anti-semitism, and the revisionist archaeology which has supported them.[2]

Much of this resurgence has only received very superficial reporting in the Australian media. There has been little comprehensive analysis of a social and political force which is common in Central and Eastern Europe, and becoming increasingly common in the West. Even allowing for local differences, it is possible to see an emphasis on mystical notions of ethnic essentialism which are strongly reminiscent of nineteenth-century romanticism. It is also possible to see in this resurgence of the irrational a tendency to revise history so that it might cease to buttress opposing views, for example, that ethnic groups are not timeless essences but are instead the products of real historical forces. Discussion now turns on this debate between history and non-history, between change and timelessness. This discussion has the very clear purpose of either supporting or rejecting the notion that different racial and/or ethnic groups must inevitably be in conflict, and that such conflicts are fuelled by a history of racial or ethnic struggle for domination.[3]

It is difficult to contemplate these events without despair. Surely the history of the Third Reich should provide ample justification for burying anti-semitism forever and refusing to allow the print media to promote gross distortions of archaeological pasts because they glorified the nation, but this is not the case, especially in Eastern Europe and in the former Soviet Union. The Slovenian archaeologist Bozidar Slapsak has recently provided an example of this last activity from Bosnia in the mid 1980s, at a time when this 'model' multi-ethnic state officially favoured no particular nationality. He relates the case of a Mexican amateur historian who seriously argued that the medieval fort of Gabela in the Neretva Valley, Bosnia, was in fact the site of Homer's Troy. Even though the Mexican was vigorously attacked by archaeologists and linguists, the Bosnian Government (and the press) showered him with honours and steadfastly declined even to debate the matter with scholars.[4] The Bosnian Government (and by extension the Bosnian people) wanted their link to the glorious Classical past for precisely the same reasons that Geoffrey of Monmouth derived his Britons from Troy in a British history published over 700 years earlier.[5]

The sense of history repeating itself, of the veneer of tolerance and understanding being so easily stripped away even after we have all seen ample evidence of the terrible consequences of racism, is difficult to avoid. But if the European Association of Archaeologists is to succeed in defending European societies against what it terms misuses of archaeology, it must first concentrate on resolving a particularly thorny problem. Re-reading Gordon Childe's passionate attacks on the misuses of archaeological concepts and categories by Nazi archaeologists,[6] one is struck by the fact that the real difference between the Nazis and Childe was not methodological but interpretative. Many of the assumptions which underwrote Kossinna's Teutonocentric prehistory of Europe were also central to Childe's quite different vision of European society. I am referring to those assumptions which flowed from the core claim of archaeology that race, language, and culture are intimately linked, and that this model of linkage powers most of the inferences of social and cultural process during prehistory. It is worth noting that even in 1933 this was a false assumption—indeed, in 1865 the philologist Max Mueller demonstrated that there is no necessary link between these elements.[7]

This chapter is not the place for a detailed exegesis about why Mueller was ignored, but I can assert that twentieth-century sociocultural archaeology would have been stopped dead in its tracks if the linkage had been denied and its implications pondered. An unintelligible European past would have weakened the claims of nations and ethnic groups, and historicised Europe in a way which

would have made it impossible to incorporate archaeological knowledge into what was then conventional knowledge about Europe.
However, one of the consequences of ignoring Mueller's advice (and
of accepting Childe's vision of Europe) was that concepts central
to that vision (ethnicity, for example) remained grossly under-
theorised, and hence extremely difficult to assess archaeologically.[8]
They remain so today, notwithstanding their crucial interpretative
role and the 'abuses' which have flowed from such over-determina-
tion.

Thus, the thorny task for the European Association of Archaeologists is to accept that much of the public plausibility of
archaeology has been built on untenable assumptions about ethnicity and history. If they do this then they also have to accept that
if they are to assist Europe in defending itself against fascism and
racism, they will have to underwrite a thoroughgoing re-evaluation
of archaeology itself. Whether they have the courage to do this—to
gamble the support they have from a public which has hitherto
been well-pleased with an intelligible and accessible European past
so that they can excise its most unsavoury expressions—remains to
be seen. Perhaps they will conclude that the price may be too high
to pay and that archaeology might simply have to define itself in
terms of this antinomy between its dark and light sides, just as
Europe may have to.

Turning from the problems encountered when one seeks to
re-evaluate the archaeology of Europe to those raised by writing
the archaeology of Aboriginal Australia, one is struck by a sense
of similarity rather than of difference. In both cases practitioners
have engaged in writing the archaeology of timeless essences, either
ethnic or Aboriginal. In both cases the need for knowledge about
the past which does not challenge the authority of contemporary
experience has meant that history has become a hostage to the
present.

In this chapter I want to reflect on these issues of identity and
history and, by doing so, explore some of the intellectual and
political terrain of a post-Mabo archaeology of Australia. I will do
this by first establishing what I consider to be the two most
important goals for that archaeology, and then by outlining some
of the obstacles which will have to be overcome before we can
reach them. Much of what I will say will turn on the power of
archaeology to provide counter-intuitive information about pre-
European aboriginal Australia, and the challenge this poses to
Aboriginal and non-Aboriginal people in framing meaningful defi-
nitions of Aboriginality. For my present purpose I will characterise
that power as both 'another way of telling', and as an open field
of discourse about the meaning of the human history of Australia.

This challenge is only partially captured by debate about the human history of Australia. Of equal importance is the challenge posed by the ownership of culture, specifically the questions raised by an Aboriginal control of access to items and contexts defined as being Aboriginal heritage and by the repatriation of that heritage to Aboriginal communities.[9] My discussion of these matters will be necessarily brief and anecdotal because our understanding of these implications of the post-Mabo environment is still quite rudimentary.[10] Nonetheless, it is clear that significant differences of opinion have begun to arise among archaeologists (and between archaeologists and Aboriginal people) about major issues such as censorship and academic freedom, and whether Aborigines' power to destroy items and contexts defined as being part of Aboriginal heritage should be limited by the State. These obstacles have to be overcome too, and it is a core claim of this essay that both types of obstacles are made all the more difficult when both archaeologists and Aboriginal people trade in the currency of essentialism.

I have begun this discussion with Europe for two reasons: first, because so much of the conceptual fabric of Australian archaeology is European and was designed to serve European ends. Although it seems certain that Australian archaeology has also served Australian ends (in the sense that it has been a part of a cultural apparatus which dominated Aboriginal Australia), it has done so without transforming the basic conceptual package it inherited. Second, because in Europe archaeology and identity are so closely linked, and the conflict between history and essentialism being re-encountered there is also being experienced in Australia. Part of the reason for this has to do with the common set of concepts and categories deployed by archaeologists in either place, another (perhaps more important) part is the difficulty of avoiding teleology when discussing identities.

Given our own pressing need to create an archaeology capable of critical self-reflection about its place in Australian society there is no reason why we have to recommit to the traditions of colonial science and wait for Europe to find a pathway through these very challenging problems. I will argue that both archaeologists and Aboriginal people have to avoid falling into the trap of conceptualising cultures with long historic and prehistoric traditions as essences, which in remote antiquity exhibited all the distinguishing features of Australian societies noted at contact. It will be my broad contention that notwithstanding some very positive outcomes—the timeless essence frequently being claimed for 'the world's oldest culture' has served as a basis for pride and recognition for both European and Aboriginal Australia, and acted to connect the survivors of the holocaust of the European conquest of Australia to their forebears—this local essentialism has a significant downside. This contention leads me to the goals of a post-Mabo archaeology of Australia.

First, such an archaeology will allow us to comprehend the archaeology of the continent (both pre-European and contact) in a way which acknowledges that Aboriginal societies have histories, and which also acknowledges that despite the fact that there were very real differences between the Aboriginal world of the eighteenth and nineteenth century and that of previous millennia, this is all properly the heritage of contemporary Aboriginal people. Second, this archaeology will be founded on the recognition that Aboriginal people will have custodial rights over the physical remains of past human action, and play the principal role in the management of Aboriginal heritage. It will also be founded on the recognition that other groups have rights and interests in that heritage, especially in its interpretation and explanation. A post-Mabo archaeology of Australia will be polyvocal, then, and the Australian public will be able to make an informed choice between competing accounts of the past; one that will not be founded on the censorship of unpopular views.

It goes without saying that as yet these goals are not generally held either by Aboriginal people or by archaeologists. Indeed, we are still a long way off creating an environment conducive to attaining them. I have already mentioned that the major obstacles in our path are the unresolved conflicts among archaeologists, and between Aboriginal people and archaeologists. I shall now deal with aspects of each in turn.

Rethinking the archaeology of Australia

In the past eight years our understanding of the archaeology of Australia has changed beyond recognition. Antiquity of occupation has been pushed back to between 50 000 and 60 000 years (although this is being vigorously debated within the profession),[11] hundreds of sites have been excavated and clear evidence of regional variation from 30 000 years ago has thereby come to light,[12] and a much needed refocussing of attention onto the Aboriginal archaeology of the nineteenth and twentieth centuries has begun.[13] These discoveries and re-orientations have also created stress within the conceptual fabric of Australian archaeology. Some practitioners have responded to the longer chronology by simply arguing that Aboriginal people have been doing Aboriginal things for even longer. Others have taken a much more radical view that a high level of variability and regionalism, when allied to a much clearer understanding of the extent to which northern Australia has been open rather than isolated, leads us to rethink the history of Aboriginal Australia as being marked by discontinuities as much as by continuities.[14] The latter view has also led to more intensified attacks on the viability of contact ethnographies, ethnohistories, and ethnoarchaeology as reliable bases for direct extrapolation to the deeper past.[15] Finally, an intensified interest in the historical archaeology of Aboriginal Australia is forcing a reconsideration of the almost talismanic power of 'old' sites and the search for high human antiquity in Australia.[16]

I have previously remarked that Australian archaeologists have been much less active in exploring changing images of Aboriginality than have anthropologists or historians.[17] This is particularly evident when one notes the lack of attention paid to the historical archaeology of Aboriginal Australia, where an archaeological dimension to pathbreaking Aboriginal histories has largely been non-existent. Given the fact that the issues raised by carrying out that archaeology have rarely been discussed, it is difficult to produce a definitive explanation for the lopsided profile of archaeological activity in Australia. Nonetheless, when we consider the traditions of Australian archaeology, some obvious points can be made which might bring us closer to our goal.

The first point stems from a still widespread view that the most interesting archaeological problems are those associated with charting the very long human history of the continent. These are problems (and this is history) on the epic scale—matters of colonisation, settlement, changing ecologies and technologies, and real variations in material culture and subsistence patterns. The great tradition of discovery archaeology begun in the 1960s gave rise in some quarters to a view that the most interesting archaeological problems were those solved primarily by excavation rather than by recourse to written documents, as if somehow the presence of such additional sources of information was 'cheating'. Historical archaeology generally has suffered from this view, which is now collapsing because fewer archaeologists accept the absurd proposition that written documents used by archaeologists are not also archaeological data.

The second point is rather more significant and deals with the problem of identifying aboriginal people after the initial phase of contact has occurred. This reflects the fact that (as noted in examples from North America) on the basis of material culture it is thought to be extremely difficult, if not impossible, to differentiate between post-contact aboriginal assemblages and those of poor Europeans. Thus, after the phase where new materials (such as ceramic insulators, bottle glass or steel hatchets) have been adopted by people still leading substantially 'traditional' lives, it has been thought that Aboriginal people literally became archaeologically invisible. However, although substantive tests of this view have not yet appeared, some archaeologists have acknowledged that the possibility of tracking the cultural trajectories of aboriginal societies from the last thousand or so years through the contact phase should, in theory at least, allow a more long-term perspective to the investigation of aboriginal responses to contact. Thus, the distinction which has been created between archaeology and pre-contact aboriginal people on the one hand, and historical archaeology and post-contact aboriginal people on the other, now seems to be losing definition.

The third point relates to the fact that up to recent times the international discourse of world prehistory has been most interested in charting the settlement of the globe by fully modern human beings and in documenting behavioural variability within that species. Indeed, the early human history of Australia has gained great world significance as part of that primarily European discourse. But this research programme too is now changing and developing a broader focus to include investigations of the historical archaeology of indigenous peoples on a global scale. Depending on one's viewpoint this development might be seen as a positive consequence of indigenising archaeology, or simply as another form of colonialist discourse as the successors of European empires possess their indigenous populations anew.

The final point derives from the fact that the practice of ethnoarchaeology, which was flourishing at the same time as the discipline of archaeology was professionalised in Australia in the 1960s, has meant that the ethnographic image of contemporary aboriginal societies has played a fundamental role in the interpretation of the deeper Aboriginal past of Australia.[18] I am by no means the first to observe that this focus on ethnography, as providing an exemplar of the scale and detail of knowledge required to underwrite a meaningful reconstruction of past societies, has created significant tensions within Australian archaeology. Not only are there now real questions about whether archaeologists can ever sensibly reconstruct to that level of detail; there remains the more vexed question of whether we can approach the archaeology of Australia as if it were all a long prelude to the creation of the kinds of aboriginal societies noted at contact. Archaeologists are growing increasingly comfortable with the notion that there was significant change in pre-European Australian history, brought about as much by factors which we might consider to be internal to those societies, as by more large-scale external factors such as climatic and environmental change. The notion that members of aboriginal societies of very high antiquity may well have exercised choice about a whole range of matters from subsistence to technology has begun to have a profoundly liberating effect on the imaginations of Australian practitioners.

These aspects of archaeological discourse about the deeper past of Australia raise questions about how archaeologists of previous generations could conceptualise change beyond models of population replacement and mass migration. These models implicitly accepted the notion of a discontinuous Aboriginal past, but at the same time their understanding of such societies was based on the contemporary aboriginal experience as revealed by ethnography. Although loudly protesting that contact societies were not pristine exemplars of an unchanged state, these archaeologists have in fact treated them as such. There is an obvious (and unresolved) paradox here which could only be accommodated if the need for a pristine end-point to the pre-European human history of Australia overcame the fact that change was self-evident in those societies. Perhaps too, there was an unconscious response to dispossession in that it was thought that the very Aboriginality of those who had survived the holocaust had been hopelessly compromised, and they were therefore of no further interest. Perhaps there was also the view that as the present was firmly non-Aboriginal, the only future was non-Aboriginal too. The search for the essential aborigine might thus be seen as a denial of Aboriginal history, a denial of a sense of 'survival through transformation' wherein surviving Aboriginal people could reconstitute their Aboriginality and thus continue into the future.

It is possibly only a straightforward case of synchronicity that archaeological approaches to the Aboriginal past are beginning to be sensitive to history at around the same time that the social and cultural contexts of archaeological knowledge have changed too. Nonetheless, we should be very clear that one of the major reasons for this rethinking of the archaeology of Aboriginal Australia are the discoveries of archaeologists themselves, discoveries which are not as plastic or as socially constructed as the opinions of cultural theorists. It is also worth emphasising that this sensitivity to history also carries with it a much more developed understanding of the very great differences between the kinds of histories archaeologists can write about pre-contact aboriginal Australia, and those produced by historians and anthropologists of the contact and post-contact periods. Thus, the potential for archaeology to destabilise the concepts and categories of others now extends into the constitution of history itself.

However, there are ideas and practices which act to undermine this attack upon the essential Aborigine and the authority of contemporary images of Aboriginality as reliable guides to the deeper past. There are significant numbers of archaeologists who still believe that the object of archaeology is to write the histories of Aboriginal societies noted at contact. There are also valid reasons to emphasise continuity and the notion of 'the world's oldest culture', especially if one is seeking to establish the world heritage significance of major sites or regions such as Mungo (where the skeletal remains of one of the oldest known human cremations are held) or Stage III of Kakadu National Park. Indeed the notions of continuity and timelessness are still central to the public perception of Aboriginal Australia, and changing these will require a willingness to accept that archaeologists can frequently produce counter-intuitive information about the human history of Australia and to use this information rather than to reject it as simply the creation of positivist colonial science.

Aspects of ownership and control

In many instances an atmosphere of fear and suspicion clouds relationships between Aboriginal people and archaeologists, and between archaeologists and heritage managers. However, at the level of contact between individual archaeologists (or departments of archaeology) and Aboriginal communities, close consultation has acted to resolve some conflicts. Professional archaeological associations such as the Australian Archaeological Association and the Australian Association of Consulting Archaeologists have codes of ethics which explicitly state that archaeologists acknowledge that Aboriginal people own their pasts. Legislation is now predicated on this principle, and institutions such as the Australian Heritage Commission have devoted considerable effort to improve access by Aboriginal people to government heritage bodies.[19]

Among practitioners there is substantial disagreement about whether 'ownership of the past' means that Aboriginal people also own the interpretations, explanations, theories, concepts, and categories which actually create pasts. Most academic (research) archaeologists insist upon the difference between archaeological data and Aboriginal heritage, in the sense that they need not necessarily be the same, a difference which simply reflects the fact that what counts as 'archaeological data' or 'Aboriginal heritage' is a reflection of two systems which do not necessarily respond to the same imperatives, although they can and frequently do. Increasing numbers of archaeologists actively involved in the management or assessment of Aboriginal heritage (including the now very large number of consulting archaeologists) hold a different view, however, which asserts the primacy of Aboriginal interest. In their reading, whatever differences there are between 'archaeological data' and 'Aboriginal heritage' are of minor importance, with the latter essentially comprising the former.[20]

For their part, many Aboriginal people still have difficulty with the notion of others studying and debating a past which they feel is already understood by the experts, that is, Aboriginal people themselves. On this basis it is hardly surprising that it is sometimes stated that money drives archaeological discourse in Australia and that an Aboriginal past is further commodified as salaries for non-Aboriginal people. And although it might be pointed out that this discourse increasingly also means salaries for Aboriginal people too (either in heritage management or in cultural tourism), an Aboriginal input into the management of heritage has not necessarily translated into an input into the management of interpretations. Such statements might be taken as *prima facie* evidence that archaeologists have not been able to effectively justify their existence to Aboriginal people, and that we should lift our games in this arena. But these statements might have much more to do with a real tension between archaeologists and Aboriginal people about the power of the past (and of the constitution of heritage) to define Aboriginality. In this sense, assertions of ownership of the past also imply an ownership or control over discourse about Aboriginality.

In Tasmania, the place whose Aboriginal heritage guidelines I know best, this tension frequently expresses itself in proposals for banning archaeology which is 'irrelevant' to Aboriginal needs or does not 'benefit the Aboriginal community'. There are also Aboriginal proposals for vetting research papers before publication and of claiming a right to add commentary to these publications or to censor 'unacceptable' interpretations. In some cases there are even proposals for banning archaeological research by non-Aboriginal people altogether. In recent times these tensions have been expressed in terms of tighter restrictions on the export of Aboriginal cultural heritage to the Australian mainland for study, and an associated push to repatriate cultural properties to the sites from which they were excavated or collected. There have even been unconfirmed reports of cultural properties being destroyed in the course of repatriation. I shall further consider the implications of these recent developments in the closing sections of this chapter, but it is worth noting at this stage that these heritage guidelines have been set for archaeologists by members of the Tasmanian Aboriginal community without consultation or negotiation with archaeologists.

These all might be considered to be predictable responses to a situation in which Aborigines fear that a plastic Aboriginality might slip from their control simply because one major area of discourse about the Aboriginal past is an expression of the traditions of a dominant European culture which constructs pasts and uses them for a wide variety of ends. It is significant that some Aboriginal communities feel that these ends have little benefit for Aboriginal people while also potentially carrying a high cost in the sense of making Aboriginal identity both unstable and prone to interference from non-Aboriginal sources. As a result, it is conceivable that Aboriginal communities may well require a quite different kind of archaeology than that which is currently being done under the rubric of research and cultural resources management. This archaeology, which would constitute an element in the total package of heritage management, would be concerned with creating inventories of sites of significance to Aboriginal people, mitigating developments which threaten the integrity of such sites, and creating registers of sites and properties. An additional aspect of this archaeology would be the control of access to such registers and inventories, which might be considered to be a partial (but still very important) database for the pursuit of other forms of archaeology.

At the present time many registers (maintained by State and Federal heritage agencies) have restrictions on public access. These restrictions were first introduced to protect sacred and secret sites and to encourage Aboriginal people to list sites which they might otherwise wish to keep out of the public eye. But in recent times, especially in the southern portions of the continent, there is an increasing tendency to apply these restrictions to a much wider range of sites, many of which have been recorded by non-Aboriginal people. Thus, the kind of archaeology which is driven primarily by Aboriginal interest may well support a case for distinguishing between the interests and rights of Aboriginal people and other Australians.

In this scenario, the fact that the existing framework of research and discourse is a very significant way for non-Aboriginal Australians to gain an understanding of the history of Aboriginal Australia is of marginal interest to such Aborigines. I have already mentioned that in the southern portions of the continent Aboriginal people frequently question the justification for doing the archaeology of Aboriginal Australia, seeing it either as a commodification of their identity or a direct attack on their authority as interpreters of their past. In the terms of their separatist reading, the conventional answer to the question of 'why study the past'—that archaeology provides one culturally meaningful way in which a kind of understanding of that past can be achieved by non-Aboriginal people—simply does not wash. White Australia, they believe, should understand black Australia in terms laid down by Aboriginal people or not at all. This said, it is highly unlikely that all Aboriginal communities share these extreme attitudes. Indeed, it should be expected that there be a very wide range of opinion on these matters within both the non-Aboriginal and Aboriginal communities, just as there is among practising archaeologists and heritage managers.

But what are we to do with the understandings derived from archaeology? There are great dilemmas here: Do non-Aboriginal Australians need the aboriginal history of the continent in order to be able establish their identities or create an Australia which might be viable into the twenty-first century, or be able (if only minimally) to understand, respect, and be reconciled with Aboriginal people? Or is this knowledge of the same order as understanding what makes bandicoots tick, or why drought features so prominently in our lives, but of no greater moment than this in defining self and community. Is not this history (as distinct from its material manifestations in stones, bones and sites) largely a non-Aboriginal creation in the first place? Can Aboriginal Australians achieve self-determination if their histories (and by extension substantial elements of their identities) are shared with others? Is it not the case that in a very real sense Aboriginal and non-Aboriginal Australians define each other through their shared histories?

Undoubtedly, one response to these dilemmas is to engage in the kinds of separatism which are beginning to surface in relations between Aboriginal people, archaeologists, and heritage managers under the guise of strategies for empowerment. Certainly, separatism is an easier option to follow than to participate in the messy and difficult conversation about identities, and the meanings of both Aboriginal and non-Aboriginal histories. But will putting the Aboriginal past into quarantine empower Aboriginal people and aid them in the drive for self determination? Further, will such separatism aid the decolonisation of Aboriginal Australia and foster reconciliation between white and black Australia?

Decolonising the archaeology of Australia

I have remarked elsewhere that the archaeology of Australia has been, and to some extent still is, a colonialist creation. Many observers have echoed the accusation made by Aboriginal people that archaeologists purvey a softer, but generally much nastier, form of colonialism. In this analysis archaeologists are seen to be the creators of an archaeology of Aboriginal Australia which answers more to their needs than to those of Aboriginal people (particularly those from the south and the south-east of the continent for whom the archaeological component of heritage has particular potency). I have also remarked that until recently Australian archaeologists have generally been hostile to calls for critical self-reflection about the role of archaeological knowledge in the constitution of Australian society, both past and present, although John Mulvaney has been a notable exception.[21] The significant point here is that although it might be possible that archaeological knowledge has been (and still is) a significant force in the domination of Aboriginal Australia, the fact is that detailed analyses which might allow us to assess this possibility have not been done.

But there is a more fundamental construal of the issue than this exploration of how archaeological knowledge is complicit with the state. Whether or not archaeological knowledge produced and controlled by (non-Aboriginal) archaeologists has supported (or still supports) the subjugation of Aboriginal Australia, it is a distinct possibility that some Aboriginal groups believe that true self-determination cannot come without complete control over their culture. In their reading, it is simply not enough for archaeology to 'reform' itself through critical self-reflection and to thereby allow other voices, other pasts, to be heard and experienced. It is also not enough that the research priorities of this archaeology (such as the increasing attention being paid to Aboriginal historical archaeology) have been changed as a result of requests by Aboriginal people to take a more active role in the management of their heritage. Complete control in this more fundamental sense has less to do with negotiation or with democratising access to archaeological information than it does with a control over what research might be done, who might undertake this research, and to what ends this research might be put.

I have already argued that the potential for archaeological investigations to actively destabilise conventional views about the human history of the continent and to provide an additional source of information for constructing Aboriginality, has made them seem threatening to those seeking to control discourse about Aboriginal identity. What is for archaeologists an abstract debate about the nature of Aboriginal history is far from an abstract discussion for Aboriginal people. But the fact that such discussions go to the heart of identity does not logically necessitate or warrant the adoption of a separatist position which claims that the achievement of self-determination requires the curtailment of access to (or perhaps even the destruction of) material culture which is seen variously as 'heritage' or 'archaeological data'.

This aspect of separatism rests on the proposition that as sites and material culture are aspects of the heritage of a living culture then they need have no greater status than any other aspect of contemporary Aboriginal culture. Thus, it is entirely possible that such cultural material can be considered to be expendable, so long as its destruction serves the cause of Aboriginal advancement in the present. It is worth noting that this basically ahistorical approach to heritage defines both Aboriginality and heritage essentially in the present. On the one hand it makes a very clear statement that for some sections of the Aboriginal community, history is expendable in the creation by Aboriginal people of an Aboriginal present. On the other it condemns future generations of Aboriginal people to that past which survives such acts of destruction.

It seems sufficiently clear today that these more extreme elements of Aboriginal separatism will have a permanent impact on Aboriginal heritage, but it is also true that even in its milder forms a separation of Aboriginal pasts from non-Aboriginal people might well condemn much of what is left to destruction. If we are not allowed to know about the existence of sites, or to come to value them for their own reasons, then there will be no incentive to ensure their preservation—the survival of Aboriginal heritage depends on non-Aboriginal people as well. Thus, the cause of separatism does not resolve the dilemmas posed by the existence of shared pasts and presents; indeed, it makes them worse.

I do not want to minimise the significance of this fundamental construal of colonialism, but there is another view which might possibly go towards a more rounded understanding of the very real differences which arise between archaeologists and Aboriginal Australians, and which might foster communication rather than division and exclusion. This view states that the practice of archaeology in Australia is colonialist for two interlocked reasons: first, archaeology has answered a number of colonialist agendas. It was, until recently, mainly undertaken by people who felt themselves to be only temporary exiles from Britain, and who pursued the research objects of metropolitan archaeology in Australia. Second, that the methods and perspectives used by Australian archaeologists have few indigenous attributes, and that the bulk of the conceptual armoury of Australian archaeology is made from a wide variety of overseas sources. So, while Aboriginal people may with some justification argue that *they* need to decolonise Australian archaeology, in the sense of it pursuing the goals of western science, Australian archaeologists also have a grave need to actively reconsider the central tenets of anthropological archaeology as it has been developed in the United States and Europe, and to establish whether they are sufficiently robust to deal with the kinds of data regularly encountered by archaeologists working in the deeper past, or with societies that did not climb the conventional ladder of social evolution. I have already identified a reliance on ethnographic analogy as one area of concern because of its tendency to be used badly, and when used badly to reinforce the kind of essentialism which needs to be rejected. Having said this it is worth emphasising that ethnographic analogy can be used in a way which allows an exploration of both the similarities *and* differences between present and past Aboriginal societies. The end of the 'essential Aborigine' holds great fears for archaeologists as well as for Aboriginal people. A commitment to writing history poses significant methodological and theoretical problems, as well as making categories which were previously thought to be stable and natural become unstable and cultural. But it also holds out tremendous possibilities to us all, both as an intellectual challenge of considerable moment, and a source of perspectives which Aboriginal people can use to recreate themselves. Freeing Aboriginal Australia from the constraints imposed by the needs of European history in the nineteenth and twentieth centuries might well be the greatest benefit flowing to all Australians from a post-Mabo archaeology of the country.

In this chapter I have traversed some of the terrain of a post-Mabo archaeology of Australia and in doing so I have briefly considered matters of essence and identity, and advanced the cause of history. These are just a few elements of a complex process. Other developments in improving communication between archaeologists and Aboriginal people through publication, discussions with communities, the employment of Aboriginal people in archaeological research, and the training of Aboriginal people in heritage management are also of great significance. My point has been simple—to attain to the kind of archaeology I am here advocating will be a tough business, and it will be ultimately unsuccessful if these elements are not represented and given equal weight in the future.

6

Between Mabo and a hard place: race and the contradictions of conservatism

Andrew Markus

This chapter reviews the positions taken by those opposed to the Mabo decision in the public debate which erupted in June 1993, sparked by the release of the Federal Government's discussion paper on Mabo[1] and the subsequent negotiations between the Commonwealth and heads of State governments. The inability to reach agreement, and the lodging of a number of extensive land claims by Aboriginal groups, fuelled a heated debate which raged for more than two months. My analysis is focussed on the stance of conservative spokespersons, or perhaps more correctly with the stance adopted by those publicly opposed to the High Court decision, which does not appear to have included people on the left of the political spectrum. My primary aim is to analyse the basis of the criticism of the Mabo decision, in particular the role, if any, of racism in that critique.

Public debate—the contest for the 'hearts and minds of middle Australia'—is of great consequence in setting the political agenda and parameters of government action on Aboriginal issues. Aboriginal Australians have little with which to bargain. Comprising under two per cent of the population, they are too few in number to be of direct political significance—there is no 'Aboriginal vote' to play a role in the calculations of political strategists. Further, the vast majority of Aboriginal people do not command economic resources which would necessitate political groups treating their views and demands with respect; rather, the task, as understood by some vested interests, is to prevent Aborigines obtaining resources—seen primarily in terms of control over potentially rich mineral lands—which would give them such influence. Thus, for the demands of

Aboriginal groups to be taken seriously they must appeal to the
white electorate; and so the power to persuade the wider society
of the justness of their claims—the power to appeal to what Tim
Rowse has termed the 'moral community'[2]—is of vital importance.
Defenders of the status quo must of necessity counter the
arguments on which Aboriginal claims rest. While recognising that
Mabo presented a challenge to the self-concepts of those on the
right, threatening to undermine their world view (a position elo-
quently argued by Bain Attwood in this book), this chapter is
concerned with the perceived threat to material interests and with
tactics adopted in the attempt to gain ascendancy in the public
debate: with arguments designed to win over the 'moral community'
to a rejection of Mabo and to endorsement of legislation to overturn
the High Court decision.

I

The immediate response to the Mabo decision was muted. For
nearly twelve months criticism was limited; in some, perhaps unex-
pected quarters, there was even support. Certainly there was little
to indicate the ferocity of the attack that was to be mounted and
maintained over a period of months. There were five major themes
in this response, concerned primarily with: the consequences of the
Mabo decision; views of history; the position of Aborigines in
Australian society; the High Court decision; the nature of Aboriginal
people and of their civilisation.

The first theme concerned the devastating consequences which
would follow from the High Court's decision. Leading conservative
politicians in Victoria and Western Australia asserted that much
property title had been thrown into question, encompassing even
the backyards of the average citizen.[3] The possibility of an end to
the country's territorial integrity, even of the sovereignty of the
Australian people, was also canvassed. The historian Geoffrey
Blainey wrote:

> we could well end up with two permanent systems of land tenures
> and the genesis of two systems of government . . . Aboriginal lands
> form almost a continuous corridor from the Arafura Sea to the
> Southern Ocean, with only tiny breaks in the continuity . . . One
> large Aboriginal area has the rainfall and general capacity to sup-
> port a nation of many millions at East Asian standards . . . To
> extend land rights is also to weaken . . . the real sovereignty and
> unity of the Australian people.[4]

The mining executive Hugh Morgan spoke in a similar vein to the annual conference of the Victorian Returned Servicemen's League, where he was accorded a standing ovation:

> Ian McLachlan [Opposition frontbencher] has told us that Mabo is the most important issue Australia has faced since the War, and he is right. It has already led to increasing racial tension and resentment. Unresolved it can lead to very rapid economic decline and to a partitioning of the continent . . . Mabo directly threatens the unity of Australia. It brings in a separate law for one group of Australians. It encourages aboriginal Australians to think of themselves as separate and distinct from their fellow citizens. It promises racial tension. It guarantees economic stagnation. I call on all of you to stand up for the ideals of federation—one nation—one continent; one law, one people, one destiny.[5]

Subsequently in a speech at Bond University, he declared that the Mabo decision carried 'the seeds of territorial dismemberment of the Australian continent and the end of the Australian nation as we have known it'.[6]

The second theme comprised two elements. First, what may be described as a realistic, non-sentimental view of the history of nations. There were many exemplars of this perspective; Morgan, for example, argued that: 'because the Europeans had the ships, the navigation skills, the weapons, the technology, the wealth, the people, the ambition; the future of Australia was going to be either a French or an English future, not an aboriginal one . . . The English got here before the French, and the rest is history.'[7] A variant of this argument counselled Aboriginal people against living in the past; in the past everybody had been dispossessed, for example the Anglo-Saxons had to contend with the Norman conquest. Aborigines should concern themselves with the present. They should congratulate themselves that it was the British who got here first; they had been treated no differently to other indigenous populations, indeed much better than most.

The third theme concerned the status of Aborigines in contemporary Australia and was based on the proposition that Aborigines, far from being a disadvantaged group, were privileged. The newspaper columnist and media celebrity, Alan Jones, put forward a forceful exposition of this perspective:

> For some time now, a small group of Australians—our indigenous people—have been seeking the spoils of Australia's hard-won gains out of all proportion to their numbers or their entitlement . . . No other Australian seeks or qualifies for such largesse. Aborigines, important Australians that they are, still only constitute a mere 1.5 per cent of the population. Yet, they already own 15 per cent of Australia . . . Many Australians have never had a cent from government. Many struggle to afford any sort of title to anything . . .

These people are being asked to work and pay taxes so that other, heavily subsidised Australians, who apparently have greater legal rights than they, can receive extraordinary benefits funded by someone else. It is not only unjust. It is un-Australian.[8]

The fourth theme concerned the nature of the High Court decision. A criticism was mounted that the judges, on a number of counts, had betrayed the demands of their high position. Their decision gave insufficient weight to the body of legal precedent which should have guided their deliberations, and they invoked principles of dubious validity. In sum, they had embarked on a legal revolution. The logic of their decision, in the words of the Western Australian Premier, Richard Court, was 'fatally flawed'.[9] Some argued that the judges stepped outside the bounds of their position and had assumed the role of legislators. Barrister and Liberal Party frontbencher, Peter Costello, argued: 'Once upon a time, Parliament made the law and the courts interpreted it. But all that has changed . . . You've got unelected, and maybe unrepresentative, people making the rules that we all have to live under. And if you don't like what they're doing, you can't vote them out.'[10] Blainey encapsulated the argument in one sentence: 'In effect, the High Court has become a parliament, an unelected parliament.'[11] In a key passage of the High Court decision, Justice Brennan argued that the law should not be allowed to remain 'fixed in an age of racial discrimination'; a failure to adapt to changing social values would be unacceptable to the Australian people. How, the critics asked, had the learned judge come to this view; what basis did he have for statements about public opinion? Morgan commented that as far as he was aware 'the only public record . . . of Justice Brennan's investigations into contemporary Australian values' were conversations he held with his son, Fr Frank Brennan, 'over a glass of cleansing ale'.[12] Instead of discharging its obligations, the court, in the view of Morgan, had embarked on a path of 'naive adventurism' with its 'perverse and politically driven logic', bringing about 'a legal, political and constitutional crisis'.[13] In the view of the prominent Western Australian Liberal Bill Hassell, 'the High Court of Australia has clearly become political'.[14] In the past some of these same critics had themselves challenged the legal wisdom of their day, for example, in the sphere of industrial relations, but now they professed a view of the law as non-problematical: the legal 'facts' were there for all to see, parallel with the 'facts' of history. The role of the judge, as of the historian when chronicling the story of Australia, was presented as one of neutrality, one of simply establishing the correct reading of the law or ordering of facts, not of embarking on a highly complex interpretative exercise, involving the evaluation of contradictory principles and precedents (see Rosemary Hunter's chapter).

The last major element in public discussion was the critical commentary on Aboriginal culture and civilisation, voiced by the leader of the Country Party, Tim Fischer, the Liberal–Country Party Chief Minister of the Northern Territory, Marshall Perron, Hugh Morgan, and the former head of the National Companies and Securities Commission and government adviser, Henry Bosch. The views of these individuals received prominent media coverage across the nation. Fischer commented that 'at no stage did Aboriginal civilisation develop substantial buildings, roadways or even a wheeled cart as part of their different priorities and approach . . . Developing cultures and peoples will always overtake relatively stationary cultures'.[15] Perron observed, in the context of a comment on Aboriginal health standards, that 'part of the problem is they really are centuries behind us in their cultural attitudes and their aspirations in many respects'.[16] Morgan, with a long record of commentary on Aboriginal culture, made the following statement during this period of intense debate:

> Guilt industry people have great difficulty in accepting, or recognising, that aboriginal culture was so much less powerful than the culture of the Europeans, that there was never any possibility of its survival. They also cannot understand that this statement has nothing to do with individual morality. Human nature is the same regardless of race . . . The necessity of choice forces us, in the end, to accept that cultures are not equal, that some cultures will wither away, and some cultures will expand and grow . . . The indisputable fact . . . is that throughout human history many cultures have died out because they were not strong enough to survive in competition with more powerful cultures.[17]

Lacking Morgan's high profile as a commentator on Aboriginal culture, Henry Bosch nonetheless won media attention with his remark that Aborigines were 'a Stone Age people' who were 'the most backward one per cent of the population'.[18] He clarified his position in a subsequent newspaper interview. Aborigines were:

> the most backward by any objective set of achievements by which I can think. I realise that this is not a politically correct thing to say. I have the utmost contempt for political correctness, the white-washing of Aboriginal people who are a Stone Age people . . . [The High Court decision recognising native title was] regrettable, entirely regrettable. I think we should forget completely about any concept of Aboriginal land rights and if that requires legislation, then let's do it . . . I don't want reconciliation, I don't believe it's necessary, nothing should be done, let's get on with something

serious. Aboriginal reconciliation is a complete waste of time and a
diversion from important things.[19]

II

The time of Mabo madness was remarkable for the extent of what
I take to be irrational argument: the degree of overstatement of the
significance of the High Court decision, the re-appearance in the
leading pages of the national press of arguments denigrating Aboriginal people and their culture, the lack of proportion, balance, and
reasoned leadership within the ranks of the critics of the Mabo
decision.

The conservative over-reaction may be understood, at least in
part, in terms of the anxiety that if the decision was not reversed
by some means, significant economic interests, notably the mining
industry, would incur serious costs. It is not coincidental that the
major locus of opposition was in Western Australia, the state with
the largest proportion of its territory open for claim under the Mabo
principles. However, their over-reaction may also be understood in
broader terms: the perceived weakness of the conservative position
and the fear that the public debate would be irretrievably lost.

The issue of land rights—which brings into prominence the act
of dispossession upon which existing land title rest—has always
presented conservatives with potentially greater problems than those
on the left, who are more comfortable with the idea that property
is not sacrosanct, that wholesale expropriation by the state may be
justified in certain cases. The left will more readily apply principles
of general utility in deciding right to land. Those on the right,
however, pay much less regard to obligations which supposedly go
with land ownership, and are much more ready to defend the
absolute or near absolute rights of property as an inviolate principle.
This situation may be clarified through consideration of a hypothetical situation: suppose there was a family whose fortune rested
on a large land grant in the early period of colonial history; this
family was notorious, down the generations, for lives of idleness
and dissipation supported by income from their property, which
they neither cultivated nor developed; to all intents the family made
no 'useful' contribution to society. Did they, through their actions,
forfeit their property rights? Few conservatives would concede that
they had, while those on the left would be at least likely to consider
the proposition seriously.

The decision of the High Court added a further complication
to what was already a disquieting issue for conservatives. Prior to
Mabo a successful campaign had been waged to prevent the

enactment of national land rights legislation, but with Mabo the difficulty of winning the 'moral argument'—important for the maintenance of the status quo—was heightened. Why is this so? Let us step back and take a long-term view of what happened in this, the highest court in the country. The court, after very lengthy deliberation, handed down a ruling that one group of people had rights in land: the court found, in a very limited and narrow (not revolutionary) sense, for what it determined to be an old class of land holders as against the interest of a new class. That, one might say, should have been the end of the matter; the court had, in a fundamental sense, handed down a conservative decision, re-establishing the rights of an old class. Perhaps of equal importance, the court had ruled and that should have been the end of the matter for conservatives, at least in terms of public debate. As Fred Chaney, a former Minister for Aboriginal Affairs and member of the Liberal Party frontbench, stated: 'Being pro or anti-Mabo is not the point. The decision is there . . . The importance of the rule of law to a free society demands that the law found in the Mabo judgement be given the same respect as any other binding law.'[20] But it seems that some felt there was too much at stake to remain silent.

However, in opposing the decision in the public forum, conservatives faced the problem that the potentially contradictory elements of their arguments could be brought into sharp relief insomuch as, first, the firmest defenders of property rights were placed in the position of arguing for expropriation of property rights—by referendum if necessary—of a section of the population (while seeking to explain that what seemed like expropriation was not in fact expropriation). Second, the firmest defenders of the existing order, of Australia's British derived institutions (such as the monarchy, the constitution, and established national symbols such as the flag), were found to be attacking the highest court in the land, often in unmeasured words. Third, the defenders of evolutionary social change were attacking the High Court decision as revolution, while denying the revolutionary act of their forebears in the dispossession of Aboriginal people by their seizure of a continent. There was thus the danger that the much vaunted *principles* of conservatism would come to be seen as little more than empty verbiage deployed in the service of privilege. Furthermore, while clearly there is a widely held view that the Mabo decision is seriously flawed, the legal critique faces the problem, already noted, that there are major difficulties in raising complex issues about the law for a lay audience: between contending legal principles; between native title and other forms of rights in property; between the legal meaning of *terra nullius* and the more readily grasped literal understanding of the term.

Key conservative arguments, as outlined above, came under

criticism in a number of major newspapers, which sought to explain the basic principles of the decision and to clarify its limited scope.[21] The argument that 'might makes right' seemed to be of limited efficacy in 1993. As Keith Scott wrote in the *Canberra Times*, in response to the proposition that superior force justifies conquest:

> To take the point to its extreme, if it is acceptable, then surely it's acceptable for Serbs to march into Muslim villages in Bosnia and take whatever land they want. If it is not, then it is not acceptable to deny . . . Aboriginal and Torres Strait Islander people title where they can prove it today under the High Court's ruling. This is not guilt, it is social progress.[22]

The advice to Aborigines to stop living in the past was at best of rhetorical value; it certainly lacked the power to persuade in the face of evidence that many Aborigines have never accepted their dispossession, which in some parts of the country took place not in some distant past but within living memory. The view that Aborigines are privileged members of Australian society, as propounded by commentators such as Jones, may strike a responsive chord with some but is unlikely to make much impact in the heartland of the 'moral community', which is frequently presented with the findings of social science surveys showing Aboriginal people to be the most disadvantaged group in the community in terms of practically all social indicators, such as life expectancy, income, qualifications, and employment status. Likewise, the view that Aborigines now own 15 per cent of the Australian land mass is unlikely to be persuasive. In an economic sense, and that is presumably the ultimate criterion of proponents of this view, the land regained by Aborigines, being largely semi-arid and arid (otherwise it would have passed into white hands) would not amount to 0.1 of the monetary value of Australian real estate. More striking, however, are the socialist implications of such a perspective: are critics arguing that no people should own land out of proportion to their numbers, so that after depriving Aborigines of the 13.5 per cent of the land which has passed into their control to bring their holdings in proportion to their numbers, governments should then redistribute the wealth held by the top one per cent of the population and then work their way down the ladder of wealth?

The above argument demonstrates, I believe, the weaknesses inherent in the conservative position and response to Mabo and, more generally, to the demand of Aboriginal people for restitution of their land. These weaknesses are essential to an understanding of what I have interpreted as gross overstatement and irrationality. Furthermore, it is an important factor in at least partially explaining why the conservative attack moved from the High Court and legal principles to *ad hominem* arguments directed against the judiciary and Aboriginal people.

In these circumstances it is not surprising to find the re-appearance of what closely resembles, if it does not equate with, racism. Before proceeding further it is necessary to clarify my understanding of 'racism', a term commonly confused in public discussion. There is a popularly accepted notion, more implicitly understood than articulated, which sees 'racism' in terms of acts of violence, verbal harassment and abuse. Given this frame of reference, there is resistance to the idea that a person adopting a moderate tone, disclaiming any pretence to superiority and defending 'commonsense' propositions, irrespective of the substance of the position adopted, can reasonably be labelled racist. Such an approach confuses demeanour with meaning, tone with substance. The narrow definition of racism also avoids the essential elements at the heart of the racial value system.

Racism is based on the proposition that culture is a function of biology. It holds that there are biologically distinct human populations, called races, whose genetic character determines physical, intellectual and moral qualities. Race, as a genetic attribute, is seen as the most important defining characteristic of a human being. Race is held to shape the individual's cast of mind and orientation to life, and the racial collectivity's destiny. Capacity for 'civilisation', loyalty to the fatherland, and ability to engage in abstract reasoning are all as inescapably linked to racial origin as skin colour, hair type and eye shape. Behavioural characteristics supposedly change as a consequence not of social processes but of racial interbreeding, which alters the gene pool. Where genetic stock is kept 'pure', the character of a 'race' remains constant from one generation to the next; where it is 'tainted', the race and its way of life will die out.

The form of racism—the words through which the core ideas are expressed—takes on new features over time, as with all value systems. The problem facing those wishing to maintain a racist perspective in the second half of the twentieth century has been that for a complex of reasons their belief system gradually lost its legitimacy: the support for overt racial discrimination and the dissemination of racial dogma became politically untenable in much of the western world. Yet there were, and continue to be, attempts to maintain the essential elements of racism behind a facade from which claims of racial superiority are excised, indeed replaced by professions of respect for all peoples. The essential element retained is a form of racial, or ethnic, determinism, described by some as 'essentialism' or 'new racism',[23] which maintains that as a result of some (deliberately undefined) 'natural' process, peoples (read 'races') have certain inborn ('essential') qualities which will never alter; thus, for example, it may be argued that 'Asian' people in Australia will maintain distinctive non-physical characteristics (to do with the mind, with orientation to life) which will forever set them apart from 'Australians'; and there are inherent characteristics in groups of people ('races') which interpose barriers against harmonious co-existence, not least against inter-breeding of populations; there is an allegedly intrinsic characteristic to form 'a bounded community, a nation, aware of its differences from other nations'.

Examples of this 'new racism' were evident in Australia in the 1950s, as they were throughout western culture, indicating a similarity of response to common pressures to remove from view the unacceptable elements of racism. In attempts to defend the 'White Australia' immigration policy in the postwar period, government spokespersons argued that 'racial prejudice' was never a factor in the development of policy, that there was 'not the slightest suggestion that Europeans are a superior race to others', and that 'few people are less conscious of differences of race and colour than contemporary Australians'.[24]

Similar themes of 'new racism' were evident in the mid 1980s in the context of debate over immigration policy and in comments on the place of Aboriginal people in Australian society. Critics, at least in the mainstream media, sought to emphasise that they were not to be understood as disparaging Asian and Aboriginal people, for all people were worthy of respect. But nevertheless 'Asians', unlike immigrants from Europe, presented a threat to Australian institutions and values which had to be addressed by adoption of what amounted to a racially discriminatory policy. There were certain supposedly inherent non-physical qualities which, it seems, would forever prevent their full absorption, a legacy which would be passed on to their descendants. Comparable attitudes are evident in parts of Australia towards Aborigines, where they are dismissed as lazy, undisciplined, shiftless and irresponsible, insensible to the work ethic, content to live on social welfare. In other words, they are seen as a category of people with essential and invariable characteristics.

The negative views of Aboriginal culture expressed in the course of the 1993 controversy, often brief comments picked up by the media, were ambiguous and cannot be simply labelled racist. This is so even though references to a 'Stone Age people', 'relatively stationary cultures', a people, *qua* Social Darwinism, destined to 'wither away'[25] (while failing to make clear precisely why Aboriginal culture should have been so incapable of 'development'), recalled a time when ideas of biological determinism were dominant in the western world, and betrayed a simplistic, unilinear view of 'evolution' long discredited in the academic world, and so seemed more akin to the 'old' variants of racism than to the newer manifestations.

It is not entirely clear how the manifestation of such views in 1993 is to be explained. Several possibilities will be canvassed. It seems that some critics of Mabo identify closely with the values of the nineteenth century, including elements of its racial outlook; while these elements are rarely on public view the heat of the debate brought forward such sentiments, in some cases perhaps because unguarded statements were made. It is also possible that some critics deliberately couched arguments in a form calculated to appeal to prejudice and bigotry within the Australian electorate, although on this point evidence is necessarily slim. One of the country's leading political analysts, Laurie Oakes, wrote following the Fischer episode:

> The real allegation about Fischer is not that he is prejudiced and a redneck but that he is calculatedly appealing to those who are. Hewson implied as much when, trying to defend his coalition partner, he said: 'Look, Tim Fischer presents the views of a particular constituency . . . He uses words that we wouldn't use to make a point'. It is reminiscent of the coalition's attempts to play the so-called 'Asian immigration card' under both John Howard and Andrew Peacock. Howard and Peacock were diminished by what was seen as an abandonment of principle and it did not work as an electoral ploy anyway.[26]

One might conclude, then, that denigration could not be pushed too far, even if some felt a strong desire to do so. It could perhaps confer political benefits and be seen as a weapon in the battle to undermine Aboriginal moral legitimacy, but the appearance of racism also had the capacity to spark a reaction against those who mounted such an attack; beyond a certain point it could prove to be counterproductive.

Further, racism, in both its older and newer manifestations, I would contend, is an exclusionary device, a device for drawing boundaries, whether as functioning to control immigration or to establish lines of differentiation in a labour market. Such exclusionary mechanisms would be counterproductive in the context of Mabo: an argument stressing innate differences of Aboriginal people could form the basis for separation and land rights for the people separated, not for its denial. Thus, a key element of the successful anti-land rights campaign which defeated proposed legislation in Western Australia in the period 1983 to 1985, and present in a muted form in 1993, stressed the assimilation of Aborigines and their position as equals in contemporary Australia.[27] The essence of this position is the argument that all Australians are equal. All should have the same right to land, no one group should have special privileges. In the words of the Western Australian Premier: 'None of us want the land, the law, or the people divided. All of us want the same fair go to apply evenly to all. Australian culture is based on recognition that we all love the land that is our home—whether we were born here or came here.'[28] There was, it seemed, little that was distinctive about the Aboriginal people's attachment to the land which could form the basis for rights in law. In the words of Fischer:

> There are families in Australia who have held land for generations. Their forebears worked the land and were buried on the land. They live in the same homesteads as their forebears and there is an extremely strong bond with their land . . . I think [it] is a relevant consideration to recognise that there is attachment by a lot of Australians to their land—be they black, white or otherwise.[29]

Of course, there was a possible contradiction between the stress on the inferiority of Aboriginal civilisation (with the potential for the argument to be understood as pointing to biologically determined characteristics), the innate attributes of the 'race', and the view that Aborigines were no different from other Australians, but there is no difficulty with the espousal of contradictory positions in a public debate. Indeed, as I have argued, contradictions ran throughout the attack on Mabo.

To summarise the interpretation here presented, the Mabo debate was about maintaining the position of vested interests. The High Court decision was seen as having the potential to damage seriously those interests, and certainly weaken the capacity to argue against land rights. In part I have interpreted the disparaging of Aboriginal culture as indicative of this weakness, a reflex reaction to the weakening of the critics' position; it may also have been a calculated move, at least on the part of some, seen as useful in maintaining standing within a section of the electorate and a valuable, if potentially counterproductive tool in the ongoing battle for moral ascendancy.

7 Mabo, Australia and the end of history[1]

Bain Attwood

In this chapter I will argue that the sense of national crisis provoked by Mabo was largely due to it being perceived as a profound challenge to a traditional notion of Australian nationhood and national identity.[2] More specifically, I will argue that since the meanings of 'Australia' and 'Australian' are primarily grounded in and formed by historical narratives,[3] Mabo (or, more generally, the new history of which it is an integral part) is considered revolutionary because, inasmuch as it questions a long established and once dominant history, it threatens many Australians with the loss of their customary narrative and thus the loss of identity and nationhood. To express this another way, I believe that Mabo forms part of a new historical narrative which portends for conservatives[4] the end of (Australian) history as they have conceived it and, therefore, the end of their Australia.

My argument rests on a particular meaning of history—not history as the past but rather history as a narrative discourse which constructs a past in the present. I assume, in other words, that the past (like the present) is known only through an interpretive act which not only comprehends the past but also constitutes it, and that this interpretive act conventionally assumes the form of a narrative. Thus, I follow Jerome Bruner, as well as other theorists of narrativity such as Louis Mink and Hayden White, inasmuch as I assume that histories, like any narrative, 'do not exist, as it were, in some real world, waiting there patiently and eternally to be veridically mirrored in a text';[5] instead, the past only has the form of narrative insofar as 'we give it that form by making it the subject of stories'.[6] Narratives are constructed in two ways, Bruner suggests.

First, through the selection of 'events' and 'protagonists' and the arrangement of these in an appropriate order. In this process, just as certain events and protagonists are highlighted, others are suppressed or at least subordinated, and particular relationships between events and protagonists are created whereas other possible ones are not. Second, the events and protagonists themselves are discursively constituted, and, moreover, this only occurs with reference to the narrative itself; in other words, events and protagonists are constructed in terms of the putative story. Simultaneously, the formation of the narrative whole depends on its appropriate constituent parts—those constructed events and protagonists; thus, the 'parts and wholes in a narrative rely on each other for their viability', and 'a story can only be "realised" when its parts and wholes can, as it were, be made to live together'.[7]

To relate this process (which Bruner calls 'hermeneutic composability') to the Australian context, I would suggest that in the late nineteenth and early twentieth centuries the Australian nation was created by 'narrative accrual'—a process whereby a corpus of connected and shared narratives constitute something which can be called either a myth, a history, or a tradition. Furthermore, it was only as the people came to comprehend and know this story that they came to realise and be conscious of themselves as Australians.[8] This history of the nation constituted the British, the Australians and the Aborigines as its principal protagonists, and discovery, settlement and pioneering as its principal events. And this narrative—which is also to say Australia—assumed a particular content only in terms of these constituents. There was, consequently, a textual interdependence between each of the protagonists, 'the British', 'the Australians' and 'the Aborigines', as well as between these and the foundational events. This is to argue, then, that each category of the history, for example 'Australians', was and is profoundly dependent upon the maintenance of a particular relationship with the other (categories), for example, 'Aborigines', as it was realised in the narrative whole of 'Australia', whose meaning, in turn, both shaped and was shaped by its constituents and their particular relationship with each other. Consequently, as these internal relationships change, the meanings of Australia are severely disrupted, and this is the case, I will argue, with Mabo.

I

At the turn of this century historical narratives in Australia were coalescing into a myth which could be summarised thus: following its discovery by Captain James Cook in 1770, Australia was founded by the British in 1788 when Governor Phillip declared British sovereignty and took possession of the entire continent. This was in accordance with legal convention because prior to the coming of the white man the continent was inhabited by a relatively small number of nomadic savages whose culture was simple and unevolved and who did not cultivate the land and who therefore forfeited any right to it. The process of colonising the new land was, by and large, peaceful, and although Aboriginal society was more or less destroyed this was largely an unforseen consequence of introduced diseases and tribal conflict, and inasmuch as there was any conflict between settlers and Aborigines the latter were treated in accordance with British justice and their suffering was alleviated by humanitarian endeavour. Besides, the Aborigines' decline was inevitable because they were a weak, inferior, archaic and unprogressive race which was incapable of adapting to the presence of the white man—in short a dying race who would pass away. By contrast, British settlers, drawing on the knowledge of intrepid explorers, settled upon the strange and alien continent, and with enormous courage, fortitude and hard work came to possess it by transforming it into flourishing pastures and the like, so that the countryside prospered, great cities were created, and the Australian colonies became a working man's paradise. Not only British people, but also British values such as equality, liberty and justice, and venerable British institutions, especially political and legal ones, were successfully transplanted. In time, a new nation was born whose defining characteristics were the landscape ('the bush'), its Britishness ('the crimson thread of kinship'), and a new people who were typified by white racial purity, egalitarianism and mateship.[9] Thus arose modern Australia: 'one continent, one nation, one people'.

Most importantly, this historical narrative fashions a particular relationship between 'Australians' and 'Aborigines' in relation to the space and time of Australia. First, a homology of Australians and the land of Australia is created and naturalised; in other words, an unmediated and apparently organic relationship between these parts (and, therefore, the narrative whole of the Australian nation), is produced in which 'Australians' are present and the possessors and Aborigines are absent, not even being accorded the status of the dispossessed. Second and simultaneously in this history, Australians symbolise the modern and Aborigines the past. Consequently, it is believed that Australia can only be modern (and progress) provided that its space is unambiguously Australian and not Aboriginal.[10]

This history became the dominant narrative of the nation at

the turn of the century and is still the conventional 'truth' of many Australians, especially conservatives whom in recent years have strenuously sought to uphold it. Those such as Leonie Kramer, Hugh Morgan, Ken Baker, Gerard Henderson, and, most importantly, Geoffrey Blainey, insofar as he claims authority as a professional historian and influences other conservatives, regard this history as a national tradition or heritage. It is a source of what is variously called 'unifying core values', 'shared attachments', 'the accumulated wisdom of past generations', and 'precedents' they wish to preserve and inculcate in the young because they believe that 'the sense of having inherited a worthy past is essential to . . . feel[ing] part of a national community'.[11] Evidently, history, in their view, has the distinct purpose of nationalising the people—forging a common understanding of the self and community—and so creating the nation. The conservatives' renewed emphasis on this national tradition or heritage has occurred in a context in which various parts of this history and therefore the nation, is seen to be at risk because it has been challenged by another series of narratives (which I will call the new Australian history), whose most recent manifestation is Mabo.

What is the nature of this new history? At the most fundamental level this narrative is characterised by the return of an Aboriginal past which had been suppressed by, and repressed in, the dominant history I have outlined—what W.E.H. Stanner called 'the great Australian silence' and a 'cult of disremembering'. This very simple change, the return of the Aborigines to the national history, has profound consequences for Australian history: it both dramatically overturns its chronology—as D.J. Mulvaney notes, 'the two centuries since Captain Cook's arrival dwindle into insignificance' and become 'no more than 0.5 per cent of the human story of Australia'—and subverts the foundational events and protagonists: the first 'discoverers, explorers and colonists' of Australia become Aborigines instead of Europeans.[12] Thus, the relationship between the British, the Australians and Australia, which was realised by the traditional history, is sundered (while simultaneously a particularly close relationship between the indigenous peoples and the land of Australia tends to be posited by the new history). More particularly, as a consequence of the return of the Aborigines and the corresponding acknowledgment that they were prior to the British, the foundational event of British colonisation is construed as an invasion rather than discovery and settlement, and so the legitimacy of the British claiming of the land of Australia, if not their assertion of sovereignty, is brought into question. Furthermore, and as a consequence of the legal doctrine of settlement being challenged, this new Australian history represents the coming of the British in terms of the dispossession of Aborigines, and, moreover, asserts what the 'cult of disremembering' had denied: the violence, racial discrimination and neglect which accompanied it. Thus it undermines the theory of peaceful settlement as well as the notions of British justice, humanitarianism and egalitarianism which were central to the Australian nationhood and identity constructed by the earlier history.

Insofar as the High Court's majority judgment presents such a narrative, it might be regarded as merely another element, albeit a prominent one, in the process of 'narrative accrual'—constituting a new national history or tradition and, therefore, forging a new Australia. However, it has a special potency because of what it represents as the originating act of the nation: the prior existence of native title, and thus *terra nullius* as a legal fiction. This is immensely significant because the conventional historical narrative of Australia, like that of any nation, is teleological—outcomes are immanent in and are an expression of their beginnings—and so a change in the origins alters all that follows. Conservative spokespersons are acutely aware of this. Not only do conservatives like Morgan, Executive Director of Western Mining, vehemently insist that 'the first European settlement in Australia *was* properly, lawfully, and peacefully constituted, not only in accordance with British law, but also . . . with international law'; they also bitterly complain that 'the free, prosperous and dynamic nation that our forebears built here . . . and which we have inherited, is irremediably tainted by [the imputation of the] unlawfulness and immorality of settlement', that 'this version of Australia's foundation as illegitimate sets the tone for the new history'.[13]

As a new history of the beginnings of Australia, however, Mabo does not only subvert the conservatives' narrative in a cognitive or intellectual sense; more importantly, it also threatens conservatives in a psychic sense, and it is this which largely explains their panic and hysteria in relation to Mabo.[14] To understand this, one must note that since history is not uncommonly understood as a representation of the past that is complete and unalterable, it often provides, particularly in the context of change, an illusory sense of meaning, order and composure, and thus a comforting psychological escape from the contingency of the present and future shock. Mabo threatens to deprive the conservatives of just such a familiar and comforting map of the past, and thus it provokes angry denunciations of the perpetrator of this loss, the new Australian history, which is accused of *rewriting* the past (as if history is not always written anew by each generation). For instance, an Australian Mining Industry Council advertisement in 1993 called upon Australians to 'Take a good look at this map', asking, 'Does it look anything like the one we studied at school?'.[15] In numerous conservative assaults upon the High Court's Mabo decision (and even, as Andrew Markus notes, the High Court itself), it is similarly manifest that they are unsettled by the fact that the question of how the British appropriated Aboriginal land—settlement or conquest—is no longer settled. Liberal Party senator Peter Durack, for instance, wrote: 'It is the *disturbing* feature of the case that six out of the seven judges have been prepared to change the *foundations* of the land law in Australia after that law has been *settled* for two hundred years . . . The High Court was quite clearly changing what had been *settled* law.'[16] This disturbance is also revealed in the irrational statements of Morgan, for example: 'Mabo is a challenge to the legitimacy of Australia . . . We must . . . restore our legitimacy, as a nation. If we fail in this Australia will soon [be] . . . no longer in undisputed possession of this island continent';[17] and of Blainey, who believes that 'there is no excuse for any Australians casting doubts on their own nation's legitimacy', and who accused Prime Minister Paul Keating of a series of 'veiled attack[s] on the legitimacy and history of the nation'.[18] What is only too apparent in this hysteria is the refusal or the inability of these conservative spokespersons to come to terms with a new history which represents Australia's foundations in terms of an invasion and not settlement.[19]

Mabo, like the new history of which it is a part, is all the more disturbing, though, because it not only dislodges the traditional origins of Australia, but also seems to weaken if not destroy the connection with the British past, which is *the* traditional Australian past. The degree to which Mabo subverts this treasured tale of a particular past becoming the national present is evident in conservatives' emphatic criticisms of the High Court's rejection of the conventional history as it has been expressed in legal precedent. For instance, a professor of constitutional law and adviser to the Western Australian Government on native title, Colin Howard, commented: 'The law as it previously stood was based on a line of *English* decisions . . . Mabo . . . lacks a sense of history . . . The philosophy of the common law is above all evolutionary in character, not revolutionary. Mabo is above all revolutionary in character, not evolutionary.'[20] And in the heat of the Mabo debate in mid 1993, National Party leader Tim Fischer accused Paul Keating of 'an obsessive hatred of the British origins of Australia's political institutions, law and language'.[21]

The loss of the British Australian past provokes a disproportionate fear, however, because of the conservative anxiety as to what might replace this traditional past—not an 'Australian' past but the past of Aborigines. Thus, they are anxious that symbols of the British Australian past will be abandoned or severely eroded, for instance, that the Union Jack will be replaced by a symbol of the Aboriginal presence, or the Constitution will be undermined by the insertion of a passage acknowledging the prior occupation of Australia by Aborigines (see John Morton's chapter for a consideration of this). And, more generally, conservatives believe that the new history not only 'fails to give due recognition to the British contribution to Australia's heritage, [but] it singles out the history and contribution of the Australian Aborigines . . . for special attention', instead.[22] Such a representation or rather misrepresentation of the new Australian history reveals the conservatives' assumption that the mere return of the Aboriginal past necessarily entails the displacement of the British one, and so betrays the extent to which their traditional history depended and depends upon the silencing of Aboriginal narratives.

The loss of the British past is considered to be all the more serious because, in the absence of a deep non-Aboriginal past in Australia and the corresponding presence of a narrative which (correctly or incorrectly) represents the Aboriginal past as being very long and continuous, this British past constitutes a principal source of legitimacy for the conservatives' Australia. Thus, Morgan, for example, in the context of contemplating what is barely one hundred years of Australian federation, bemoans the High Court's decision in terms of it having 'overturned the *centuries old* legal doctrine of *terra nullius*'.[23]

Mabo and the new Australian history threaten conservatives' psychic equilibrium all the more since they not only seem to displace the traditional Australian past but also present, as I have noted, a new set of historical truths about what can be called the Aboriginal colonial past. In response, many conservatives have tended to deny the violence of colonial frontiersmen, the racism of the colonial order, and the role played by government in the dispossession of Aborigines. Morgan, for instance, has dismissed 'the claims of pre-meditated genocide, systematic and widespread massacres', calling them 'total nonsense', while Tasmanian Premier Ray Groom claimed that the decimation of the aboriginal people of Van Diemen's Land did not constitute genocide. Furthermore, Morgan, along with other conservatives, have argued that Aborigines 'were unable to mount anything but local and sporadic resistance to British settlement', that 'more than any other factor the cause of aboriginal death and decline during the nineteenth century was disease', and that 'vengeance killing . . . exacted a far greater toll on the Aboriginal population in the nineteenth century than any depredations by the Europeans'.[24] They validate these claims by invoking the scholarly reputation of Blainey who has repeatedly advanced such arguments.[25] Morgan, moreover, reiterates the conventional historical narrative when he notes that 'some white men were hanged for murdering Aborigines' (thus disguising the uniqueness of the 1838 Myall Creek Massacre trial), and portrays 'continuing missionary endeavour' as 'one of the most uplifting and heroic chapters in Australian history'.[26]

A second and more important form of denial of the Aboriginal colonial past is evident in statements like those made by Fischer, who acknowledged that 'there has been horrific massacres [and] horrific dimensions of white policy applied since 1788' but also insisted that 'the horrors of the past were not caused by this generation of Australians', a position also enunciated by Howard who claims, quite tendentiously, that 'everyone associated with [the conquest of Australia] has long since died'.[27] This refusal to accept any responsibility or to admit any association with their forebears is usually accompanied by an assertion that the past is past. 'That's in the past', Fischer says; 'the facts of the eighteenth century are what they are, and cannot be changed retrospectively', Morgan preaches; these are 'long past historical events', Howard opines.[28] In a somewhat different fashion, Blainey also dismisses the ongoing importance of this past by attacking the High Court's suggestion that 'injuries done 200 years ago . . . are the main determinant of their plight today', and by deriding it as 'nothing but the fashionable fad for enthroning the victim'.[29]

In doing so, Blainey, like the other conservatives, is not only denying the determinative role of the Aboriginal colonial past (and simultaneously erasing one of the most salient markers and sources of Aborigines' difference), but also its explanatory power with reference to the Aboriginal present. In effect, then, these conservatives acknowledge this past only to deny its significance. Indeed, their claims can be read as the utterance of a wish to separate the past and the present, rather than an expression of a belief that any such disjunction actually exists. Hence, Fischer testily complains: 'You cannot right every [past] wrong by Mabo and you should not attempt to do so'; Howard implores us to believe that 'nothing will ever right the wrongs done'; and Lachlan McIntosh, executive director of the Australian Mining Industry Council, similarly proffers some 'commonsense' advice: 'We can't keep looking back and trying to fix up the past. It's time for Australians to stop beating their heads against the unalterable facts of history.'[30] Simultaneously, then, these conservatives direct our attention in the opposite temporal direction: 'We ought to be looking forward. Mabo is an opportunity to look to our future relationships, not . . . the past', McIntosh instructs us; 'there certainly should not be any good purpose served by . . . dwelling on the past. Surely . . . we must look to the future of this country', Fischer pleads.[31]

This denial of the past (or responsibility for it)—which bears a marked similarity to those Germans who desperately seek to 'revise' their nation's Nazi past[32]—is nowhere more evident than in the conservatives' angry attacks upon the so-called 'guilt industry', such as Fischer's retort, 'I'm not filled with guilt but I am filled with pride for what it is to be an Australian and white Australians should not have to apologise for the country's past'.[33] What is apparent here is the inability of conservatives to maintain pride in being Australian at the same time as they acknowledge any shameful deeds in the past, which makes one mindful of the Nietzschean aphorism, '"I have done that", says my memory. "I cannot have done that", says my pride, and remains adamant. At last, memory yields'.[34] Thus, the pride that is articulated by their mythic narrative is predicated upon suppressing (or destroying) or denying other remembrances of the colonial past.[35]

In a more general sense, Mabo and the new history has apparently robbed Australian history of the central role conservatives have conceived for it, that of providing 'the nation's own sense of itself and where it is going'.[36] Conservatives have complained, ironically enough, that the new history seeks to 'transform Australia into a new country unconnected with its past', and have attacked it as 'the falsification of Australian history' and an 'Orwellian reconstruction of our history'.[37] It is, they allege, a history which 'rejects the notion of a national interest' so that 'little sense is conveyed of what is distinctive about being Australian', and which portrays instead 'a nation of varied cultures and origins, but without a unifying core', even emphasising that which tends 'to divide the nation'.[38] Furthermore, what Blainey calls 'the Black Armband view of history' is deemed to have 'assailed the generally optimistic view of Australian history', and has deprived young Australians of their inheritance by denying they have anything of which they can be proud. Similarly, Morgan alleges that there are those 'seeking to recreate our history in such a way that we [can] . . . no longer regard our pioneers, our forebears, with any sense of pride . . .'; indeed, the High Court judges, he railed, 'seem to have no pride in their country and they strive mightily to melt it down and recast it, furtively, in a new self-deprecating and much diminished mould'. The new historical narratives of 'destruction and persecution', Baker frets, 'will ultimately undermine the legitimacy of existing institutions [and values] inherited from the past'. Indeed, 'Australians [will] come to accept that the society they and their forebears have established is not worth defending . . . [and] the message will not be lost on Australia's potential rivals and enemies'.[39]

The attitude of these conservatives to the (Australian) past is inconsistent if not contradictory, however. While denying the relevance of the colonial Aboriginal past to the present, they assert in their narrative of the nation the vital importance of the British Australian past (as I have noted), and at the same time they allow for one other past. This other past which is conceded and even articulated by some conservatives is the pre-colonial Aboriginal past. The principal exponent of this is Blainey, especially in his journalism but also in his *Triumph of the Nomads*. This book seems to contradict the thrust of his other historical writings and is therefore a source of puzzlement, but this is perhaps solved once it is appreciated that for Blainey, like other conservatives, the Aboriginal and Australian pasts are incommensurate. Blainey writes, for example: 'My view is that we should be proud of much of the *ancient* Aboriginal history of this land; we should be proud of much of the British history of this land'.[40] In other words, he is quite content to valorise the Aboriginal past as long as it does not occupy the same time as the Australian past of his traditional narrative. As a case in point, Blainey writes a eulogy to Aborigines' traditional linguistic skills as a vehicle for arguing that 'some Aboriginal peoples would gain more if [they were] proud of their traditions' rather than conceiving of themselves as 'permanent victims or puppets of a tragic past'. Hence, Aborigines are encouraged to use the coinage of the pre-colonial past just as they are discouraged from trading upon a particular representation of the colonial past. And, at the same time as Blainey advocates this strategy, he emphasises that most of the 250 or so Aboriginal languages once spoken are 'now silent'.[41] This suggests that Blainey's allowance for this pre-colonial past is relatively unimportant, for it is either deemed to be already past or it is assumed that it will eventually become so in effect, and so is incommensurate with the British Australian past which, by comparison, is conceived of as part of the ongoing Australian present.

II

This conservative construction of the Aboriginal past, and thus the Australian present, derives from a particular historical discourse, and is fundamental to the fevered conservative misperception that Mabo represents the end of history and hence the end of Australia. Conservatives have inherited many of the assumptions which underpinned the discourse of history in the nineteenth century, *the* century arguably of both history and the nation. In particular they assume that history has an evolutionary trajectory, and is invariably the story of progress.[42] The most important exponent of this view is Blainey, who renders the history of the British colonisation of this continent in terms of a natural process of evolution and thus one whose course is inevitable:

> The *old* way of life survived [before 1788]. But that way of life was doomed, even if the Papuans, the Javanese or the Maoris had been the first outsiders to settle in Australia . . . What happened to the Aborigines after 1788 had probably happened a few thousand years earlier to all our ancestors . . . All over the world, the relatively *simple* way of life of hunters and gatherers was wrecked by the coming of people who domesticated plants and animals . . . Everywhere, groups of people lost their vast sweeps of land . . . Such a form of land use was bound to be overthrown or undermined. The world's history [i.e., progress] has depended heavily on the eclipse of this *old* and wasteful economic way of life . . . There is no way it could be preserved. The miracle is that it survived until 1788 and later.[43]

Blainey's denial of any historical agency and therefore moral responsibility for the consequences of British colonisation reiterates the historical accounts produced in the late nineteenth and early twentieth centuries (see pp. xi–xii), as Henry Reynolds has noted,[44] and is echoed by other conservatives today in a similarly crude fashion. Howard, for instance, bluntly pronounced that non-aboriginal populations have, 'throughout history, [always] supplanted [their] predecessors'; Fischer claimed that 'rightly or wrongly, dispossession was always going to happen'; as did Morgan (see pp. 90, 92).[45]

The logic of this history of progress quite obviously rests upon another of those nineteenth-century historicist assumptions: that Aborigines or Aboriginality are more or less unchanging. Thus, Fischer instructed 'those in the guilt industry . . . to consider that developing cultures and peoples will always overtake relatively stationary cultures', while Blainey claimed that 'Aborigines, more than most other peoples, found it unusually painful and slow to adjust to the regime of their displacers and conquerors'.[46] This unchangingness is construed by conservatives as a function of Australia's geographical location:

> There is little doubt that the coming of Europeans to Australia's shore had a detrimental impact on the culture of the Aborigines. As Geoffrey Blainey has written, the Aborigines may well have been happier if they had been able to continue to live in isolation from the outside world. But such a proposition is unrealistic in the *modern* world . . . There is no turning back the clock to recreate the insularity on which the survival of Aboriginal culture was ultimately dependent.[47]

Implicit in such an argument is a contention that Aborigines were not only isolated in space but were also, as a consequence of this, suspended in time. This construction of Aboriginality, which also derives from the nineteenth-century historical discourse, is very apparent in Blainey's writings about what he has called 'oldtime Aboriginal Australia':

> The Aborigines missed out on the most important chain of events in all economic history [the neolithic revolution]. These momentous events had begun at least 10,000 years ago but, for some reason not easily explained, they did not reach here . . . These economic changes did not penetrate this continent until the British brought them . . . [Australia was one of] the remaining regions where the old way of life survived.[48]

It is quite evident, then, that conservatives believe the widely held conception (I noted in my introduction to this volume), that while Aborigines exist in the contemporaneous present they are inherently representatives of the ancient human past. This representation of Aborigines as the old, the traditional and the past, can only be understood in a context where Europeans, especially Anglo-Australians, are simultaneously conceived of as being the new, the modern and the present (future). In other words, in this myth of the modern, Europeans figure themselves as modern while they invent the Aborigines as ancient or traditional. Thus, in this narrative discourse, Aborigines were and are conceived to be the temporal place which Europeans left behind in order to enter into modernity, and progress is adjudged to have occurred inasmuch as Australians move away from this time. Blainey writes: 'there was a deep gulf' between Aborigines and Europeans because Aborigines 'lagged several millennia behind'; they belonged to 'a world almost as remote, as different as outer space'.

> Here were the citizens and outcasts of the world's latest economic revolution—the industrial revolution and the age of steam—confronting Aborigines who had not yet experienced the first economic revolution [i.e., pastoralism]. Here were the inhabitants of the land that had just invented the steam engine meeting folk who could not boil water.[49]

This conception of Aborigines was startlingly evident in what were regarded as the most notorious expressions of racism during the Mabo debate of last year, which Andrew Markus discusses in his chapter (see p. 92).

The currency of this construction of Aborigines as an old and unchanging people owes much to the late nineteenth century when, as I have noted, the national history and the nation of Australia were founded. Both these discourses, the historical and the national, omitted Aborigines. While Aborigines were conceived by historians as being ahistorical subjects because, as I remarked in the introduction, they were seen as unchanging, other historicist assumptions—that Aborigines were of the past or were passing away and so not part of the present (future)—dictated that they could not be subjects of the nation. And so Aborigines were not only effectively omitted from the new national history, they were also excluded from the new nation, namely in the founding document, the Australian Constitution of 1901, those who had been the first to be called Australians were not to be counted in any census of the peoples of Australia. These people were denied the status of Australian, and they were not to be the responsibility of the new Australian State but rather to be that of what were the old colonies. If this symbolically removed Aborigines from the time of the nation, the States themselves sought to remove Aborigines from the central spaces of Australia by confining them to marginal areas, and inasmuch as their segregationist–protectionist policies (along with the representation of Aborigines as being 'outback') succeeded in achieving this object, the illusion of Aborigines being of another time was perpetuated.

This temporal separation of Australia and Aboriginality, the present and the past, was, it can be argued, integral to the image of Australia as a modern nation in the first half of this century. It was maintained, moreover, in the postwar period when Australian governments abandoned their segregationist–protectionist policies and adopted the policy of assimilation. No longer were Aborigines to pass away in the manner that had been eagerly anticipated; instead they were to simply pass as Australians and thus enter into the nation—they were indeed to become citizens, but as Australians (or at least as Australian Aborigines first of all), not as Aborigines. Assimilation, then, was premised on the notion that Aborigines were going to be modernised. Little had changed, for while Aboriginal bodies were no longer considered to be disappearing into the past, Aboriginal culture was still posited as being of the past and therefore incompatible with modernity. Hence, Aborigines could only be granted a place in the nation if they abandoned their past—their Aboriginality—in order to enter into its time zone.

These notions of Australia and Australianness could only be sustained, however, if Aboriginality, as a symbol of past time, had a tenuous relationship to what was conceived of as Australian space. But since the 1960s and, more particularly with Mabo, this nexus has been threatened, even severed, in the eyes of conservatives, and thus their Australia is deemed to be at risk. This is evidenced by a consideration of conservative responses to the granting of land to Aborigines. Conservatives are not opposed to land rights for Aborigines *per se*; instead they are quite evidently prepared to grant land to so-called 'traditional Aborigines', that is, the 'real' Aborigines who are authentic because they are deemed not to have changed,[50] but only when and where this does not threaten the symbolic time of Australia, that is its present (future). Therefore, while conservatives oppose land rights they do so because they assume that Aborigines are of times past—primitive hunter-gatherers who have not reached that economic and cultural stage of pastoralism, agriculture or commerce which allegedly ensures a progressive nation—and so they believe that granting important Australian spaces will mean that Australia either stops or regresses in time. Thus, one concerned Australian construed Mabo as an 'attempt to turn back time', while another claimed its champions were 'trying to lead Australia backwards'.[51] More prominently, Blainey contended that the solution of 'massive land rights essentially looks backwards . . . [and] almost tries to restore [an] archaic and untenable way of life'; Morgan described 'Aboriginal land rights . . . [as] a symbolic step back'; Perron predicted the land will become 'a frozen asset'; and a financial analyst warned that 'Australia could go back to being a Stone Age culture of 20,000 people living on witchetty grubs'.[52] Australia, they assume,[53] cannot 'develop', which is to say progress, at the same time as Aborigines have land. In other words, according to these conservatives, Aboriginal places cannot be coterminous with Australian time. So, in exactly the same terms as British colonisation was justified by the conventional narrative, the present and the future of the nation effectively depends upon Aboriginal dispossession. For Australia's future, the (Aboriginal) past cannot be present and the present cannot be the (Aboriginal) past, any more than Aborigines can be both Aboriginal *and* Australian since the conventional narrative has imagined (modern) Australia in contradistinction to the (antique) Aboriginal other.

While native title and other Aboriginal land claims are held to endanger Australia because it threatens the temporal dream of conservatives, it also wreaks havoc in the conservative unconscious because it challenges the way they have invented Australia in spatial terms. In their historical narratives, Australia is imagined as an indivisible and possessed whole, enclosed and complete, its 'Australianness' thus residing in its exclusive possession of the continent. This fantasy is evident in Morgan's remembrance of the forthcoming centenary of Federation, 'our first hundred years as . . . a nation occupying, entirely, a great island continent. The great ideal of federation was "one nation—one continent". That ideal was . . . fractured, badly fractured, by . . . the . . . Mabo judgement'.[54]

Mabo is represented as an act of cannibalism upon this Australia: Morgan speaks of Aboriginal land being 'carved out of Australia'; Perron refers to Aborigines 'demanding large slices of the continent'; Fischer claims there are Aboriginal claims to 'large chunks of Australia'; Blainey believes Mabo 'could even cut the nation in half'; and the *Herald Sun* warns that Mabo has 'the potential to split the nation'.[55] Other spokespeople misrepresent native claims as covering all or nearly all of Australia.[56] Durack claimed that 'no part of Australia will be exempt', and Opposition spokesman on infrastructure and national development, Ian McLachlan, contended that 'the High Court decision . . . imposes the possibility of claims for native title over a great part of Australia'.[57] Mabo is also represented as something akin to a tidal wave or flood emanating from *outside* Australia. Thus, Fischer alleged that there were 'strident outlandish claims sweeping across . . . Australia'; Sir Arvi Parbo, chairman of Western Mining Corporation, warned of 'a very fundamental change which has arisen out of the decision which the High Court made in relation to two very small islands off the coast of Australia and which has now had a sort of spillover effect onto the mainland'. Blainey's atlas suggested 'these tiny . . . [and] remote islands . . . [were] closer to Papua than the Australian mainland'; and *Australian Business Monthly* journalist Trevor Sykes claimed that what he called 'three specks of coral [are] so far out in the ocean that most Australians would hardly think they were within its territorial waters'.[58] The validity of applying such a margin to 'mainland Australia'[59] is questioned most of all, however, in Morgan's implication that Mabo is akin to an 'invasion of our continent', similar to the danger constituted by the Japanese during World War II.[60]

The 'one nation, one continent' of Australia is deemed to be at risk in much the same way as other nations have been in the past. Thus, *The Australian* columnist Frank Devine claimed that 'the delineation of Aboriginal "homelands" gives the [Australian] map the crowded look of a map of nineteenth-century Europe'. Others were more specific in their historical analogies: Morgan and Perron invoked the India of 1947 when they referred to 'a partitioning of the continent'; Howard referred to the possibility of 'the emergence in Australia of our version of the notorious South African homelands'; and Blainey conjured up Germany (and Poland) when he claimed that there is 'a wide corridor of Aboriginal land [which] now runs almost across Australia', and in another version, that 'you can travel over Aboriginal lands for five-sixths of the way—if I have read my atlas correctly. In that north-south corridor of Aboriginal lands there are only a couple of gaps of any size, and each gap is narrower that a crossing of Bass Strait'.[61]

These areas of land are immediately conflated, in the conservatives' imagination, with nations. Blainey says that 'one Aboriginal block of land is about as large as Portugal, another is as large as Austria, another as large as the Netherlands . . . [and another is] larger than South Korea', and quite explicitly claims that his 'corridor could be the nucleus of a nation'. 'If too much land is given', he claims, 'we could end up with . . . the genesis of two systems of government'. In apocryphal terms, Blainey warns that 'the ever-increasing grants of land to Aborigines is probably a step towards . . . two nations, or worst of all, two half-nations', while Morgan prophesies that 'Mabo . . . carries the seeds of territorial dismemberment of the Australian continent and the end of the Australian nation as we've known it'.[62] Australia is only deemed to be facing its end, it should be emphasised, because these conservatives bear the burden of a narrative discourse which was only able to imagine Australia as 'one nation—one continent' by symbolically dispossessing and denying the existence of Aborigines, and thus they assume that Australia cannot survive as a nation when there is a return of the Aboriginal other to the continent: Aboriginal space cannot be Australian any more than Australian space can be Aboriginal.[63]

Mabo is also deemed to augur the end of Australian history and therefore the end of Australia since it is construed as dividing the people of the nation. Australia can only *be* if Australians are 'one people', the same as each other. Blainey conflates ethnic or racial identity with 'racial separateness', and fears we are being forced to 'countenance two ways of life and two separate Australias', while Morgan pronounces that:

> the fate of the nation depends, in the long term, on the common
> beliefs which unite the people and provide the foundation for
> national sovereignty . . . Mabo directly threatens the unity of Aus-
> tralia . . . It encourages aboriginal Australians to think of
> themselves as separate from their fellow citizens. It promises racial
> tension. It guarantees . . . stagnation.[64]

Morgan reiterates this logic when he claims that 'the distinction that is being asked for [between Aborigines and the rest of Australia on grounds of culture, tradition and descent] is impossible in a *modern* society'.[65] This reasoning is made more explicit in other conservatives' writings. Tim Hewat describes Aboriginal society as 'a mass of small tribes . . . all jealously guarding their individuality'; Institute of Public Affairs anthropologist Ron Brunton represents the demand for Aboriginal self-determination as a 'push for retribalisation'; Fischer claims that any recognition of Aborigines' prior occupation of this continent would be 'an enormously retro- grade step because it would mean the acknowledgment of some sort of tribalisation of our society'; and Blainey sees it as akin to the policy of multiculturalism which threatens 'to disperse this nation into many tribes'.[66] 'Tribes' and 'tribal' are signifiers for the past, aligned with the 'primitive' or the 'savage' as the antithesis of modernity. It is not surprising, then, that Blainey insists that:

> the future of the Aborigines lies in looking to the 21st century, not to the 18th century. Even if a minority of Aborigines succeed in keeping alive parts of their traditional culture, their future and success will be more as Australians than as Aborigines . . . The nation should certainly help and foster them, not because they are Aborigines, but because they are Australians.[67]

It is thus evident that the conventional historical narrative cannot conceive of Australia being modern *and* Aboriginal, or Aborigines being Aboriginal *and* Australian. Instead, its future is predicated upon the destruction of the racial other as the symbol of the past, and the defence of the Australia of the foundational myth: 'I call on all of you', Morgan appealed in 1993, 'to stand up for the ideals of federation—one nation—one continent; one law, one people, one destiny. Let us go forward then, together . . .'[68]

Mabo, I have argued, has threatened conservatives, not because it presages a revolution in Australia but rather because it offers a new history which has threatened to overturn the traditional narrative constitution and comprehension of Australian nationhood and identity. The anguish of conservatives has been especially profound for two major reasons, I have suggested: first, Mabo and the new Australian history ends the historical silence about the Aboriginal pre-colonial and colonial past upon which the conservative invention of Australia and Australianness was founded, and since their Australia was realised through and rests upon that conventional historical narrative, the end of this history constitutes for them the end of Australia. Second, the historical changes Mabo portends in the space of Australia challenge a narrative of the nation which has measured its progress relative to an Aboriginal absence or dispossession in that space while simultaneously constructing Aboriginality as the past, and so Aboriginal possession of the land of Australia symbolises for conservatives the end of progress and thus the end of history.

8 Aboriginality, Mabo and the republic: indigenising Australia

John Morton

Near the beginning of each Australian Football League (AFL) Premiership Season the *Age* asks a number of prominent personalities for their predictions for the coming football year. In 1993, the International Year for the World's Indigenous People, nobody managed to predict the teams to be involved in the season's Grand Final (the victorious Essendon and the vanquished Carlton), yet two predictions came true. Ted Whitten (Mr Football) nominated Mandawuy Yunupingu to sing before the Grand Final crowd, on the grounds that 'you can't get more Australian than that', while Paul Keating foretold of Gavin Wanganeen winning the Brownlow Medal, the AFL's premier annual award.[1]

Wanganeen was one of a number of Aboriginal players who helped Essendon take honours in 1993. Another was Michael Long, who was presented with the Norm Smith Medal for being the best Grand Final player, in front of a crowd who had listened to the National Anthem sung by Aboriginal singer Maroochy Barambah. This same crowd at half-time listened not only to Mandawuy Yunupingu and his band Yothu Yindi's combined rendering of 'Djapana' and 'Treaty', but also to Archie Roach's 'Jamu Dreaming'. In addition, with Icehouse's 'Great Southern Land' creating a musical background, scores of young indigenous Australians treated the gathering to a spectacular visual representation of Australia covering a substantial part of the Melbourne Cricket Ground (MCG). This representation placed the Aboriginal flag at the very centre of Australia, flanked on the right (as seen by the crowd) by the Torres Strait Islander flag and on the left by the more familiar emblems of the Australian flag. With the production and display of

indigenous totemic effigies to match those representing Essendon
(the Bombers) and Carlton (the Blues), this was a day when
reconciliation between black and white Australians was literally
brought to dramatic fruition. It was fitting that the Bombers, with
the largest contingent of Aboriginal players in the AFL, were 37
points in front at half-time. It was fitting, too, given the historical
reality of 'the great Australian silence', that the red, white and blue
of (white) Australia had moved left from centre stage, making way
for the gold, red and black of Aboriginal Australia and leaving the
propitious right side[2] open for occupation by the green, blue, black
and white of the Torres Strait Islands. Like Carlton, white Australia
was ostensibly humbled this day.[3] Yet, simultaneously, Australia was
heavily promoted.

What we make of these kinds of events, with their stark
appropriations of indigenous themes in the name of the nation, is
always intensely personal, and this is certainly true of myself. But
my own background as an English migrant to Australia has also
led me to light upon something general in the Mabo era, namely,
the indigenisation of Australia as correlative to its un-Anglicisation.
As we know, the High Court's Mabo decision in June 1992 came
as the long-term outcome of a widespread interrogation of Australian history. Later the same year Paul Keating made his famous
confessional Redfern speech to open the International Year of the
World's Indigenous Peoples, frankly admitting a history of
'dispossession' and 'national shame'. The Mabo judgment, he
averred, was therefore just, because it overturned the 'bizarre'
doctrine of *terra nullius* and recognised the 'fundamental truth' of
the 'oldest culture in the world'—a truth embodied above all in a
'timeless' association with 'the land'.[4] Prime Minister Keating's
dedication to this truth was profiled again when he later moved
responsibility for Aboriginal Affairs to his own Department of Prime
Minister and Cabinet in order to give himself 'a key role in
consultations over the landmark Mabo High Court decision on land
title, the reconciliation process, the issue of a treaty, and Aboriginal
aspirations to be recognised in the Constitution'. The Aboriginal
chairperson of the Aboriginal and Torres Strait Islander Commission
(ATSIC), Lois O'Donoghue, welcomed this 'recogni[tion] that the
rights of indigenous Australians are central to the issue of our
country's national identity and its place in the world'.[5]

The other question involving the Constitution which the Prime
Minister himself sees as central to national identity and the country's
international standing is that of the possibility of forming an
Australian republic. This possibility is not entirely unconnected to
the indigenisation of the nation. As historian Don Watson, the Prime
Minister's adviser and speech writer, has recently argued, the logic

behind the call for an Australian republic is not so much that we are a young nation which, in order to mature, needs to cut the umbilical cord with the 'motherland', but more that we are already far, far too old to maintain that tie: 'The great myth about Australia is that we are young. We're not. Not only is this the oldest continent and Aboriginal Australia the oldest society on earth, this white Australia or multicultural Australia, or whatever you like to call it, is also old.' In this regard, Watson found it useful to quote Henry Lawson: 'I am Australian—I know no other land.'[6] Similarly, it made sense for Lyall Munro Jnr to underline the Prime Minister's logic during the latter's Redfern speech by claiming that Aborigines have been in Australia 'since time immemorial—not for 40,000 years as some anthropologists have decided. We are not a 40,000-year-old people. We come from the time that the land and the world was made. We come from the beginning'.[7] One way to 'know no other land' than Australia is to acknowledge this fact and at the same time deny the nation's previous links to Britain. This conversion of knowledge is generally known as 'rewriting history': it is a normal, if highly contested, aspect of the creation of national genealogies (and it reminds us that it is *knowledge* that creates a nation as an 'imagined community' or as 'collective conscience').[8] Equally normal, and equally contested, is the corresponding process of the passing over of history into myth.

Symbolic substitution

Myths are symbolic narratives. When histories change and harden into myths, so too do narrative sequences, which go through processes of logical transformation. One such process is symbolic substitution, which I argue characterises the relationship between current debates over Mabo and the republic. As Dennis Altman has argued, if Paul Keating's recent republican bid is to be successful, then the Prime Minister needs to 'tell Australia exactly why we should change the present structures, and what symbols of nationhood are available to replace the monarchy'. An Australian republic will not become a reality, suggests Altman, until an alternative myth is advanced which can rival the one already in place, and the only concrete candidate is Aboriginality. As Altman says:

> Some people, and maybe the Prime Minister is among them, see the reframing of the Constitution as an opportunity to recognise the prior existence of Aboriginal Australia, to incorporate reconciliation into a symbolic statement of nationhood. If the republic debate were to concentrate on this last point it would, I suspect, have more chance of success.[9]

I would argue that there is not much doubt that the Prime Minister has grasped the connection. O'Donoghue, as Aboriginal Australia's premier bureaucrat, has been hailed in regal tones as 'the Mother of the Nation'.[10] She is a member of the Federal Government's Republic Advisory Committee and has enunciated her belief that constitutional recognition of the prior existence of Aboriginal Australia would be a condition of Aboriginal people accepting constitutional reform in the direction of a republic. There is even 'growing currency' in the suggestion that she will be Australia's next Governor-General 'or even its first President'.[11] This, then, is the 'chessboard' logic of symbolic substitution, in which 'black queen' takes 'white queen'. It is a logic which makes some sense of Keating's emergence from his native title legislation triumph in December 1993 with his arm around O'Donoghue, familiar treatment which the Prime Minister had previously reserved for the Queen.[12]

Examples of the logic of symbolic substitution are often deeply personal as well as political. For example, in 1993 I attended two Mabo discussions held at La Trobe University. In one of these, consideration of questions of identity and the space Aboriginal people might occupy in the nation's collective conscience provoked a non-Aboriginal person to declare that she had a problematic identity as a white Australian and was critical of the directions of Australian society, but she looked to Aboriginal people and Aboriginal knowledge as a way of finding alternative inspiration. At the other forum, another non-Aboriginal person proclaimed something similar. She was concerned that the debate about Mabo was getting submerged by legal details. For her, it was the symbolic and historic dimensions of Mabo that mattered most, particularly at a time when the nation was moving towards a republic, which meant that it should no longer look towards Britain for cultural inspiration. Indeed, she suggested, it should look to its own indigenous people.

These remarks are good examples of what has happened in recent years as a result of the shattering of 'the great Australian silence'. As a result of the revolutions in history that began in the 1960s and have culminated (for the time being at least) in the Mabo judgment, Aboriginality in Australia—its archaeology, its indigenous racial and cultural forms, and its encounters with imperialism—has been very much 'talked up'. In other words, an Aboriginal absence has turned into an Aboriginal presence.[13] The remarks are also enough to alert us to a certain redemptive function being performed by Mabo and all that it stands for by way of anti-colonial sentiment, reconciliation and the elevation of Aboriginal history. Whether the focus is on the individual person, who looks to Aboriginality as a kind of therapeutic antidote to modernity, or on the nation as a whole, which looks to reconciliation as a sign of its increasing independence and maturity, Aboriginal identity plays its part in a utopian projection of the future. Such twinning of the individual personality and the nation's character, couched in terms of idioms of salvation, is well-known and well documented through recent studies of Euro-Australian appropriations of Aboriginality.[14] In broad outline, there is a widespread view that Aboriginal values can in some sense come to fill a vacuum in the soul of (white) Australia. It is precisely this sentiment which has in recent decades made many white Australians ashamed to say that they have never met, let alone come to know, an Aboriginal person. Most probably, these same people who yearn for Aboriginality would support Mabo, and possibly a republic as well.[15]

The symbolic substitution of Aboriginality for the monarchy informs a number of discursive movements. For example, Jesuit priest, lawyer and campaigner for Aboriginal rights, Frank Brennan, has recently updated his call for 'greater reconciliation with the descendants of the traditional owners of the land',[16] and advocated a number of post-Mabo constitutional reforms: were Australia to become a republic, there should be 'a Council of Elders to advise the Head of State, and also choose or sack the Head of State', and this should have Aboriginal representation guaranteed; and we should also 'change the system of land titles so the radical title is held by the traditional owners instead of the Crown'.[17] In a profound sense, therefore, Brennan advocates the replacement of the Crown with Aboriginality.[18]

Then again there is the question of the future of the Australian flag. It is clear that Keating supports the removal of the Union Jack from Australia's premier symbol, although how he might replace it is not known. However, at the end of 1993, just prior to the passing of the Federal Government's native title legislation, *The Australian* announced the result of a competition it had held to find an alternative design. The winning entry, judged as such by eight prominent Australians, including the then deputy chairperson of ATSIC, Sol Bellear, was virtually identical to the one that was placed second. It combined the familiar Southern Cross and Commonwealth Star motifs with the red, white and blue of the old flag to produce a new design incorporating Ayers Rock, the ancient 'heart' or 'navel' of the nation to which thousands of Australians and overseas visitors make a pilgrimage every year to experience the 'magical Dreamtime'.[19] Of the two designs which tied for third place and were coincidentally created by the same person, one, depicting the Southern Cross, was simply black and white, evoking the reconciliation of racial distinctions that has been emblematic of Australia at least since the choosing of the national capital's coat of arms;[20] the other was a slightly modified form of the Aboriginal flag, with a telling white stripe separating the black (people) and the red (land) behind the golden yellow of the sun.[21] But while these playful symbolic constructions only implicitly engage a logic of substitution, that logic is far more explicit in the design of a flag which I first encountered as a postcard in 1993. This representation bore the familiar current format of the Australian flag, except that the Union Jack was missing. In its place was the red, black and gold of the Aboriginal nation—together, one assumes, with everything that the Aboriginal flag stands for in terms of anti-imperialism. This representation has since become more widespread and can now be found emblazoning its message as stickers and on T-shirts.[22]

What this substitution naturally achieves is the replacement of Australia's British heritage and history with that well-known, deceptively simple and ambiguous message: 'white Australia has a black history'. This is the same history which Midnight Oil very recently alluded to in a song whose lyrics spoke ironically about monarchist sentiment amidst dejected images of Aboriginality in the shape of Truganini and Albert Namatjira. It is a message that makes sense if we understand that the massively burgeoning field now known as Aboriginal history, which hardly existed before the 1960s, has brought British history seriously into question. This has had important repercussions, which can be measured by the tone of Keating's Redfern speech, as well as the judgment of Justices Deane and Gaudron in the Mabo case, which described Aboriginal dispossession as 'the darkest aspect of the history of this nation', which must 'remain diminished' until a 'national legacy of unutterable shame' is acknowledged.[23] Of course, whether or not the nation 'remains diminished' by keeping its ties with Britain and the monarchy is also what is at stake in the debate over the republic. We may say, in fact, that not only does the reconciliation project match the call for a republic in terms of the nation's developing maturity, but the Mabo judgment itself, together with the movement towards reconciliation, comes to answer the requirements of a republic, as one pre-1788 heritage (a *British* heritage) is conveniently replaced with another (some 40 000 or more years old). To the extent that this depends upon a moral questioning of Imperial history, it should also be the case that a republic can come to answer the requirements of Aboriginal people.[24]

In this respect it is necessary to underline again the ambiguity of the slogan, 'white Australia has a black history'. This statement is, of course, condemnatory. It depends on viewing the past darkly and therefore provokes counter-narratives: 'This is a great country with a great history', and 'If ever we have been governed by airy fairy trendies whose main ambition in life is to denigrate anything that is British, that is what we now have in Federal Parliament'.[25] However, the statement is also celebratory. As has long been stressed in debates about reconciliation, recognition of Aboriginality is supposed to be of benefit to 'all Australians', with Aboriginal people being, as it were, prepared to donate 40 000 or more years of their heritage to the nation. Notwithstanding the counter-narratives, the nation seems increasingly accepting of this gift, thereby extending its 'authentically Australian' genealogy. In all states, as well as at the Federal level, there is legislation designed specifically to protect Aboriginal heritage, and the ever expanding possibilities of embarking on Aboriginal cultural tours ensure that we can 'experience what life was like in Australia 40 000 years ago'—and even 'take it back' home.[26]

Now, however, the nation celebrates its birthday on 26 January, with the parturition having fictitiously occurred in 1788. This fiction seems less and less appropriate as the nation extends its genealogy and heritage so as to become founded on 'the oldest living culture in the world'. We were reminded of this by the Aboriginal protest march held in Sydney on Australia Day in 1988, the bicentennial year, when Galarrwuy Yunupingu told an assembled crowd that 'Australia's too old to celebrate birthdays'.[27] But this logic was also behind the recent call by Federal Minister for Aboriginal Affairs, Robert Tickner, to change Australia Day from 26 January, often known in Aboriginal circles as Invasion Day, to some date more acceptable to Aboriginal people.[28] While there has been at least one suggestion that *no* date would be acceptable to Aboriginal people, on the grounds that 'Australia has *always* been our land',[29] one possible scenario for a solution to the problem would be to sign a treaty between black and white Australians on 26 January. Australia Day could then become Treaty Day or Reconciliation Day, and, at a stroke, Australia really could, in line with Don Watson's wishes, move from being a young nation to an ancient one grounded in a 'timeless' past.[30] Being 'the first Australians', it follows that Aborigines, notwithstanding the historical presence of the First Fleet and its convicts, would become the ancestors of us all.[31]

One family, one nation, one blood

A sense of kinship between white and black Australians is, I believe, what accounts for the popularity of works like Sally Morgan's book, *My Place*, and Jimmy Chi's musical, *Bran Nue Dae*. As Marcia Langton has speculated, the popularity of the best-selling *My Place*, which tells of its author's determined, but surprising, detection of her Aboriginal roots, may well lie in the fact that it 'raises the possibility that the reader might also find, with a little sleuthing in the family tree, an Aboriginal ancestor'.[32] It takes little imagination to see that, with sales approaching record proportions, *My Place* may eventually convert the whole of Australia.[33] Such conversion is, incidentally, how *Bran Nue Dae* comes to a conclusion. After a beginning marked by a mocking rendition of 'God Save the Queen', absolutely everybody in the cast, both black and white, is overjoyed to find that they are all related, and they sing that 'there is nothing they would rather be than to be an Aborigine'.[34] This idea of relatedness is also what underwrites the Christian projects of Frank Brennan, whose writing aims to reconcile differences so that 'every Australian [can] proudly call this land "My Place"'.[35] One might add, as well, that white Australian writers are beginning to construct more figures akin to those depicted in films like Peter Weir's *The Last Wave* and Paul Hogan's *'Crocodile' Dundee*—figures with Aboriginal ancestry. As one such writer has said: 'Bless the koories [*sic*] . . . Let's honour their heritage and join them in their future. We are not Europe. If we stay here long enough the country will have its way and we'll all be its Aborigines.'[36]

What should we make of this fictive kinship, evidently sensed from both sides of the 'racial' and 'cultural' divide? A clue was given in 1993 in an edition of the *Age Good Weekend* magazine, which had a story titled 'Aboriginal Reconciliation: Time to Get Serious'. This was accompanied by a stylised Aboriginal map of Australia that encompassed the Aboriginal flag and was surrounded by Aboriginal hands reaching inwards, in the midst of which two hands, one black, one white, were firmly and mutually clasped in an image of reconciliation.[37] Furthermore, the edition was led by a cover image, headlined 'It's Time', of a young Aboriginal man and a young white woman kissing. This explicitly sexualised public image of reconciliation, with its conjunction of black man and white woman, is quite new in terms of the history of Australian race relations and says something about the revolutionary nature of the Mabo era. Yet, as some recent advertising of a similar or related nature would suggest, we might have expected to see more of it on the horizon.[38] This expectation was fulfilled when the Australian Broadcasting Corporation screened its series *Heartland* in early 1994, depicting, against a complex backdrop of Australian race relations, the problematic creation of a loving relationship between an Aboriginal man and a white Australian woman.

Why this might be the case is, I believe, connected to metaphorical ideas about kinship, affinity and blood that have always characterised nationhood. Anthropologists, for example, have long been aware that, perhaps universally, marriage and affinity in 'the elementary structures of kinship' carry with them the multivalent sense of a reconciliation between opposing forces. This reconciliation can be viewed in terms of the symbolic opposition between man and woman, or it may be viewed in terms of biological or genetic mixing. Interestingly, however, a major emphasis has been on the fact that marriage symbolises an alliance between two groups, whose 'reconciliation' is ideally cemented over the generations by ongoing exchange, particularly by what is androcentrically viewed as the 'exchange of women'. Such alliance and exchange (not simply of women, but also of goods and services) can and do go wrong. And, when exchange is negated, it is replaced by mistrust, hostility and sometimes outright warfare, which has at various times and in various places been characterised by both territorial conquest and the stealing of women.[39] This picture, although far removed from its initial anthropological application to small-scale (including Aboriginal) societies, has important implications for a post-Mabo view of Aboriginal history and its place in national reconstruction.

Although still contested, it goes without saying that Europeans invaded Australia,[40] and while its extent should not be over- or under-emphasised, there was also an unrecognised war (or series of wars) between Aboriginal people and the white invaders who came to take land and consolidate new modes of production. Furthermore, while efforts to exchange with or by Aboriginal people were made, tension between indigenous and non-indigenous peoples nevertheless often manifested itself in disputes over access to women, which led to persistent acts of rape, murder and theft. Eventually, the whole formal and informal framework of racism in Australia came to be buttressed by the implicit idea that white men taking black women was permissible (if not always officially approved of), while black men taking white women was subject to the strongest prohibition. This attitude came to be entrenched in the White Australia Policy, which was allied to aspects of the so-called assimilation policy designed to 'breed out' Aborigines by 'thinning' Aboriginal blood and steering mixed-race children to their paternal 'white side'. It is no coincidence that these genocidal and ethnocidal impulses (which added a strange and macabre twist to anthropological ideas about Aboriginal 'virgin birth' and 'ignorance of physiological paternity')[41] officially died at about the same time that Aboriginal history emerged to re-create an Aboriginal presence in the 1960s and 1970s.

Up until that time, a sexualised image of 'making up' or 'getting serious' about reconciliation simply could not take root in a public context. The emotional climate had been reinforced by typically racist fears and desires concerning the sexual potency of black men, fears and desires clearly related to what Freudians call 'castration anxiety'.[42] For example, during Charles Perkins' freedom rides in New South Wales in the mid 1960s, one white man justified the exclusion of blacks from the Moree spa baths on the basis of his belief that all blacks had a secret desire to impregnate white women and that one masturbatory effort in the pool would be enough to impregnate hundreds of white female bathers.[43] This, of course, could hardly be further from a sexualised image of reconciliation, although there is, I believe, reason to believe that the new image is derived from the old one. For example, Aboriginal actor Ernie Dingo lampoons the sexualisation of racism in one of his comedy routines in which he carries with him a white vacuum cleaner pipe, comments on it being the only thing 'this long and white', and plays it as a didgeridoo. The logic of this humour is once again that of inversion, since this 'signification of the phallus'[44] explicitly compares black and white to the latter's cost; in addition, a white pipe that 'sucks' and is used to eradicate 'dirt' becomes in Dingo's hands a 'horny' instrument with which to 'trumpet' Aboriginality and betray the 'shortcomings' of white Australia. I would suggest, then, that while an earlier racist ideology rendered Aboriginal people impotent, the clear intention of sexualised images of reconciliation is to (re)assign power. This bestowal is surely the same as that which has occurred in the acknowledgment of Aboriginality in Australian history that determined the High Court's Mabo judgment—and nowhere has it been symbolically worked through more thoroughly than in *Heartland*.

Sovereign parentage from Windsor to Barunga

There could be much to say about *Heartland* as an allegory of reconciliation, but here I will only sketch a partial framework of its symbolism. We may be sure, I think, that this framework deals with an issue central to (at the *heart* of) the nation (or *land*). As one mid-1993 newspaper headline to a story about Eddie Mabo and the repercussions of his people's claim to Murray Island, screamed: 'Mabo's cry from the heart land that echoed around Australia.'[45]

Heartland 'echoed around Australia' over a three-month period in early 1994. With significant Aboriginal input into its production, the television series portrays the reconciliation process as a difficult romance between Ernie Dingo's Vincent Barunga and Cate Blanchett's Elizabeth (or Beth) Ashton. The two meet and the always-in-doubt reconciliation of their very different backgrounds occurs on neutral ground. Vincent hails from Western Australia, from a remote, strongly traditional community he left after a broken marriage and an apparent infraction of Aboriginal law. Beth, for her part, hails from a harbourside area of Sydney, whose community is decidedly 'yuppie'. The potential romance between middle class Australia and traditional Aboriginality is primarily played out in a place called Brooklyn Waters, on the northern New South Wales coast, which, unlike the communities from which Vincent and Beth originate, is depicted as multiracial, as befits the miscegenation that their romance would entail. It is also a place of considerable strife.

The names of Vincent Barunga and Elizabeth Ashton give us the first clue as to the nature of their romance inasmuch as they suggest a working through of the relationship between place and sovereignty, between land and law. Barunga is, in fact, a place in the Northern Territory every bit as remote as Vincent's Western Australian homeland. It is also the place where, in June 1988, Galarrwuy Yunupingu and Wenten Rubuntja, the then respective chairpersons of the Northern and Central Land Councils, presented Prime Minister Bob Hawke with a statement which, amongst other things, called 'on the Commonwealth Parliament to negotiate with us a Treaty or Compact recognising our prior ownership, continued occupation and sovereignty and affirming our human rights and freedoms'. Hawke responded by promising a treaty to be 'negotiated between the Aboriginal people and the Government on behalf of all the people of Australia', and later hung what came to be known as the Barunga Statement in Parliament House as a reminder to future leaders that it must be honoured. It seems that Vincent Barunga makes the same statement concerning Aboriginal sovereignty, which is presumably why he is in strongest dialogue with a woman who shares her name with the Crown. Barunga as 'land' or 'place' and Elizabeth as 'law' or 'sovereignty'—these are the initial terms of exchange in *Heartland*. However, as their respective other names might suggest, these terms will need changing for reconciliation to take effect. Vincent, after all, comes from the Latin *vincere*, which means 'to conquer' and is related to words like 'convince' and 'convict'. Just whom Vincent may aim to 'prosecute' in this array of meanings is indicated by Beth's surname, Ashton, which I interpret as part of the 'spirit of place' in *Heartland*, corresponding to Vincent's Barunga. The conquest and destruction of 'her place' is conveyed by the pun on 'Ash Town', perhaps making Beth a transformation of Cinderella (or 'Cinders'), awaiting her suitor prince. *Heartland*, I wish to argue, will therefore serve to 'convince' white Australia of the importance of the Barunga Statement, and this 'conviction'—this assertion of burning black desire—will be directed towards the Crown.

Brooklyn Waters, the site of reconciliation, is really two communities: the town itself and the nearby old mission settlement. As outsiders, Vincent and Beth must negotiate their way across this division. The mission is now owned and occupied by Aboriginal people, who are polarised in their relations with white townsfolk, most prominently represented in the form of the police. This symbolic geography is mediated by a property close to the mission, across which runs a pathway connecting the Aboriginal settlement to the town. The property belonged to Beth's recently deceased grandfather. She is not only potentially his heir, but also, as it turns out, a blood relative of a number of the local Aborigines, some of whom had been her grandfather's consorts. But while Beth occupies this mediating position between black and white in respect of land and blood, lying closer to the mission than to the town, Vincent inverts this situation. He is a police aide, has no blood ties to the Aboriginal community and, in spite of working closely with his fellow Aboriginal people, does not live on the mission. Vincent, therefore, although black and explicitly acting as a mediator, lies closer to the white side of the local landscape, where his link is not so much with the land as with the law. As if to complete the symmetry, we are eventually obliquely informed that Vincent is drawn to a career in the police force because it is 'in the blood'.

Brooklyn Waters, then, is the site of a symbolic 'crossing over'. As in a conventional yin/yang representation, white participates in black and black participates in white. This logic of mutual invasion and the reconciliation of opposites is framed in terms of Vincent and Beth's relations to their respective home communities and to the leading characters representing the inside communities at Brooklyn Waters. At home, in Western Australia, Vincent's Aboriginal identity is shown to be problematic in terms of his capacity to embrace the law, yet he travels there with Beth, who consequently learns, with some difficulty, the sources of his actions—his history, family and identity. The same situation occurs in reverse when Vincent accompanies Beth to Sydney, where Beth's middle class identity is also in question, largely in relation to her estranged spouse and their circle of bourgeois friends. But these steps backwards, to ascertain identities anchored in the past, are matched by Vincent and Beth's steps forward to the established communities at Brooklyn Waters, since both will leave their histories behind there and move to a new future. At Brooklyn Waters, they will both work through important relationships with the mission's leading character, Alf Dyer, usually referred to as 'Uncle', and the corresponding 'boss' of the white community, head policeman Phil McCarthy.

Phil is Vincent's 'best mate', but he is also Vincent's competitor for Beth's favours. Phil, in spite of himself, heads a thoroughly racist town, whose primary signification is the wrongful prosecution of Ricky Dyer, Alf's grandson, for murdering his girlfriend. In point of fact, the murder was committed as part of a series of rapes and killings of Aboriginal women by a pair of redneck whites, and it is Vincent's task to uncover the truth of this situation. In so doing, he not only guarantees the prosecution of those who live by a racist code, but inadvertently brings about the dramatic death of his best mate, Phil. In addition, in reciprocally guaranteeing the release from gaol of Ricky Dyer, he also assists Alf, the only surviving elder with traditional knowledge, in the transmission of local Aboriginal law. This transmission had always been in doubt, since Ricky, who in the end sits down with Alf to learn the 'old ways', had previously complained that these ways were no longer relevant to his life. The message seems clear. For reconciliation to occur, racist white law must die: this in turn opens up the space for the transmission of Aboriginal law. This is no easy task and ends with certain tragic consequences, since Vincent must be obliquely instrumental in his best friend's death, in fact triggering it with an 'unintended' remark: 'Leave him! He's not going anywhere.' The fact that some of his best friends are racist is not going to stop Vincent 'getting somewhere'.

In all this Beth plays a complementary role. While Vincent actively secures the law, Beth must guarantee the land. As has already been indicated, Beth comes to Brooklyn Waters because of a property interest, although her intentions are moulded by the market place: she aims to renovate her grandfather's property in order to sell it. Initially, she nearly sells it to Ben Lovell or Eddie Dyer, whose dual naming reflects the fact that he was one of 'the stolen generation' taken away from his Aboriginal mother and brought up white, with all knowledge of his Aboriginal heritage denied. His new identity as an Aborigine takes shape only after Beth's arrival in Brooklyn Waters: Eddie, as the illegitimate son of her grandfather, is her 'uncle'. In the end, however, Eddie is shown to be neither 'fish nor fowl'—a man who admits that 'I'll never be one of them; but, now I've met them, I'll never be what I was either'. He withdraws his interest in Beth's property, due largely to the fact that, as an ex-real estate agent, he cannot help but view it in monetary terms, which is against the (confused) spirit of his Aboriginality. Following this, the question arises as to whether Beth might lose the property to her white husband, a media personality in Sydney, as part of their settlement. But in the end, Beth neither sells the property, nor has it taken from her through divorce. Indeed, all suggestion of monetary interest in, and alienation of, the land dissolves as Vincent moves into the property to share it with Beth, at the same time fully Aboriginalising it by adorning its walls with 'Aboriginalia'. In the meantime, however, thanks largely to the acumen of Eddie Dyer, the nearby mission secures its economic and

social future through a business deal. Just as Beth and her land will
be married to Vincent and his law, so too will there be a marriage
of Aboriginal law and economic enterprise at Brooklyn Waters.

The reconciliation of black and white embodied in Vincent and
Beth's union is evidently a complex process of exchange. At all
stages of the story, appropriations are mutually constituted. At the
end of *Heartland*, after Vincent's career in the police force has been
placed in question, we find that he will, after all, stay with the law
at Brooklyn Waters—no longer as a police aide, but as a full
member of the local force. He will fully replace his mate Phil and
represent the law in a non-racist manner. And while Vincent, in an
inversion of the function attached to his (place) name Barunga,
symbolises the law, Beth symbolises the land—land which is Aboriginal in spirit and which embodies, against the spirit of her (regal)
name, Aboriginal sovereignty. The question of a future for this 'law
of the land' is considered in the very last scene of *Heartland*, in
which Vincent and Beth finally say confidently that they are a part
of each other, so recognising that they may at last have reconciled
their differences. This, in turn, raises the question of continuity, as
Vincent enquires of Beth about the possibility of children. The last
words are Vincent's, who declares his ulterior motive: 'It's all part
of a plan to breed you mob out.'

We should treat this ostensibly amusing remark seriously. Earlier forms of racism aimed at 'breeding out' Aborigines can be taken
as metaphoric of the relationship between white law and Aboriginal
land.[46] *Terra nullius* depended on the full presence of the Crown
and the symbolic absence (emptiness) of the land. Just as white
invaders came to dispossess by 'penetrating', occupying and settling
'virgin territory', so did the same hierarchical opposition between
man and woman characterise processes of miscegenation. In *Heartland* the law remains masculine and the land remains feminine, but
the use of Vincent and Beth as signifiers serves to reverse the
white/black polarity. This is fitting for the Mabo era. If *terra nullius*
is dead, it is not inaccurate to see this death as a victory, however
partial, over racism. This means, in effect, that recognition of native
title is a recognition of Aboriginal law—a conversion of an Aboriginal absence into an Aboriginal presence, which *Heartland* deals
with as an archetypal shift in masculine and feminine values relative
to those of black and white. Black law, then, in resisting, surviving
and even to some extent vanquishing white law, proves to be potent
and 'superior'. This is partly what I see encoded in Vincent's joke
about 'breeding out' white people, which is the natural outcome of
the long-term affirmation of Aboriginality that has occurred steadily
since the 1960s, at least from the time of the 1967 referendum, the
conventional benchmark taken to signify Aboriginal people's full

Australian citizenship, through to the present Mabo era, which looks forward to a treaty that seems to some of us as inevitable as a republic and the demise of the Crown.

So, if 'white Australia has a black history', does it also have a black future, as heralded by the possibility of 'breeding out' white people? At this point it might be pertinent to return to Ernie Dingo's 'signification of the phallus' and his 'trumpeting' of Aboriginality thereby. For, in *Heartland*, Vincent, and all he stands for, are constantly alluded to by a didgeridoo accompaniment: so when he gets 'horny', this display of potency is evidently meant to make Australia sit up and take note of a new form of power that has moved from the margins to centre stage. This shift, which is part of a global movement in the politics of identity, 'is from a narrative of dispossession, the narrative which demands justice for people already placed as defeated, to a narrative which asserts out-and-out sovereignty'.[47] From another angle, we might say that Aboriginality, as the author of the law, is coming to assume the role of 'the name of the father',[48] which in *Heartland* just happens to be Barunga. Should Vincent and Beth marry, she would, one assumes, become Elizabeth Barunga. And if she, in line with her English regal namesake and perhaps anticipating Lois O'Donoghue's role, should become 'Mother of the Nation', all her children will be Barungas too. Naturally, if a republic, as well as a treaty, is on the horizon, it is appropriate that Beth and her offspring will be assimilated to the new House of Barunga. Here, with Vincent as 'Father of the Nation', there is definitely no question at all of 'ignorance of physiological paternity'.

Perhaps it is important to point out that one thing is missing from *Heartland's* plot. If Vincent signifies the law, and Beth the land, then this would appear to reverse, and thereby mask, the fact that, at every stage of the gradual appearance and affirmation of Aboriginality in Australian history, progress has been dependent on concessions from the sovereign law of white Australia—law based on British justice and the rights of the Crown. This was illustrated in the Mabo judgment, since the High Court could not deal with the issue of sovereignty without undermining its own authority. Of course, in the end it is the Australian state that polices or defends, as well as ignores or acknowledges, all forms of Australian law, indigenous and non-indigenous. As Noel Pearson has remarked:

> Colonial law has been a reality in Australia since 1788. Aboriginal law has always been a reality and we are unanimous in our resolve that it continue to be so. Colonial law is part of our indigenous reality here in Australia; it determines and controls our ability to exercise our law, enjoy our rights, maintain our identities.[49]

What opportunities remain within this framework for the further expression of Aboriginal sovereignty is very much a question for the future, but it is clear that such expressions will paradoxically depend, as in the Mabo judgment, on ongoing concessions and recognition from white Australia. In other words, Aborigines and their heritage will continue to belong to the nation. Even in the era of self-determination, it follows that Aboriginal people will in some sense remain dependent, subject to the law. It could (and no doubt will) be argued that *Heartland*, with its resolution of all the contradictions, too comfortably endorses this ongoing dependency. The danger of such criticism is that it might deflate Vincent's potency and lead him a long way from the etymological roots of his name and back to the role of victim. Is this though, I wish to ask, too high a price to pay for the encouragement of ongoing 'resistance'?

A Fourth World 'real Australia'

It has been argued that Mabo and the subsequent *Native Title Act* represent the consolidation of *terra nullius* rather than its end: after all, the authority of the High Court and the Federal Parliament depends *absolutely* on the fact of invasion, and without a treaty in place *terra nullius* must in some sense remain intact.[50] This point continues to underwrite the claim of Yothu Yindi's 'Treaty', which Mandawuy Yunupingu sang to the crowd at the 1993 AFL Grand Final, claiming that Australia was never surrendered by Aboriginal people and that British sovereignty changed Aboriginal law not a whit. Yet British sovereignty most certainly did change Aboriginal law, since it guaranteed that claims for that law's recognition must always afterwards depend on the goodwill of those whose rights paradoxically depend on Aboriginal dispossession. In the absence of any foreseeable effective revolution by Aboriginal people, and any subsequent violent displacement of the Crown, it is clear that Aboriginal rights can only be secured through the liberal democratic process inherited from Britain. It follows that Aboriginal people's only prospect for getting what they want is in the Aboriginalisation of that process, which, in a liberal democracy, must partly entail an effective mobilisation of its discursive regimes of representation. *Heartland* is a case in point;[51] the promotion of Aboriginality at the 1993 AFL Grand Final is another.

The public display at the MCG in 1993 was undoubtedly a national appropriation of Aboriginality, which was thus placed in the service of the state—the same state which ironically owes its origin to Aboriginal dispossession. As Patrick Wolfe has observed, 'in order to produce a narrative that can bind it transcendentally to its territorial base—to make it, as it were, spring organically from the local soil—the settler stage is obliged to appropriate the symbolism of the very Aboriginality that it has historically effaced'. Thus, 'internal contradictions reduce the invader to seeking salvation from the dispossessed'. Fictive kinship with the native then comes to express 'the coloniser as the legitimate heir and successor to the colonised'.[52] But what precisely does 'appropriate' mean in this context?

The word 'appropriate' is often used in a diacritical fashion to mark what Meaghan Morris has called the 'radical credibility' of a critique. By this usage, she argues, predatoriness becomes 'the universal rule of cultural exchange. As reified token of rapacious relations, "appropriation" is a lexical mini-myth of power'.[53] But it is insufficient to approach 'appropriation' by only looking at the interests of the state. That these interests are important, and even by definition paramount, is not in doubt. Neither is the fact that the construction of a national Aboriginality must continue to serve the state.[54] Yet, in spite of its own rhetoric, the Australian state is no more a timeless monster feeding on its 1788 victory celebrations than is Australia's Aboriginal constituency destined to forever continue some kind of mystical walkabout at the 'dawn of time'. The state is, in fact, an organised political community with government recognised by the people. As such, it must be responsive to the wishes, needs and will of the people, and not always in such a way as to coerce, repress and call forth resistance.[55] In this sense, it is not surprising that a logic of salvation or redemption pervades the appropriation of Aboriginality in contemporary Australia, since, increasingly, through effective resistance, persuasion and accommodation, the will of the people and the rhetoric of the state have come to demand that something be done to make amends for past injustices. *Heartland*, being more than some simple romance of the primitive, demonstrates that this movement, including its expression in Mabo, is not based exclusively on 'imperialist nostalgia'[56] for some 'Eternal Dreamtime'.

Much depends on 'appropriation' and there are many ways to lend support to the 'lexical mini-myth of power' by stressing distortion, inequality, theft, repression and coercion, and when these happen appropriation certainly becomes a one-way street that one can only blindly follow or block. However, appropriation remains an aspect of *exchange*. One does not necessarily judge exchange by considering only the advantages reaped by one side, thus relegating the other to an agentless subject position.[57] *Heartland* could be taken as a model of this truth, as it moves its characters through a series of uncertain negotiations of identification between black and white. This recovery of native agency calls into question the whole logic of 'imperialist nostalgia' and indeed presents the possibility that imperialism might be transcended. Hence it is important to stress again how reconciliation necessarily entails a logic of redemption. This logic is, at the same time, personal and political, not simply subject to 'discourse'. In imagining Australia, and ourselves as Australians, we cannot only look back to an original imperialist creation of those realities. Instead, we must also look forward into that utopian space ('heart-land') in which it will be possible to work out a mutually satisfying future, and where 'Aboriginal knowledges . . . will constitute a revolution of thought we can only begin to imagine'.[58]

If 'appropriation' is too often a dirty word, 'assimilation' and 'colonisation' are even grubbier. In each case, lexical defilement obscures possible shades of meaning. To appropriate something merely means to take it unto oneself and devote it to a special purpose; to assimilate is to liken and absorb something into oneself; to colonise is to occupy and settle new terrain. Making these processes mutual is what we should be looking towards and creating in the nation's future. In the post-Mabo era, a struggle for a treaty and a republic should help to secure that reform. This is not just:

> an issue of removing colonial thinking from European thought . . .
> It is rather a question of repositioning European systems of know-
> ledge so as to demonstrate the long history of their operation as
> the effect of their colonial other, a reversal encapsulated in Fanon's
> observation: 'Europe is literally the creation of the Third World'.[59]

In a republican future, governed by the 'House of Barunga', one might equally well say: 'Australia is the creation of the Fourth World.'

This finally takes us full circle to the AFL and to the time when indigenous people really did create Australia at the MCG. In that same year, during a match with Collingwood, St Kilda's Nicky Winmar faced not only the black and white colours of the Magpies, but also the racist taunts of Collingwood fans. In response, he lifted his shirt and pointed to his black body, to proudly call attention to his intact black soul. The event surely embarrassed the Magpies' most famous supporter, Paul Keating, and this must have been aggravated when club president, Allan McAlistair, publicly declared: 'As long as [Aborigines] conduct themselves like white people . . . everyone will admire and respect them.'[60] Yet Winmar had already taken the initiative by moving from the margins to act like the territory was black.

In the event, the matter was resolved by another Fourth World creation of Australia, when an Aboriginal All-Stars team, decked in green and gold, a map of Australia and the Aboriginal and Australian flags, played and beat the Magpies in a special 'peace' match in Darwin. Keating, who attended the match, said that the event was one step further towards reconciliation. It was also part of Collingwood's formal apology for the behaviour of its fans and the imprudence of its president.[61] Since then, the All-Stars captain, Brisbane Bear, Michael McLean, has been seen sporting a mouthguard carrying the Aboriginal flag.[62] That same flag now also appears regularly at Collingwood's matches, waved by a Magpie fan. And Winmar has linked the whole event to Mabo, saying: 'What the Mabo story shows is that if the Aboriginal people want something they can get it.'[63]

What a pity it would have been if a too punitive attitude towards the Prime Minister's and Collingwood's appropriation had stopped Aboriginal people from putting their identity where their mouths are; from convincing at least one Collingwood fan of the moral bankruptcy of racism; and, in general, from getting what they want.[64] In other words, what a pity it would have been if too negative a take on power and appropriation had led straight to another 'great Australian silence'.

Notes

Introduction

1 I am indebted to Graeme Davison, Tom Griffiths, John Hirst, John Morton, Tim Murray, Gillian Robinson and Deborah Bird Rose for their comments on an earlier version of this introduction.

2 *The Death of the Past*, London, 1969, pp. 11, 15, 14.

3 See D. Lowenthal, *The Past is a Foreign Country*, Cambridge, 1985.

4 G. Davison, 'A Sense of Place', in B. Attwood (comp.), *Boundaries of the Past*, Melbourne, 1990, p. 28.

5 My reason for classifying anthropology thus will become apparent later in this introduction.

6 While the past is undoubtedly a permanent dimension of human experience and consciousness, and history is universal inasmuch as all peoples tell stories about the past, History (as distinct from history) is a distinctive form of knowledge which is peculiar to the modern culture of Europe. It is marked, at the very least, by a sense of anachronism, that is, a sense that the very nature of the past is *different* to that of the present; a doctrine of linear development or evolution, or, more particularly, a notion of progress; and an emphasis upon human agency and autonomy. (See Plumb, *Death of the Past*, pp. 13–14; E. Hobsbawm, 'The Social Function of the Past: Some Questions', *Past and Present*, no. 55, 1972, p. 3; J. Le Goff, *History and Memory*, translated by S. Rendall and E. Claman, New York, 1992, p. 5; P. Burke, *The Renaissance Sense of the Past*, London, 1969, ch. 1.)

7 *A Place for Strangers: Towards a History of Australian Aboriginal Being*, Cambridge, 1993, pp. 2–4. Swain overstates the case, and serious objections have been made to his thought-provoking argument (see I. Keen, 'Ubiquitous Ubiety of Dubious Uniformity', *Australian Journal of Anthropology*, vol. 4, no. 2, 1993, pp. 96–110; R. Tonkinson,

'Review of *A Place for Strangers*', *Australian Historical Studies*, vol. 26, no. 103, 1994, pp. 312–13; J. Morton, '*A Place for Strangers* and a Stranger Out of Place: Towards a History of Tony Swain's Aboriginal Being', *Social Analysis* (forthcoming)). Morton has argued that Swain adopts an allochronic and relativising approach whereby he casts Aborigines as a radical other—as having a sense of time *fundamentally* different to that of Europeans. I concur with this criticism but would assert, as does Morton, that it is none the less valid to argue that pre- (and post-) colonial indigenous societies have had a different (as well as a similar) sense of time and history to that of Europeans. Our disagreement with Swain, then, lies in how one should generally characterise difference.

8   As Johannes Fabian has noted, imperialism had a temporal dimension as well as the more commonly recognised spatial one (*Time and the Other: How Anthropology Makes its Object*, New York, 1983, ch. 1).

9   One might also argue that History was coterminous with the encounter between 'Europe' and the New World of the Americas. The possibility that History was constituted in this (among other) contexts is tantalisingly raised by Peter Burke and John Hale (Burke, *The Renaissance Sense of the Past*, p. 149; Hale, 'Geographical Horizons and Mental Horizons', in D. Hay (ed.), *The Age of the Renaissance*, London, 1967, pp. 333–43, *The Civilisation of Europe in the Renaissance*, New York, 1994, ch. 1).

10 This is not to argue that there were no other important motives; there obviously were, as Alan Frost and others have argued (see G. Williams and A. Frost (eds), *Terra Australis to Australia*, Melbourne, 1988).

11 See B. Smith, *European Vision and the South Pacific*, 2nd edn, Sydney, [1984]; D. Mackay, *In the Wake of Cook: Exploration, Science and Empire 1780–1801*, London, 1985; J. Gascoigne, *Joseph Banks and the English Enlightenment*, Cambridge, 1994.

12 The French explorer La Perouse, cited in Fabian, *Time and the Other*, p. 8.

13 See Fabian, *Time and the Other*, pp. 2–21; S. Toulmin and J. Goodfield, *The Discovery of Time*, Harmondsworth, 1967, especially ch. 7; M. Hughes, 'Philosophical Travellers at the Ends of the Earth: Baudin, Péron and the Tasmanians', in R.W. Home (ed.), *Australian Science in the Making*, Melbourne, 1988, pp. 23–44; R. Jones, 'Images of Natural Man', in J. Bonnemains *et al.* (eds), *Baudin in Australian Waters*, Melbourne, 1988, pp. 35–64; P. J. Marshall and G. Williams, *The Great Map of Mankind*, London, 1982, ch. 9.

14 See A. Frost, 'New South Wales as *Terra Nullius*: The British Denial of Aboriginal Land Rights', *Historical Studies*, vol. 19, no. 77, 1981, pp. 513–23.

15 This paragraph draws heavily upon the argument of Nancy Williams' *The Yolngu and their Land: A System of Land Tenure and the Fight for its Recognition*, Canberra, 1986, chs 7 & 8; see also R. Dixon,

The Course of Empire: Neo-Classical Culture in New South Wales 1788–1860, Melbourne, 1986, ch. 1.

16 Cook wrote in his journal: 'We are to Consider that we see this Country in the pure state of Nature, the Industry of Man has had nothing to do with any part of it' (*The Journals of Captain James Cook: The Voyage of the Endeavour 1768–71*, edited by J.C. Beaglehole, Cambridge, 1955, p. 397).

17 The phrase is Locke's. He wrote: 'there are still *Great Tracts of Ground* to be found, which (the Inhabitants thereof not having joyned with the rest of Mankind . . .) *lie waste*, and are more than the People, who dwell on it, do, or can make use of, and so still lie in common . . . Thus in the beginning all the World was *America* . . .' (*Two Treatises of Government* (1690), edited by P. Laslett, 2nd edn, New York, 1967, pp. 317, 319, Locke's emphasis).

18 *The Yolngu*, p. 109.

19 See R.L. Meek, *Social Science and the Ignoble Savage*, London, 1976; D.L. Spadafora, *The Idea of Progress in Eighteenth-Century Britain*, New Haven, 1990, ch. 7.

20 Williams, *The Yolngu*, pp. 127, 129.

21 For a contrary interpretation of the basis upon which the British declared their ownership of all the lands of New South Wales, see Henry Reynolds' chapter, and his *The Law of the Land*, Melbourne, 1987. In the latter he does concede that 'their [the Aborigines'] occupation, their possession was overlooked for two distinct reasons—European ignorance and European philosophical and political ideas' (pp. 22, 28).

22 The word 'aborigine' predates this time, of course, but it would seem that 'aboriginal' did not and that 'aborigines' had little if any currency previously. See W.S. Ramson (ed.), *The Australian National Dictionary: A Dictionary of Australianisms on Historical Principles*, Melbourne, 1988, pp. 1–3.

23 For other reasons for their failure, see L. Ryan, 'Aboriginal Policy—1838—A Watershed?', *Push From the Bush*, no. 8, 1980, pp. 14–22; S.G. Foster, 'Aboriginal Rights and Official Morality', *Push From the Bush*, no. 11, 1981, pp. 68–98.

24 'Amicitia', letter to the editor of *Sydney Gazette*, 19 August 1824, in H. Reynolds (comp.), *Dispossession: Black Australians and White Invaders*, Sydney, 1989, p. 71, original emphasis.

25 *Southern Australian*, 8 May 1839, in ibid., pp. 71–72.

26 H. Reynolds, *Frontier: Aborigines, Settlers and Land*, Sydney, 1987, pp. 171–72.

27 Both John Mulvaney and myself have cast doubt upon some aspects of Reynolds' interpretation on this matter (Mulvaney, 'Review of *The Law of the Land*', *Overland*, no. 111, 1988, pp. 94–95; Attwood, 'Aborigines and Academic Historians: Some Recent Encounters', *Australian Historical Studies*, vol. 24, no. 94, 1990, pp. 130–31); see also G. Partington, 'The Aetiology of Mabo', in *Upholding the Australian Constitution: Proceedings of the Fourth Conference of the Samuel Griffith Society*, Melbourne, 1994, pp. 18–21.

28 See T. Griffiths, 'Past Silences: Aborigines and Convicts in Our History-Making', *Australian Cultural History*, no. 6, 1987, pp. 18–32.

29 *The History of Tasmania* (1852), edited by A.G.L. Shaw, Sydney, 1971, pp. 330–32.

30 Sutherland, *Victoria and its Metropolis*, Melbourne, 1888, vol. I, p. 29; Turner, *A History of the Colony of Victoria* (1904), Melbourne, 1973, vol. I, p. 218.

31 'Progress, Morality, and the Dispossession of the Aboriginals', *Meanjin*, vol. 33, no. 3, 1974, p. 309.

32 J. Beckett, 'The Past in the Present; the Present in the Past: Constructing a National Aboriginality', in J.R. Beckett (ed.), *Past and Present: The Construction of Aboriginality*, Canberra, 1988, p. 196.

33 J. Beckett, 'Aboriginality in a Nation-State: The Australian Case', in M.C. Howard (ed.), *Ethnicity and Nation-Building in the Pacific*, Tokyo, 1989, p. 124.

34 W. Murdoch, *The Making of Australia: An Introductory History*, Melbourne, [1917], p. 9. Many years earlier, Sutherland had argued likewise, insisting that:

> A truly savage race can have nothing that we may narrate as history . . . It is only when such a degree of civilisation is reached that the race becomes welded into a solid nation; when wandering tribes consolidate and own some unifying authority, that we can tell its story as a history (*Victoria*, p. 15).

35 See Ramson (ed.), *Australian National Dictionary*, pp. 19–21.

36 See Fabian, *Time and the Other*, ch. 1. The associated distinction between 'written' and 'oral' societies was also important; Sutherland, for example, wrote:

> There is no history anterior to [the arrival of the first white men. The Aborigines] have left not a trace for the historian to dwell on, of the time before the settlement of the European. They have left material for the antiquarian, their bygone ages may offer scope to the geologist, but of history they have none (*Victoria*, p. 15).

37 'The Past as Power: Anthropology and the North American Indian', in I. McBryde (ed.), *Who Owns the Past?*, Melbourne, 1985, p. 34.

38 *The Arunta: A Study of a Stone Age People* (1927), Oosterhout, 1966, p. vii. See D.J. Mulvaney and J.H. Calaby, *'So Much that is New': Baldwin Spencer, 1860–1929*, Melbourne, 1985, especially ch. 9.

39 Fabian, *Time and the Other*, p. 31.

40 Beckett, 'The Past', p. 195. The classic exposition of this can be found in W.E.H. Stanner's famous 1953 essay, 'The Dreaming':

> If we put these four facts about the Aborigines together—1) an immensely long span of time, 2) spent in more or less complete isolation, 3) in a fairly constant environment, 4)

> with an unprogressive material culture, we may perhaps see
> why sameness, absence of change, fixed routine, regularity,
> call it what you will, is a main characteristic of their
> thought and life. Let us sum up this aspect as leading to a
> metaphysical emphasis on abidingness. They place a very spe-
> cial value on things remaining unchangingly themselves . . .
> Absence of change . . . seems to be a good thing in itself
> . . . The value given to continuity is so high that they are
> simply a people 'without a history': they are a people who
> have been able, in some sense, to 'defeat' history, to become
> a-historical in mood, outlook, and life' (in Stanner, *White
> Man Got No Dreaming*, Canberra, 1979, pp. 37–38).

41 'Aborigines and Anthropologists', *Australian Aboriginal Studies*, no. 1, 1986, pp. 2–11.
42 See B. Hodge and V. Mishra, *Dark Side of the Dream: Australian Literature and the Postcolonial Mind*, Sydney, 1991, and B. Attwood and J. Arnold (eds), *Power, Knowledge and Aborigines*, Melbourne, 1992, where 'Aboriginalism' is treated as a series of discourses akin to Edward Said's Orientalism.
43 In 1959 the eminent Australian historian John La Nauze had remarked that 'unlike the Maori, the American Indian or the South African Bantu, the Australian Aboriginal is noticed in our history only in a melancholy anthropological footnote' ('The Study of Australian History, 1929–59', *Historical Studies*, vol. 9, no. 33, 1959, p. 11).
44 *After the Dreaming*, Sydney, 1969, pp. 7, 25, 24, 53, 56.
45 ibid., pp. 17, 27.
46 Stanner, 'Foreword', in M. Reay (ed.), *Aborigines Now*, Sydney, 1964, cited Reynolds, 'Violence, the Aboriginals and the Australian Historian', *Meanjin*, vol. 31, no. 4, 1972, p. 476; see also Reynolds (comp.), *Aborigines and Settlers: The Australian Experience 1788–1939*, Melbourne, 1972, p. ix.
47 Reynolds to author, personal communication, 16 February 1995; for Reynolds' own reflections on this, see his 'History From the Frontier', in Attwood (comp.), *Boundaries of the Past*, pp. 22–27.
48 See P. Burke, 'History as Social Memory', in T. Butler (ed.), *Memory: History, Culture and the Mind*, Oxford, 1989, pp. 97, 110.
49 'History From the Frontier', pp. 23, 26.
50 The most widely read archaeological texts are probably D.J. Mulvaney, *The Prehistory of Australia*, London, 1969; G. Blainey, *Triumph of the Nomads: A History of Ancient Australia*, Melbourne, 1975; J.P. White and J.F. O'Connell, *A Prehistory of Australia, New Guinea and Sahul*, Sydney, 1982; J. Flood, *Archaeology of the Dreamtime*, Sydney, 1983; and J.P. White and D.J. Mulvaney (eds), *Australians to 1788*, Sydney, 1987.
51 See A. Markus, *Governing Savages*, Sydney, 1990, ch. 10; G. Cowlishaw, 'Helping Anthropologists', *Canberra Anthropology*, vol. 13, no. 2, 1990, pp. 1–28.
52 The High Court decision has been well documented elsewhere. P.

Butt and R. Eagleson, *Mabo: What the High Court Said*, Sydney, 1993, summarises the decision, and M.A. Stephenson and S. Ratnapala (eds), *Mabo: A Judicial Revolution: The Aboriginal Land Rights Decision and its Impact on Australian Law*, St Lucia, 1993, and M. Goot and T. Rowse (eds), *Make a Better Offer: The Politics of Mabo*, Sydney, 1994, discuss its legal and political dimensions.

53 This contention is neither inconsistent with the fact that archaeological research was not drawn upon in the Mabo case and has seldom if ever been used in land claim cases, nor with the possibility that the specific content of historical research was quite unimportant in persuading the High Court judges to overturn the legal doctrine of *terra nullius*, as Henry Reynolds has argued: 'The specifically historical references occupy only a small part of the judgments. They are often little more than asides that could be removed without affecting the legal argument in any way at all' ('Anti-Mabo Arguments Past their Use-by Date', *Australian*, 17 November 1993). Elsewhere, Reynolds has proudly claimed that 'there can be little doubt that the History Department [of James Cook University] played a major role in the fundamental re-interpretation of Australia's past which found expression in the Mabo decision' ('Introduction', in Reynolds (ed.), *Race Relations in North Queensland*, 2nd edn, Townsville, 1993, p. 3).

54 See also G. Simpson, '*Mabo*, International Law, *Terra Nullius* and the Stories of Settlement: An Unresolved Jurisprudence', *Melbourne University Law Review*, vol. 19, no. 1, 1993, pp. 207, 210.

55 The appearance of such objectivity is enhanced where scholars in this field adopt the position of the omniscient narrator and tell their histories without reference to other historical scholarship, as they commonly do.

56 See, for example, R. Brunton, 'Mabo and Oral Traditions', in P. Durack *et al.*, *Mabo and After*, Melbourne, 1992, pp. 13–23; G. Blainey, 'Sitting in Judgment on History', *Australian Business Monthly*, vol. 13, no. 10, 1993, p. 44, 'Land Rights for All', *Age*, 10 November 1993, 'National Damage', *Age*, 1 December 1993; K. Baker, 'The New History', *IPA Review*, vol. 42, no. 3, 1988–89, p. 50.

57 As Patrick Wolfe has noted, historical studies such as Reynolds' have 'an insulating effect'. Because they end by and large in the nineteenth century, they insert 'a screen into Australian historical consciousness, rendering expropriation [as] a past event rather than a continuing structure' ('Nation and MiscegeNation: Discursive Continuity in the Post-Mabo Era', *Social Analysis*, no. 36, 1994, p. 96).

58 Gillian Cowlishaw has also criticised these histories: While filling 'a textual gap about our racist past', they present a view of it that fills us with horror at the same time as distancing us from it. 'How is it that in reading these accounts we position ourselves on the side of the Aborigines and identify our forebears as the enemy?', she asks

('Studying Aborigines: Changing Canons in Anthropology and History', in Attwood and Arnold (eds), *Power*, pp. 26–27).

59 'History From the Frontier', pp. 22, 24, 26; *The Other Side of the Frontier*, Townsville, 1981, pp. 2, 3. Other historians have reflected in a similar if less extended fashion in introductions to their scholarly monographs, none more so than Charles Rowley in his *The Destruction of Aboriginal Society*, significantly titled 'History and Aboriginal Affairs' (Canberra, 1970, pp. 1–9).

60 Le Goff, *History and Memory*, p. xx; A. Megill, 'Reconstructing the Past: "Description", Explanation, and Narrative in Historiography', *American Historical Review*, vol. 94, no. 3, 1989, p. 647.

61 p. 1.

62 This is what is known in legal terms as the 'history and traditions' doctrine: 'rights and privileges may be presumed to exist, and hence less easily erased, if they can be demonstrated to have been part of the "history and traditions" of the people' (J.C. Mohr, 'Historically Based Legal Briefs', *The Public Historian*, vol. 12, no. 3, 1990, p. 24). For several reasons I am less enamoured of another (problematic) doctrine Reynolds might be said to work within, that of 'original intent'. For example, Reynolds' attempt to prove that history supports a particular interpretation of 'land rights' strikes me as a very risky strategy—one that is incumbent upon lawyers, as Rosemary Hunter discusses, but not upon historians—inasmuch as if it could ever be proven conclusively that the imperial and colonial governments did *not* comprehensively endorse native title, this would require us to honour this immoral precedence (see E. Freedman, 'Historical Interpretation and Legal Advocacy', *The Public Historian*, vol. 12, no. 3, 1990, pp. 27–32).

63 *The Law*, p. xi.

64 I have explored the various possible meanings of 'Aboriginal history', in 'The Paradox of Australian Aboriginal History', *Thesis Eleven*, no. 38, 1994, pp. 118–37.

65 I discuss these criticisms in detail in ibid., pp. 132–33. I believe these criticisms are valid, but they ignore the question of whether non-Aboriginal historians can do otherwise. Surely the answer is no: as Australians who are not Aborigines it is axiomatic that we will understand the past in a manner which is peculiarly 'Australian' rather than 'Aboriginal'. This means that the problematic of this history-making lies not in its intrinsic nature but in practitioners misrepresenting their work as 'Aboriginal history' and as something other than perspectival and, therefore, partial and limited.

66 L. Coltheart, 'The Moment of Aboriginal History', in Beckett (ed.), *Past and Present*, p. 183.

67 ibid., my emphasis.

68 It should be noted that these criticisms are mostly uttered by those working outside of the discipline of history but who are drawn to its subject matter at the same time as they prophesy its imminent death as a system of knowledge, making them akin to those

colonialists who exploited Aboriginality while eagerly anticipating the disappearance of its bearers.

69 Quite clearly Aborigines have not been alone in this, for academic scholars have also been involved in the production of this new history.

70 See, for example, J. Mathews, *The Two Worlds of Jimmie Barker: The Life of an Australian Aboriginal, 1900–72*, Canberra, 1977; B. Shaw, *My Country of the Pelican Dreaming: The Life of an Australian Aborigine of the Gadgerong, Grant Ngabidj, 1904–77*, Canberra, 1977; Labumore: E. Roughsey, *An Aboriginal Mother Speaks of the Old and the New*, Melbourne, 1984; L. Hercus and P. Sutton (eds), *This is What Happened: Historical Narratives by Aborigines*, Canberra, 1986; R.M. and C.H. Berndt (eds), *The Speaking Land*, Melbourne, 1988.

71 Bennett has written:

> I see much of my current work as history painting—not as documentary history painting, but rather as painting that investigates the way history is constructed after the event; it is always mediated by someone's point of view—a one-point perspective that reflects an ethnocentric bias. My 'History' paintings aim to present other possible perspectives within other possible meanings . . . I believe in the importance of history in informing one's sense of identity in the present, and in the relationship to shaping one's perceptions for the future, both on an individual and on a national level . . .
>
> If identity is seen as an individual/collective self-image which has been defined, to a certain extent, by a succession of images that mirror a culture's sense of itself—as painting does—then I am naive enough to believe that by interrupting a complacent sense of history, and therefore of identity, I can influence a change towards a more open, tolerant and just society. Perhaps a society that is able to encompass multiple perspectives and right the wrongs of the present that are based on the great misunderstandings of the past ('Artists' Statements', in Museum of Contemporary Art, *Tyerabarrbowaryaou: I Shall Never Become a White Man*, Sydney, [1994], p. 14).

72 See, for example, Mudrooroo/Colin Johnson, *Doctor Wooreddy's Prescription for Enduring the Ending of the World*, Melbourne, 1983; J. Davis *et al.* (ed.), *Paperbark: A Collection of Black Australian Writings*, St Lucia, 1990; G. Ward, *Wandering Girl*, Broome, 1987 (published by Magabala Books, which currently has 27 titles); L. Thompson (comp.), *Aboriginal Voices: Contemporary Aboriginal Artists, Writers and Performers*, Sydney, 1990; J. Isaacs (ed.), *Aboriginality: Contemporary Aboriginal Painting and Prints*, St Lucia, 1989; A. Morgan, *Lousy Little Sixpence*, 1983; T. Moffat, *Nice Coloured Girls*, 1987, *Night Cries*, 1989; *Plays From Black Australia: Jack Davis, Eva Johnson, Richard Walley, Bob Maza*, Sydney, 1989; L. King-Smith, 'Patterns of Connection', *Arena*

Magazine, no. 5, 1993, pp. 26–29; the music of No Fixed Address, Yothu Yindi, Kev Carmody, Ruby Hunter and Archie Roach.

73 See, for example, any of the land claim books of the Northern or Central Aboriginal Land Councils; H. Goodall, '"The Whole Truth and Nothing But . . .": Some Intersections of Western Law, Aboriginal History and Community Memory', in Attwood and Arnold (eds), *Power*, pp. 104–19.

74 See, for example, C. Pardoe, 'Arches of Radii, Corridors of Power: Reflections on Current Archaeological Practice', in Attwood and Arnold (eds), *Power*, pp. 132–41.

75 See, for example, C. Edwards and P. Read (eds), *The Lost Children*, Sydney, 1989; B. Cummings, *Take this Child: From Kahlin Compound to the Retta Dixon Children's Home*, Canberra, 1990; D. Smith and B. Halstead, *Lookin' For Your Mob: A Guide to Tracing Aboriginal Family Trees*, Canberra, 1990.

76 See p. xxii.

77 See, for example, S. Morgan, *My Place*, Fremantle, 1987. For a discussion of Aborigines' present constructions of the past, see several of the essays collected in Beckett (ed.), *Past and Present*, and I. Davidson, 'Archaeologists and Aborigines', *Australian Journal of Anthropology*, vol. 2, no. 2, 1991, pp. 247–58. For an international perspective on the general phenomenon, see E. Hobsbawm and T. Ranger (eds), *The Invention of Tradition*, Cambridge, 1983.

78 Alec Kruger, audio-cassette tape, in *Between Two Worlds: The Commonwealth Government and the Removal of Aboriginal Children of Part-Descent in the Northern Territory*, exhibition curated by R. MacDonald, Australian Archives, 1993–94; Edwards, 'Introduction', in Edwards and Read (eds), *Lost Children*, p. xxi; Miller, *Koori: A Will to Win: The Heroic Resistance, Survival and Triumph of Black Australia*, Sydney, 1985, p. xvii; Mudrooroo, *Writing From the Fringe*, Melbourne, 1990, p. 25. As Andrew Lattas has noted:

> the present is partly constituted through what it is not, and
> . . . this space of otherness which allows the present to be
> differentiated and interpreted can be partly provided through
> a mythic . . . past. The past provides the imaginary alterna-
> tive ground from which human existence can reflectively
> grasp and constitute itself . . . The past is here a necessary
> fiction needed to render meaning to the present ('Essential-
> ism, Memory and Resistance: Aboriginality and the Politics
> of Authenticity', *Oceania*, vol. 63, no. 3, 1993, p. 250).

79 The Working Party of Aboriginal Historians for the Bicentennial History, 1788–1988, 'Preparing Black History', *Identity*, vol. 4, no. 5, 1981, p. 8.

80 See Hercus and Sutton (eds), *This is What Happened*, chs 17, 18 & 23; R.H.W. Reece, 'Aboriginal Community History: A Cautionary Tale', paper delivered to the Australian Historical Association Conference, 1982.

81 It is also manifest where they assume the form of legend. See my 'The Paradox', p. 131.

82 The distinctive nature of 'oral history' is seldom delineated adequately by its practitioners. See my discussion of the content of this form of history in Attwood *et al.*, *A Life Together, A Life Apart: A History of Relations Between Europeans and Aborigines*, Melbourne, 1994, pp. 197–208.

83 'Myth as History, History as Myth', in I. Keen (ed.), *Being Black: Aboriginal Culture in 'Settled' Australia*, Canberra, 1988, p. 265.

84 H. and F. Morphy, 'The "Myths" of Ngalakan History: Ideology and Images of the Past in Northern Australia', *Man* (n.s.), vol. 19, no. 3, 1985, pp. 459, 462.

85 K. Maddock, 'Myth, History and a Sense of Oneself', in Beckett (ed.), *Past and Present*, pp. 13–30; E. Kolig, 'Captain Cook in the Western Kimberleys', in R.M. and C.H. Berndt (eds), *Aborigines of the West: Their Past and Their Present*, Nedlands, 1979, pp. 274–82; D.B. Rose, 'The Saga of Captain Cook: Morality and European Law', *Australian Aboriginal Studies*, no. 2, 1984, pp. 24–39.

86 See also J. Beckett, 'Walter Newton's History of the World—or Australia', *American Ethnologist*, vol. 20, no. 4, 1993, p. 675.

87 'Critique and Remembrance', in J. O'Neill (ed.), *On Critical Theory*, New York, 1976, p. 4 (Deborah Bird Rose's work drew my attention to this essay). Similarly, Luisa Passerini has noted that 'the political value of what is forgotten reminds us of the deep connection between memory and freedom' ('Memory', *History Workshop Journal*, no. 15, 1983, p. 196). See also Lattas, 'Essentialism', p. 246.

88 Kolig, 'Captain Cook', pp. 277, 274.

89 'The Saga', p. 38.

90 C. Perkins, 'History, as Written by the Conquerors' (1982), in White and O'Connell, *A Prehistory*, p. 233.

91 R. Langford, 'Our Heritage—Your Playground', *Australian Archaeology*, no. 16, 1983, pp. 2, 6.

92 R. Layton, 'Anthropology and the Australian Aboriginal Land Rights Act in Northern Australia', in R. Grillo and A. Rew (eds), *Social Anthropology and Development Policy*, London, 1985, pp. 148–67; H. Creamer, 'Aboriginal Perceptions of the Past: The Implications for Cultural Resource Management in Australia', in P. Gathercole and D. Lowenthal (eds), *The Politics of the Past*, London, 1990, pp. 130–40; P. Read, 'Come On In, the Water's Fine: Some Reflections on AHA Proposed Code of Ethics', *Australian Historical Association Bulletin*, nos 64–65, 1990, pp. 33–42.

93 See C. Anderson, 'Australian Aborigines and Museums—A New Relationship', *Curator*, vol. 33, no. 3, 1990, pp. 165–79; R. Fraser (comp.), *Aboriginal and Torres Strait Islander People in Commonwealth Records*, Canberra, 1993.

94 Thus, when the outspoken archaeologist Rhys Jones quipped that Australian politicians were prepared 'to give Aborigines the past because we are unwilling to give them a future', it seems he overlooked the considerable opportunity this can provide Aborigines (cited Davidson, 'Archaeologists and Aborigines', p. 255).

95 There has been little research on this subject, but see T. Griffiths,

Hunters and Collectors: The Antiquarian Imagination in Australia, Melbourne, 1996, especially ch. 8.

96 See, for example, B. Anderson, *Imagined Communities: Reflections on the Origin and Spread of Nationalism*, revised edn, London, 1991; E. Hobsbawm, *Nations and Nationalism Since 1780: Programme, Myth, Reality*, Cambridge, 1990.

97 'The Past', pp. 191–92.

98 ibid., p. 194.

99 'Fear and Desire: Aborigines, Asians and the National Imaginary', *Australian Cultural History*, no. 9, 1990, p. 16.

100 ibid., pp. 16, 18; J. Marcus, 'The Journey Out to the Centre: The Cultural Appropriation of Ayers Rock', in A. Rutherford (ed.), *Aboriginal Culture Today*, Sydney, 1988, p. 256.

101 My preference for this term (rather than, say, 'non-Aboriginal Australians') will become apparent later in this introduction.

102 'Aborigines and Contemporary Australian Nationalism: Primordiality and the Cultural Politics of Otherness', *Social Analysis*, no. 27, 1990, pp. 50–69.

103 *Adelaide Advertiser*, 23 May 1989, cited ibid., p. 52.

104 There are other explanations for the appropriation of Aboriginality. First, it has been suggested by Beckett that in the late 1960s the Australian state embarked upon a new strategy in Aboriginal Affairs which had, as its rationale, the notion that Aborigines would in fact be a permanent presence in Australia, and so it increasingly sought to articulate Aboriginality. This occurred, Beckett argues, because the state recognised that the only solution to Aboriginal disadvantage was a massive increase in government expenditure on existing communities, and in order to justify this the liberal-democratic state conceived of Aborigines as a culturally distinct people who possessed a unique culture which should be preserved as part of the national heritage ('Aboriginality, Citizenship and Nation State', *Social Analysis*, no. 24, 1988, pp. 12, 14, 'Comment on Hollinsworth', *Oceania*, vol. 63, no. 2, 1992, pp. 165–66). Second, cultural tourism has become an increasingly important sector of an ailing Australian economy, and it exploits Aboriginality as one of its major drawcards.

105 See A. Lattas, 'Primitivism, Nationalism and Individualism in Australian Popular Culture', in Attwood and Arnold (eds), *Power*, pp. 45–58.

106 Hamilton, 'Fear and Desire', p. 18.

107 K. Maddock, 'Metamorphosing the Sacred in Australia', *Australian Journal of Anthropology*, vol. 2, no. 2, 1991, pp. 215, 217, 230, 218, 214; see also P. Wolfe, 'On Being Woken Up: The Dreamtime in Anthropology and in Australian Settler Culture', *Comparative Studies in Society and History*, vol. 33, no. 2, 1991, pp. 197–224.

108 'Religion, Totemism and Symbolism', in R.M. and C.H. Berndt (eds), *Aboriginal Man in Australia*, Sydney, 1965, pp. 215, 217, cited Maddock, 'Metamorphosing the Sacred', p. 214.

109 Maddock, 'Metamorphosing the Sacred', pp. 214, 222.

110 ibid., pp. 219, 222, 230. One could produce much evidence to

support this claim. I will confine myself to citing one example, a phone call to Access Age: 'Crucial to the complex Mabo debate is to have an understanding of Aboriginal spirituality expressed in the words of an Aboriginal person—"I am part of the land, and the land is part of me"' (*Age*, 22 June 1993).

111 This obviously leaves aside the question of whether it is empirically true that Aboriginal cultures in Australia have these characteristics. This is irrelevant to my argument here, given my assumption that settler Australian constructions of Aborigines do not necessarily bear any relationship to the external reality they purport to represent.

112 Maddock's account implies such a reading but does not explicate this interpretation ('Metamorphosing the Sacred', pp. 230–31).

113 G. Davison, 'The Broken Lineage of Australian Family History', in D. Merwick (ed.), *Dangerous Liaisons: Essays in Honour of Greg Dening*, Melbourne, 1994, p. 341, comparing her 1959 *The Generations of Men* with her 1981 *The Cry for the Dead*.

114 To cite a recent example:

> When Cathy Freeman [Aboriginal athlete] reaches Ubirr, in Kakadu, the years just fall away. This rock takes her back a hundred years . . . that one transports her a thousand years through time . . . Her people have been in this powerful part of the world for 50 000 years (*Age*, 15 October 1994).

See A. Hamilton, 'Spoonfeeding the Lizards: Culture and Conflict in Central Australia', *Meanjin*, vol. 43, no. 3, 1984, pp. 363–78; Marcus, 'Journey Out to the Centre'.

115 *The Past*, p. 52.

116 'The Past', p. 194.

117 Lowenthal, *The Past*, pp. 53–54.

118 'Beyond 1788: A Personal Exploration', in Attwood (comp.), *Boundaries of the Past*, p. 8.

119 ibid., p. 13.

120 St Lucia, 1990; the revised edition, 1993, bears a new subtitle: *An Indispensable Guide for Exploring Prehistoric Australia*.

121 See T. Murray, 'Aboriginal (Pre)history and Australian Archaeology: The Discourse of Australian Prehistoric Archaeology', in Attwood and Arnold (eds), *Power*, pp. 1–2, 15.

122 *Age*, 3 October 1994.

123 Lowenthal, *The Past*, p. 43.

124 Australian National Parks and Wildlife Service, *Nourlangie*, 1994.

125 See, for example, *Age*, 7 June 1993.

126 Murray, 'Aboriginal (Pre)history', p. 1.

127 Lattas, 'Primitivism', p. 45.

128 Lowenthal, *The Past*, p. 55.

129 pp. 9, 8. Part I of this book is entitled 'In the Beginning was the Dreaming'.

130 Cf. Lattas, 'Primitivism', pp. 51–57.

131 See B. Smith, 'The First European Depictions', G. Williams, 'Reactions on Cook's Voyage', J. Urry, '"Savage Sportsmen"', in I. and T.

Donaldson (eds), *Seeing the First Australians*, Sydney, 1985, pp. 21–34, 35–50, 51–67.
132 Lowenthal, *The Past*, p. 55.
133 See L. Sackett, 'Promoting Primitivism: Conservationist Depictions of Aboriginal Australians', *Australian Journal of Anthropology*, vol. 2, no. 2, 1991, pp. 233–46; J. Newton, 'Aborigines, Tribes and the Counterculture', *Social Analysis*, no. 23, 1988, pp. 53–71.
134 *The Past*, p. 57. See also his 'The Timeless Past: Some Anglo-American Historical Preconceptions', *Journal of American History*, vol. 75, no. 4, 1989, pp. 1263–80.
135 *A Place for Strangers*, p. 278. Swain is actually discussing here what he considers to be the origins (and the continuing impulses) of anthropology, which authorises these conceptions of 'the Aborigine'. One might question whether this is so true of anthropology today.
136 Hamilton, 'Fear and Desire', p. 22. Such views are not the preserve of environmentalists; for instance, businesswoman Eve Mahlab believes that 'we as a country have a lot to learn from [Aborigines]. They've lived on this land for 40 000 years. We may wipe ourselves off in a few hundred' (*Age Good Weekend Magazine*, 21 August 1993, p. 31).
137 See the comments by Mulvaney regarding conservationist perspectives expressed during the Gordon River dispute, cited T. Griffiths, 'History and Natural History: Conservation Movements in Conflict?', *Australian Historical Studies*, vol. 24, no. 96, 1991, p. 25. As Griffiths notes:

> The modern wilderness movement . . . [advocates] the stripping back of later layers of history to recover an earlier ideal time . . . It preserves or restores landscapes as Europeans supposedly found them—and as Aborigines made them—and calls them untouched, pristine . . . Just as in nineteenth-century museums, Aborigines are classified in nature. Only now it is done with reverence (ibid., pp. 22, 24).

138 'Putting Ourselves on the Map', *Age*, 23 January 1988.
139 *The Past*, p. 53.
140 Smith was well aware of this genealogy, referring to Stanner's *After the Dreaming* in the opening words of his first lecture (*The Spectre of Truganini*, Sydney, [1981], p. 9). Other exponents of the general thesis espoused by Stanner and Smith include the senior government adviser Nugget Coombs and the writer Judith Wright (see H.C. Coombs, *Kulinma: Listening to Aboriginal Australians*, Canberra, 1978, *Aboriginal Autonomy: Issues and Strategies*, Melbourne, 1994; Wright, *Born of the Conquerors: Selected Essays*, Canberra, 1991). Coombs, Wright and Stanner were closely associated, and were key figures (along with Charles Rowley) in the Aboriginal Treaty Committee (see Wright, *We Call for a Treaty*, Sydney, 1985, especially ch. 5).
141 My approach here is similar to Lattas' 'Aborigines and Contemporary

NOTES 149

Australian Nationalism', but, unlike Lattas, I do not reserve my
approbation of it.

142 ibid., pp. 7, 9, 44, 10, 30, 45, his emphasis. Veronica Brady has
argued recently in a very similar fashion (*Caught in the Draught*,
Sydney, 1994, especially ch. 1). For example: 'The crucial problem
facing us in this country may well be our relations with Aboriginal
people and their culture, and with the long and brutal history of our
invasion and occupation of this country' (ibid., pp. 278–79).

143 *The Spectre*, pp. 10, 44, 31, 34, 17.

144 ibid., pp. 52, 26, 10, 17, 9.

145 ibid., pp. 10, 26, 29.

146 ibid., pp. 16, 17, 21, 41, 44, 52.

147 ibid., pp. 51, 35, 26, 34, 28, 23, 31, 46, 49–50.

148 Smith is all the more confident this will solve the problem of 'culture,
place and morality' because, like many others, he assumes that
contemporary Aboriginal culture is 'derived from this ancient land'
and that it possesses a 'deep spirituality'. Yet, it seems that Smith's
confidence that the moral and psychological forces for convergence
are sufficient is by no means complete, for he invokes an external
force for change:

> We live in a south-east Asian world and the ways in which
> we succeed in relating to our own black minority between
> now and the end of the century will influence increasingly
> how seriously we are taken in the world's councils. That is
> not a good reason for doing the right thing; but it is likely
> to become a compelling one in the near future.

Elsewhere, Smith argues that 'the rest of the world . . . has come
to [regard Aboriginal culture] as more interesting, coherent and
identifiable as a unique human achievement than our own European-
derived culture' (ibid., pp. 45, 15, 10).

149 'Mabo v Queensland No. 2', *Australian Law Journal Reports*, vol.
66, 1992 (henceforth 'Mabo'), p. 449 per Deane and Gaudron JJ;
Commonwealth of Australia, House of Representatives, *Parliamentary Debates*, 37th Parliament, First Session, 1993 (henceforth Keating, 'Native Title Bill'), p. 2877; ATSIC, *1993 International Year of
the World's Indigenous People Speeches*, Canberra, 1992, pp. 5–6.
In his chapter, Richard Broome discusses the influence of Keating's
speechwriter, historian Don Watson. Whether Keating genuinely
believes the Watsonian lines he utters is a moot point, although there
is some evidence that he does (see p. xxxiii). Here I use 'Keating' as
a shorthand for the policies of the Labor Government. Some of the
historical themes I note were also expressed by Keating's predecessor,
Bob Hawke, as well as by Labor Ministers for Aboriginal Affairs,
Clyde Holding and Robert Tickner. See, for example, Hawke's
remarks on his last day of office (cited Hawke, 'Celebration at
Barunga was Starting Point for a Treaty', *Weekend Australian*, 30–31
July 1994), and Tickner's speech introducing the Aboriginal Reconciliation Bill in 1991 (Commonwealth of Australia, House of

Representatives, *Parliamentary Debates*, 36th Parliament, First Session, 1991 (henceforth Tickner,'Reconciliation Bill'), pp. 4498–504).
150 ATSIC, *International Year*, p. 9; Keating, 'Native Title Bill', p. 2883; Keating, *Address to the Nation, 15 November 1993*, Canberra, 1993, pp. 1, 2 (This is reproduced in Goot and Rowse (eds), *Make a Better Offer*, pp. 235–38).
151 Keating, *Address to the Nation*, p. 2; ATSIC, *International Year*, p. 6; Keating, 'Native Title Bill', p. 2877; Keating, 'Dispossessed Now Out of the Shadows', *Weekend Australian*, 30–31 July 1994.
152 This was also the conclusion of Elliott Johnson QC, who headed the Royal Commission into Aboriginal Deaths in Custody. See *Royal Commission into Aboriginal Deaths in Custody, National Report*, Canberra, 1991, vol. 1, pp. 7–12, vol. 2, ch. 10 (entitled 'The Legacy of History').
153 See pp. 100–1 for a discussion of the nature of narrative.
154 ATSIC, *International Year*, p. 7; Keating, *Address to the Nation*, p. 5; Keating, 'Native Title Bill', pp. 2877, 2880; *Age*, 29 April 1993, my emphasis. Some critics have questioned whether the Mabo judgment and the *Native Title Act* do constitute a break with the past, arguing that they do not 'constitute a historical rupture sufficient to enable a reconstitution of the relationship between Aboriginal and settler communities' (Wolfe, 'Nation and MiscegeNation', p. 93). While such scepticism might be well founded, I nonetheless believe, as do many of the contributors to this collection, that Mabo can be a means of changing the structure of relations—one might regard it as part of a *process*, rather than seeing it as a mere 'event'.
155 *Sunday Age*, 9 May 1993.
156 'Mabo', pp. 451, 499 per Deane and Gaudron JJ; *Address to the Nation*, pp. 1, 5; *Age*, 29 April 1993; ATSIC, *International Year*, p. 5.
157 'Mabo', p. 451 per Deane and Gaudron JJ; Keating, 'Dispossessed'; ATSIC, *International Year*, pp. 4, 5, 6.
158 Tickner, 'Reconciliation Bill', pp. 4500, 4501.
159 ATSIC, *International Year*, pp. 6, 4, 5; 'Exclusive Authentic Keating', *Independent Monthly*, April 1993, p. 13; Keating, 'Native Title Bill', pp. 2877, 2878; *Age*, 24 May 1993. Senior *Age* journalist Geoffrey Barker argued in 1993 that the Mabo judgment was 'a sacred cause' for Keating and that he had 'assumed the role of moral healer', referring to his 'vision of a nation at peace with its soul, because it is finally reconciled with the dispossessed Aboriginal minority'. Cartoonists Spooner and Nicholson also portrayed Keating's sense of Mabo in these terms (*Age*, 19 & 21 June, 3 September, 16 November 1993).
160 'Mabo', p. 451 per Deane and Gaudron JJ.
161 Keating, *Address to the Nation*, p. 2; Keating, 'Native Title Bill', p. 2877; ATSIC, *International Year*, pp. 4, 7; Keating, *Commonwealth Response to the High Court Mabo Judgement, 18 October 1993*, Canberra, 1993, p. 1; *Age*, 29 April & 2 August 1993; Tickner, 'Reconciliation Bill', p. 4502.

162 Beckett, 'The Past', p. 203.
163 'Mabo', p. 422 per Brennan J.
164 Keating, 'Native Title Bill', p. 2883; Keating, 'Dispossessed'; Tickner, cited J. Walker, 'Challenge Set For Reconciliation', *Weekend Australian*, 30–31 July 1994. Similarly, the critics of Mabo, reconciliation and the like are criticised, even scorned, for being 'crude and primitive'. See, for example, *Age*, 22 June 1993.
165 This is not to ignore that there are other, pragmatic reasons for the government's action. Among these is a concern for Australia's 'standing in the world' (ATSIC, *International Year*, p. 5; Keating, *Address to the Nation*, Tickner, 'Reconciliation Bill', p. 4504; *Age*, 2 August 1993), a consideration which has probably influenced every Australian government since World War II; Paul Hasluck, for example, told Federal Parliament in 1951:

> the whole Australian community has a responsibility for [Aborigines'] welfare . . . There are many reasons why we should be more emphatic . . . in this matter than we have been in former years . . . The Commonwealth Parliament is the custodian of the national reputation in the world at large. Our record of native administration will not stand scrutiny at the standard of our own professions, publicly made in the forum of the world, of a high concern of human welfare. We should be condemned out of our own mouths if those professions were measured by the standard of native administration accepted in Australia to-day. When we enter into international discussions, and raise our voice, as we should raise it, in defence of human rights and the protection of human welfare, our very words are mocked by the thousands of degraded and depressed people who crouch on rubbish heaps throughout the whole of this continent. Let us cleanse this stain from our forehead or we shall run the risk that ill-intentioned people will point to it with scorn. When we have done that we shall be able to stand up with greater pride and more confidence before the world as a self-respecting nation (Australian Parliament, House of Representatives, *Parliamentary Debates*, 19th Parliament, 1st session, 1950, pp. 3979–80).

166 ATSIC, *International Year*, p. 8; Keating, *Address to the Nation*, pp. 1, 2, 3, 5; Keating, 'Dispossessed'; Keating, 'Native Title Bill', p. 2880; Commonwealth of Australia, *Mabo, The High Court Decision on Native Title: Discussion Paper*, Canberra, 1993, p. 102.
167 ATSIC, *International Year*, pp. 5, 7, 9; Keating, 'Native Title Bill', p. 2883. This terminology was not used by Keating in his address to the nation but, just as interestingly, settler Australians are an unmarked category, perhaps reflecting a relatively pervasive confusion as to what we should be called. See also Tickner, 'Reconciliation Bill', p. 4499, Tickner, 'Party Politics Hamper Restitution', *Weekend Australian*, 6–7 August 1994.

168 'Dispossessed'; see also Keating, 'Native Title Bill', p. 2883; ATSIC, *International Year*, p. 9.
169 *Address to the Nation*, p. 5; Keating, 'Dispossessed'; Keating, 'Native Title Bill', p. 2883; ATSIC, *International Year*, p. 7.
170 Keating, 'Dispossessed'; see also *Age*, 19 October 1994.
171 See, especially, Keating, *Address to the Nation*, *passim*; but also ATSIC, *passim* and Keating, 'Native Title Bill', *passim*.
172 *Address to the Nation*, p. 2.
173 ibid., pp. 1, 3; Keating, 'Native Title Bill', p. 2882; ATSIC, *International Year*, pp. 7, 8.
174 *Age*, 14 June 1993; Keating, 'Native Title Bill', p. 2883.
175 Critics of Keating's linkage of the two issues—and there were many across the political spectrum in 1993 who urged him to treat the two separately—do not seem to have grasped this.
176 I have reached this conclusion on the basis of reading a broad cross-section of opinion expressed in three national newspapers, the *Age*, *Sydney Morning Herald* and the *Australian*. See especially 'Time to Get Serious: Black and White Australians Debate Reconciliation', *Age Good Weekend Magazine*, 21 August 1993; 'J. Walker (ed.), 'Sharing Our Future', *Weekend Australian*, 3–31 July, 6–7, 13–14, 20–21 August 1994; *Age* editorials, 1 & 26 May, 7 June, 29 July, 11 August 1993; *Australian* editorials, 5–6 June, 23–24 October, 16 November 1993; *Age*, letters to the editor, 9 July, 11 November 1993; K. Davidson, 'Mabo: Don't Let the Rednecks Rule', *Age*, 3 July 1993; M. Charlesworth, 'The Saint, Heretic, Mabo and the Spirit', *Age*, 10 July 1993; P. Coghlan, 'Mabo Points to Shame, Not Guilt', *Age*, 17 July 1993; F. Egan, 'If I Were Paul Keating', *Age*, 4 June 1993; R. Gaita, 'Mabo is Simply Humanity', *Age*, 19 November 1993; A. Ramsey, 'An Issue to Bring Out the Best in Us', *Sydney Morning Herald*, 2 October 1993.
177 See, for example, ATSIC, *International Year*, pp. 10, 11, 14; *Burnum Burnum's Aboriginal Australia: A Traveller's Guide*, edited by D. Stewart, Sydney, 1988.
178 Remote places stand as a touchstone for Aboriginality for Aborigines as much as for settler Australians. Best-selling authors Ruby Langford and Sally Morgan, and singer Archie Roach, for example, convey a sense of travelling back into the past when they visit such sites and where they 'discover' their Aboriginality. For example, Langford writes of Uluru:

> It would be the first time I'd ever seen our people in their tribal state . . . I wondered how our ancestors survived here. They must have been very strong people and I was proud to be just a portion of this race . . . It made me think of our tribal beginnings, and this to me was like the beginning of our time and culture. Time was suddenly shortened to include all of history in the present, and it was also stretched to a way of seeing the earth that was thousands of years old . . . I was thinking how someone had said it was the magnetic centre and meeting place of all the dreaming

tracks . . . I wished at that moment I'd been born fullblood instead of the degree of caste that I was. I had a longing for the relaxed tribal sense of time and of looking after the earth (*Don't Take Your Love to Town*, Melbourne, 1988, pp. 232–36).

See also Morgan, *My Place*, pp. 226, 229, 230, 232, 233; A.K. Murdoch, 'Back Home Where the Spirit Belongs', *Age*, 8 February 1995. For these and other Aborigines, as for many other Australians, Aboriginality has become a synonym for home, for a sense of place and belonging (see also *Age*, 30 July & 1 October 1994).

179 Beckett, 'The Past', pp. 208, 212.

180 ibid., p. 212.

181 See, for example, statements by Pat Dodson, Lois O'Donoghue, Darryl Pearce, Noel Pearson and Rob Riley, cited *Weekend Australian*, 30–31 July 1994, *Age Good Weekend Magazine*, 21 August 1993, pp. 26, 34, *Age*, 14 January 1993, ATSIC, *International Year*, pp. 12, 13.

182 For the fierce controversy over essentialism, see, for example, D. Hollinsworth, 'Discourses on Aboriginality and the Politics of Identity in Urban Australia' and 'Comments on Hollinsworth', *Oceania*, vol. 63, no. 2, 1992, pp. 137–71; Lattas, 'Essentialism', pp. 240–67.

183 As James Carrier has argued: 'After all, to put a name to something is to identify its key characteristics and thereby essentialise it . . . The problem, then, is not essentialism itself, but a failure to be conscious of essentialism, whether it springs from the assumptions with which we approach our subjects or the goals that motivate our writing' ('Occidentalism: The World Turned Upside-Down', *American Ethnologist*, vol. 19, no. 2, 1992, p. 207).

184 'The Past', pp. 194, 212.

185 ibid., p. 207; see J.M. Jacobs, 'The Construction of Identity', in Beckett (ed.), *Past and Present*, pp. 31–43.

186 Wolfe, 'Nation and MiscegeNation', p. 110.

187 'Portrait of an Aboriginal as an Artist: Sally Morgan and the Construction of Aboriginality', *Australian Historical Studies*, vol. 25, no. 99, 1992, pp. 312–18.

188 See *Age*, 15 October 1994.

189 'Foreword', in R. Guha and G. Spivak (eds), *Selected Subaltern Studies*, New York, 1988, p. viii.

190 For example, scientific archaeological research which established the longevity of aboriginal occupation of the continent has proved very useful to Aborigines in a culture which 'values such claims more highly than origins myths produced within Aboriginal society' (Davidson, 'Archaeologists and Aborigines', p. 253).

191 S. Macintyre, *A History for a Nation: Ernest Scott and the Making of Australian History*, Melbourne, 1994, p. 210.

192 ibid., p. 211. John Hirst has also expressed such concern ('Australian History and European Civilisation', *Quadrant*, vol. XXXVIII, no. 5, 1993, pp. 28–38).

193 In the conclusion to my *The Making of the Aborigines*, I wrote:

I think that the way the aboriginal peoples came to be Aborigines—as [a racial] group in itself and for itself—should be the subject of inquiry. This means focusing not on their 'being' but on their 'becoming' . . . We will not reach a proper understanding of the recent history of the aboriginal peoples here until we see Aborigines as a social and cultural formation, an historical—and hence changing—category arising from processes which can only be studied as they evolve over a considerable period of time (Sydney, 1989, p. 149).

Chapter 1

1   Earlier versions of this chapter were presented at the Critical Legal Conference, Staffordshire University, 1992, and published as 'Before Cook and After Cook: Land Rights and Legal Histories in Australia', *Social & Legal Studies*, vol. 2, no. 4, 1993, pp. 487–506. The chapter also draws on material from P. Mathew, R. Hunter and H. Charlesworth, 'Law and History in Black and White', in R. Hunter *et al.* (eds), *The History and Politics of Law*, Sydney (forthcoming). Many people helped in the development of the ideas presented here. I would particularly like to thank Peter Fitzpatrick, Penelope Mathew, and the Aboriginal and Torres Strait Islander staff and students at the University of Melbourne.

2   I am not here concerned with the debate as to whether pre-contact Aborigines had any sense of history. For some of the positions in this debate, see D. Chakrabarty, 'Subaltern Studies and Critique of History', *Arena*, no. 96, 1991, pp. 105–20; C. Healy, '"We Know Your Mob Now": Histories and their Cultures', *Meanjin*, vol. 49, no. 3, 1990, pp. 512–23; T. Swain, *A Place For Strangers: Towards a History of Aboriginal Being*, Cambridge, 1993, ch. 1.

3   Healy, 'We Know', p. 515.

4   P. Dodson, 'Policy Statement', in B. Hocking (ed.), *International Law and Aboriginal Human Rights*, Sydney, 1988, p. 140.

5   See E. Kolig, 'Captain Cook in the Western Kimberleys', in R.M. and C.H. Berndt (eds), *Aborigines of the West: Their Past and Their Present*, Nedlands, 1979, p. 278.

6   D.B. Rose, *Hidden Histories: Black Stories from Victoria River Downs, Humbert River and Wave Hill Stations*, Canberra, 1991, p. xxiii.

7   For chapter and verse on this point, see K. Maddock, 'Myth, History and a Sense of Oneself', in J.R. Beckett (ed.), *Past and Present: The Construction of Aboriginality*, Canberra, 1988, pp. 11–30.

8   ibid., p. 14.

9   Healy, 'We Know', pp. 515–16.

10 C. Mackinolty and P. Wainburranga, 'Too Many Captain Cooks', in T. Swain and D.B. Rose (eds), *Aboriginal Australians and Christian Missions*, Adelaide, 1988, pp. 355–60.

11 D.B. Rose, 'The Saga of Captain Cook: Morality in Aboriginal and

European Law', *Australian Aboriginal Studies*, no. 2, 1984, pp. 31–32.

12   ibid., p. 32.

13   Rose, *Hidden Histories*, pp. 138, 140.

14   Rose, 'The Saga of Captain Cook', p. 34.

15   Kolig, 'Captain Cook', p. 274.

16   ibid., pp. 276, 281. See also Swain, *A Place*, pp. 124, 132.

17   Rose, *Hidden Histories*, pp. 149ff.

18   'Additional Instructions for Lieutenant James Cook, 30 July 1768', in J.M. Bennett and A.C. Castles (eds), *A Source Book of Australian Legal History: Source Materials from the Eighteenth to the Twentieth Centuries*, Sydney, 1979, pp. 253–54.

19   'Lieutenant Cook's Official Log, 22 August 1770', in M. Clark (ed.), *Select Documents in Australian History, vol. 1: 1788–1850*, Sydney, 1950, pp. 25–26.

20   Henry Reynolds has noted that the banishment of Aborigines from Australian histories was a twentieth-century phenomenon: *The Breaking of the Great Australian Silence: Aborigines in Australian Historiography 1955–1983*, London, 1984, p. 1. It seems that in the nineteenth century, the fact that the British colonies were built on the dispossession of Aborigines was unavoidable, but by the twentieth century the process had advanced so far that the Aborigines could be dismissed altogether.

21   W.E.H. Stanner, *After the Dreaming*, Sydney, 1969, p. 25.

22   More recently, Alex Castles and Alan Frost have sought to justify Cook's action, and the treatment of New South Wales as *terra nullius*, by reference to the relevant international and English legal doctrines prevailing at the time (Castles, *An Australian Legal History*, Sydney, 1982, ch. 2; Frost, 'New South Wales as *Terra Nullius*: The British Denial of Aboriginal Land Rights', *Historical Studies*, vol. 19, no. 77, 1981, p. 523).

23   See, for example, R. Broome, *Aboriginal Australians: Black Response to White Dominance, 1788–1980*, Sydney, 1982; H. Reynolds, *The Other Side of the Frontier*, Melbourne, 1982, *The Law of the Land*, Melbourne, 1987; N. Butlin, *Our Original Aggression: Aboriginal Populations of Southeastern Australia, 1788–1850*, Sydney, 1983.

24   H. Goodall, '"The Whole Truth and Nothing But . . .": Some Interactions of Western Law, Aboriginal History and Community Memory', in B. Attwood and J. Arnold (eds), *Power, Knowledge and Aborigines*, Melbourne, 1992, pp. 107–108.

25   Maddock, 'Myth', p. 20.

26   See, for example, M.F. Lindley, *The Acquisition and Government of Backward Territory in International Law: Being a Treatise on the Law and Practice Relating to Colonial Expansion* (1926), New York, 1969.

27   See L.C. Green and O.P. Dickason, *The Law of Nations and the New World*, Alberta, 1989.

28   Castles, *Australian Legal History*, p. 16.

29   *Commentaries on the Laws of England*, Bk I, ch. 4, pp. 106–108.

30   (1847) 2 SCR (NSW) (App.) 30.
31   ibid., p. 35.
32   (1889) 14 App. Cas. 286.
33   ibid., pp. 291–92.
34   *Milirrpum v Nabalco Pty Ltd and the Commonwealth of Australia* (1971) 17 FLR 141.
35   N.M. Williams, *Two Laws: Managing Disputes in a Contemporary Aboriginal Community*, Canberra, 1987, p. 124. For a similarly ill-fated attempt to persuade a court to engage with indigenous evidence on its own terms, see *Delgamuukw v The Queen in Right of British Columbia and the Attorney-General of Canada* (1991) 79 DLR (4th) 185; 'Plaintiffs' Opening Address in *Delgamuukw v R*' [1988] 1 CNLR 17. This was a land rights case brought by the Gitskan and Wet'suwet'en peoples of northern British Columbia in Canada.
36   *Milirrpum*, pp. 153–56.
37   Chakrabarty, 'Subaltern Studies', pp. 114–15. The 'Plaintiffs' Opening Address' in *Delgamuukw* sought to provide a framework for the indigenous evidence that would be presented, by explaining Gitskan and Wet'suwet'en epistemologies and challenging Western assumptions about 'history', 'objectivity', and the relative weight to be given to different kinds of evidence. Unfortunately, this had little impact on the judge. See J.R. Fortune, 'Construing *Delgamuukw*: Legal Arguments, Historical Argumentation, and the Philosophy of History', *University of Toronto Faculty of Law Review*, vol. 51, no. 1, 1993, pp. 80–117.
38   For example, *Johnson v McIntosh* (1823) 8 Wheat. 543; *Amodu Tijani v Secretary, Southern Nigeria* [1921] 2 AC 399; *Sobhuza II v Miller* [1926] AC 518; *Adeyinka Oyekan v Musendiku Adele* [1957] 1 WLR 876; *St Catherine's Milling and Lumber Co. v R* (1888) 14 App. Cas. 46. The leading Canadian case, *Calder v Attorney-General of British Columbia*, was on appeal at the time the Gove case was decided. The British Columbia Court of Appeal had rejected the existence of the doctrine of communal native title, but the Canadian Supreme Court later reversed this decision and upheld the doctrine ([1973] SCR 313).
39   I use the term 'entitlement' to denote any relevant interest in the land. The exact nature of native title is a matter of debate.
40   There is some dispute as to the methods by which native title may be extinguished. See, for example, the various judgments in *Mabo v Queensland (No. 2)* (1992) 175 CLR 1, and M.C. Blumm and J. Malbon, 'Aboriginal Title, the Common Law and Federalism: A Different Perspective', in M.P. Ellinghaus *et al.* (eds), *The Emergence of Australian Law*, Sydney, 1989, pp. 27–43.
41   *Milirrpum*, p. 262.
42   ibid., pp. 206–52.
43   ibid., p. 255.
44   ibid., p. 256.
45   ibid., pp. 252–62.

46 See below, pp. 26–34.
47 Proclamation published in the *NSW Government Gazette*, 2 September 1835.
48 *Milirrpum*, pp. 256–57.
49 ibid., p. 268.
50 *Aboriginal Land Rights (Northern Territory) Act 1976 (Cth), Pitjantjatjara Land Rights Act 1981 (SA), Maralinga Tjarutja Land Rights Act 1984 (SA), Aboriginal Land Rights Act 1983 (NSW), Aboriginal Land (Lake Condah and Framlingham Forest) Act 1987 (Cth), Aboriginal Land Grant (Jervis Bay Territory) Act 1986 (Cth), Aboriginal Land Act 1991 (Qld).* Two earlier pieces of land rights legislation were the *Aboriginal Lands Trust Act 1966 (SA)*, which concerned former reserve lands other than the Pitjantjatjara lands in South Australia, and the *Aboriginal Lands Act 1970 (Vic)*, which effected the handover of the former Lake Tyers reserve in Victoria. Australian Law Reform Commission, *Report No. 31: The Recognition of Aboriginal Customary Laws*, Canberra, 1986. Royal Commission into Aboriginal Deaths in Custody, *Interim Report*, Canberra, 1989; *Final Report*, 5 vols, Canberra, 1991.
51 *Mabo*, p. 145 per Dawson J., footnote omitted.
52 Fortune, 'Constructing *Delgamuukw*', p. 81.
53 J. Hewson, 'Address to the Nation', *ABC Television*, 18 November 1993.
54 *Mabo*, pp. 107, 120 per Deane and Gaudron JJ, p. 178 per Toohey J.
55 G. Blainey, 'Land Rights for All', *Age*, 10 November 1993. Blainey's response is discussed in detail in Bain Attwood's chapter.
56 P. P. McGuinness, 'High Court's Role Now Irrevocably Politicised', *The Australian*, 13–14 November 1993.
57 *Mabo*, p. 104 per Deane and Gaudron JJ.
58 ibid., pp. 108, 109.
59 ibid., pp. 29, 41–42 per Brennan J.
60 ibid., p. 184 per Toohey J.
61 ibid., p. 29 per Brennan J.
62 'It is not possible, *a priori*, to distinguish between cases that express a skeletal principle and those which do not'; 'Whenever such a question arises, it is necessary to assess whether the particular rule is an essential doctrine of our legal system and whether, if the rule were to be overturned, the disturbance to be apprehended would be disproportionate to the benefit flowing from the overturning' (ibid., p. 30).
63 ibid., p. 39.
64 ibid, p. 93 per Deane and Gaudron JJ.
65 ibid., pp. 94–95.
66 See also R. Bartlett, 'Mabo: Another Triumph for the Common Law', *Sydney Law Review*, vol. 15, no. 2, 1993, p. 185. Bartlett argues that the High Court has not changed the law but merely offered the first explicit statement of native title.
67 *Mabo*, p. 111 per Deane and Gaudron JJ, p. 195 per Toohey J.
68 ibid., pp. 63, 64, 69 per Brennan J.

69   In practice it made little difference, as the advocates of compensation
     all agreed that any claim for compensation would be subject to
     ordinary limitation periods which, in virtually all cases, would have
     expired long ago.
70   *Mabo*, p. 69 per Brennan J.
71   ibid., p. 58 per Brennan J, pp. 87–88, 110 per Deane and Gaudron
     JJ, p. 187 per Toohey J.
72   ibid., p. 196 per Toohey J.
73   ibid., p. 110 per Deane and Gaudron JJ.
74   ibid., p. 60 per Brennan J.

Chapter 2

1   *Mabo v Queensland (No.2)* (1992) 107 Australian Law Reports,
     p. 92 per Dawson J.
2   ibid., p. 93.
3   ibid., p. 92.
4   ibid., p. 136.
5   J.G. Legge (ed.), *A Selection of Supreme Court Cases*, Sydney, 1896,
     vol. I, pp. 508–509.
6   *Cooper v Stuart* (1889) 14 App. Cas. 286, pp. 291–92.
7   Cited by Blackburn, J. in *Milirrpum v Nabalco Pty Ltd and the
     Commonwealth of Australia* (1971) 17 FLR 141, p. 246.
8   ibid., pp. 243, 272.
9   *Mabo*, p. 123 per Dawson J.
10   ibid., p. 106.
11   *The Law of Nations* (1760), Washington, 1916, vol. III, p. 84.
12   *Mabo*, pp. 106–107 per Dawson J.
13   Vattel, *The Law*, vol. III, p. 309.
14   *Elements of International Law* (1836), Oxford, 1936, p. 346.
15   The Bankers Case, 1690, cited by H. Broom, *Constitutional Law*,
     London, 1885, p. 225.
16   *Common Law Aboriginal Title*, Oxford, 1989, p. 300.
17   ibid., pp. 302–303.
18   *Of the Dominion or Ownership of the Sea*, London, 1652, p. 21.
19   *The Law of Nations*, 4th edn, London, 1829, p. 64.
20   *Commentaries on the Laws of England*, 18th edn, London, 1823,
     vol. II, p. 258.
21   G.I. Bennett, 'Aboriginal Title in the Common Law: A Stony Path
     Through Feudal Doctrine', *Buffalo Law Review*, vol. 27, no. 4, 1978,
     p. 618.
22   *Mabo*, pp. 126–27 per Dawson J.
23   ibid., p. 51 per Brennan J.
24   ibid., p. 109 per Dawson J.
25   ibid.
26   Cook's instructions, 6 July 1776, in J.C. Beaglehole (ed.), *The Voyage
     of the Resolution and Discovery, 1776–1780*, Cambridge, 1967,
     p. ccxxiii.

27 Portland to Grant, 26 February 1800, Australian Joint Copying Project, Colonial Office Files (henceforth CO) 202/5.

28 For discussion of this point, see my *The Law of the Land*, 2nd edn, Melbourne, 1992, pp. 31–32.

29 2 vols (1802, 1804), Sydney, 1975.

30 ibid., vol. I, pp. 122, 599.

31 *Historical Records of Australia*, series 3, vol. 1, p. 529.

32 Collins, *An Account*, vol. I, pp. 122, 497.

33 See above, note 24.

34 'Respecting Natives', King Papers, vol. 2, Mitchell Library, mss C/189; W. Walker to R. Watson, 29 November 1821, J. Bonwick Transcripts, Box 51, Mitchell Library; Military Operations . . . Against the Aboriginal Inhabitants of Van Diemen's Land, *British Parliamentary Papers*, 1831, vol. 19, no. 259, p. 83; Arthur to Glenelg, 22 July 1837, CO 280/84; Colonial Secretary to R. Milligan, 5 December 1843, Chief Secretary's Office (henceforth CSO), cited N.J.B. Plomley (ed.), *Weep in Silence*, Hobart, 1987, p. 144; Denison to Grey, 3 December 1847, Tasmanian State Archives, CSO 24/8/1318; CO 18/31; CO 202/272; CO 201/286; CO 13/6; *South Australian Gazette*, 25 July 1840.

35 C. Buxton (ed.), *Memoirs of Sir Thomas Fowell Buxton*, London, 1926, p. 361.

36 CO 323/218.

37 Report from the Select Committee on Aborigines, *British Parliamentary Papers*, 1836, vol. 7, no. 538, p. 516; Report from the Select Committee on Aborigines, *British Parliamentary Papers*, 1837, vol. 7, no. 425, p. 5.

38 James Stephen memo, 10 December 1835, CO 13/3.

39 Glenelg to Torrens, 15 December 1835, CO 13/3.

40 Memo on dispatch, Gawler to Russell, 1 August 1840, CO 13/6.

41 South Australian Colonisation Commission Letterbook, 8 January 1836, CO 386/137.

42 First Annual Report of the South Australia Colonisation Commissioners, *British Parliamentary Papers*, 1836, vol. 39, no. 426, pp. 8–9.

43 CO 13/3.

44 Correspondence Respecting the Colonisation of New Zealand, *British Parliamentary Papers*, 1841, vol. 17, no. 311, p. 51.

45 *Mabo*, p. 110 per Dawson J.

46 *Milirrpum*, p. 200.

47 Reynolds, *The Law*, pp. 127–28.

48 *Mabo*, p. 108 per Dawson J.

49 See my *The Fate of a Free People*, Melbourne, 1995.

50 *South Australian Register*, 1 August 1840.

51 London, 1926, p. 340.

52 CO 201/382.

53 ibid.

54 ibid.

55 ibid.

56 *Historical Records of Australia*, series 1, vol. 26, p. 226.
57 ibid.
58 See dispatch of Fitzroy to Grey, 11 October 1848, CO 201/400.
59 ibid.
60 ibid.
61 *Sydney Gazette*, 29 April 1850, pp. 685–86.
62 Memo on Letter of Colonial Land and Emigration Office, 17 April 1849, CO 201/422.
63 ibid.
64 Grey to Fitzroy, 6 August 1849, Mitchell Library, mss A/1308.
65 ibid.
66 Fitzgerald to Grey, 24 July 1849, CO 18/51; Grey to Fitzgerald, 22 May 1850, CO 397/9.
67 ibid.
68 ibid.
69 ibid.
70 ibid.

Chapter 3

1 Special thanks to Jeremy Goff for comments on a draft, Chantal Jackson and Kimberley Reid for discussions which helped focus my analysis, and Sally Roberts who assisted generously with the references.
2 D.B. Rose, 'Review of Marc Gumbert, *Neither Justice Nor Reason*', *Journal of Pacific Studies*, vol. 11, no. 1, 1987, pp. 185–86.
3 D.B. Rose, *Hidden Histories: Black Stories from Victoria River Downs, Humbert River and Wave Hill Stations*, Canberra, 1991, pp. 249–50.
4 M. Gumbert, 'Paradigm Lost: Anthropological Models and their Effect on Aboriginal Land Rights', *Oceania*, vol. 52, no. 2, 1981, pp. 103–23, *Neither Justice Nor Reason: A Legal and Anthropological Analysis of Aboriginal Land Rights*, St Lucia, 1984; J. Jacobs, 'Politics and the Cultural Landscape: The Case of Aboriginal Land Rights', *Australian Geographical Studies*, vol. 26, no. 2, 1988, pp. 249–63; K. Maddock, *Anthropology, Law and the Definition of Australian Aboriginal Rights to Land*, Nijmegen, 1980, 'Warlpiri Land Tenure: A Test Case in Legal Anthropology', *Oceania*, vol. 52, no. 2, 1981, pp. 85–102, *Your Land is Our Land: Aboriginal Land Rights*, Melbourne, 1983; G. Neate, *Aboriginal Land Rights Law in the Northern Territory*, vol. 1, Chippendale, NSW, 1989; N. Peterson *et al.*, 'Succession to Land: Primary and Secondary Rights to Aboriginal Estates', in *Official Hansard Report of the Joint Select Committee on Aboriginal Land Rights in the Northern Territory*, 19 April 1977, pp. 1002–14; N. Peterson and M. Langton (eds), *Aborigines, Land and Land Rights*, Canberra, 1983; N. Peterson and J. Long, *Australian Territorial Organisation*, Sydney, 1986; A. Rumsey, 'Language Groups in Australian Aboriginal Land Claims', Paper prepared

for the Fifth International Conference on Hunting and Gathering Societies, Darwin, 1988; P. Sutton and B. Rigsby, 'People with "Politicks": Management of Land and Personnel on Australia's Cape York Peninsula', in N. Williams and E. Hunn (eds), *Resource Managers: North American and Australian Hunter-Gatherers*, Washington, DC, 1982, pp. 155–71; R. Tonkinson, 'Working for the Judge: Role and Responsibility', *Anthropological Forum*, vol. 5, no. 2, 1983, pp. 182–88; M. Verdon and P. Jorion, 'The Hordes of Discord: Australian Aboriginal Social Organisation Reconsidered', *Man* (n.s.), vol. 16, no. 1, 1981, pp. 90–107.

5   See, for example, J. Avery, 'The Recent History of the Borroloola Aboriginal People and their Struggle for Land Rights', N. Ilyatjari, 'Women and Land Rights: The Pitjantjatjara Land Claims', W. Ludwig, 'Women and Land Rights: A Review', E. McDinny and A. Isaac, 'Borroloola Community and Land Rights', L. Tennant, 'Women and Land Rights: Kiuk and Wagaidj Women in the Darwin Area', in F. Gale (ed.), *We Are Bosses Ourselves: The Status and Role of Aboriginal Women Today*, Canberra, 1983, pp. 62–65, 55–61, 78–83, 66–67, 84–85; P. Nathan and D. Japanangka, *Settle Down Country*, Alice Springs, 1983; P. Toyne and D. Vachon, *Growing Up the Country: The Pitjantjatjara Struggle for their Land*, Melbourne, 1984.

6   See Gumbert, *Neither Justice Nor Reason*, for a discussion of some of the major shortcomings of the Act.

7   Toohey J., *Daly River (Malak Malak) Land Claim: Report by the Aboriginal Land Commissioner*, Canberra, 1982, p. 87.

8   ibid., p. 86.

9   See my 'Whose Confidentiality, Whose Intellectual Property?', in M. Edmunds (ed.), *Claims to Knowledge, Claims to Country: Native Title Claims and the Role of the Anthropologist*, Canberra, 1994, pp. 1–11.

10 Cf. my *Dingo Makes Us Human: Life and Land in an Australian Aboriginal Culture*, Cambridge, 1992, p. 114.

11 'Women in Land Claims', Issues Paper for the Native Titles Unit, Australian Institute of Aboriginal and Torres Strait Islander Studies, forthcoming.

12 The first land claim was heard in 1978 and the Aboriginal Land Commissioner published his report in 1979 (Toohey J., *Borroloola Land Claim: Report by the Aboriginal Land Commissioner*, Canberra, 1979).

13 In *Neither Justice Nor Reason*, Gumbert is particularly eloquent on this issue.

14 *Utopian Land Claim: Report by the Aboriginal Land Commissioner*, Canberra, 1980, pp. 13, 17. In the course of discussing descent in his report on the Willowra Land Claim, Toohey cites anthropologist Basil Sansom: 'A local descent group may be "recruited on a principle of descent deemed relevant by claimants" . . .' (*Willowra Land Claim: Report by the Aboriginal Land Commissioner*, Canberra, 1980, p. 15).

15 *Finniss River Land Claim: Report by the Aboriginal Land Commissioner*, Canberra, 1981, p. 17.
16 ibid., p. 19.
17 See also Neate, *Aboriginal Land*, ch. 6.
18 Personal field notes, 7 November 1994.
19 Cf. Peterson *et al.*, 'Succession', p. 1002.
20 See P. Sutton, 'Myth as History, History as Myth', in I. Keen (ed.), *Being Black: Aboriginal Cultures in 'Settled' Australia*, Canberra, 1988, pp. 253–55.
21 Transcript of Proceedings, North West Simpson Land Claim, pp. 647–49.
22 ibid., p. 649.
23 J. Wafer and A. Green, *The Simpson Desert Land Claim, Area 1: The North-West Simpson Desert*, Alice Springs, 1989, p. 45.
24 ibid., pp. 44–45.
25 ibid., p. 45.
26 Cited Rose, *Hidden Histories*, p. 229.
27 In *After Mabo: Interpreting Indigenous Traditions*, Melbourne, 1993, Tim Rowse develops this theme in relation to the Mabo decision, providing a superb analysis of the moral complexities of these issues.
28 Cf. P. Sullivan, *All Free Man Now: Culture, Community and Politics in the Kimberley Region, North Western Australia*, Canberra, 1995.

Chapter 4

1 *Herald*, 22 February 1951.
2 *Sun*, 24 February 1951.
3 ibid.
4 *Herald*, 6 March 1953.
5 ibid., 17 June 1954.
6 R. Ward, *Australia Since the Coming of Man*, Sydney, 1982, pp. 186–210; G. Bolton, *The Oxford History of Australia, vol. 5: 1942–1988*, Melbourne, 1990, chs 4–5.
7 For a discussion of academic writing in Aboriginal history, see A. Markus, 'Through a Glass, Darkly: Aspects of Contact History', *Aboriginal History*, vol. 1, pt 2, 1977, pp. 170–80; R.H.W. Reece, 'The Aborigines in Australian Historiography', in J.A. Moses (ed.), *Historical Disciplines and Culture in Australasia*, St Lucia, 1979, pp. 253–81; P. Biskup, 'Aboriginal History', in G. Osborne and W.F. Mandle (eds), *New History: Studying Australia Today*, Sydney, 1982, pp. 11–31; A. Curthoys, 'Rewriting Australian History: Including Aboriginal Resistance, *Arena*, no. 62, 1983, pp. 96–110; B. Attwood, *The Making of the Aborigines*, Sydney, 1989, ch. 6, 'Aborigines and Academic Historians: Some Recent Encounters', *Australian Historical Studies*, vol. 24, no. 94, 1990, pp. 123–35.
8 Cited D.J. Mulvaney, 'The Australian Aborigines, 1606–1929: Opinion and Fieldwork. Part 1: 1606–1859', *Historical Studies*, vol. 8, no. 30, 1958, pp. 132–33.

9   *The Journals of Captain James Cook on his Voyages of Discovery*,
    vol. 1, The Voyage of the Endeavour 1768–1771, edited by J.C.
    Beaglehole, Cambridge, 1968, pp. 305–306; *The Endeavour Journal
    of Joseph Banks*, edited by J.C. Beaglehole, Sydney, 1962, vol. 2,
    pp. 111–12, 123–30.

10 See B. Smith, *European Vision and the South Pacific 1768–1850: A
    Study in the History of Art and Ideas*, London, 1960, chs 3–5; A.
    Frost, 'The Pacific Ocean: The Eighteenth Century's "New World"',
    Studies on Voltaire and the Eighteenth Century, vol. CLII, 1976,
    pp. 779–822.

11 H. Reynolds, 'Violence, the Aboriginals, and the Australian
    Historian', *Meanjin*, vol. 31, no. 4, 1972, pp. 471–77.

12 K. Fitzpatrick, 'Ernest Scott', in *Australian Dictionary of Biography*,
    vol. 11, pp. 544–46.

13 *A Short History of Australia*, 7th edn, Sydney, 1947, pp. 28, 31–32,
    138, 189–91. S. Macintyre, *A History for a Nation: Ernest Scott and
    the Making of Australian History*, Melbourne, 1994, pp. 47–48,
    77–78, makes the same points.

14 *A Concise History of Australia*, Sydney, 1943, pp. 163, 327.

15 *Australia*, London, 1930, pp. 20–21.

16 For an outline of Victorian and later thinking on social evolutionism,
    see G.W. Stocking Jnr, *Race, Culture and Evolution: Essays in the
    History of Anthropology*, New York, 1968, ch. 6.

17 *Chambers's Encyclopaedia: A Dictionary of Universal Knowledge*,
    London, 1895, vol. 1, p. 591.

18 *Encyclopaedia Britannica: A Dictionary of Arts, Sciences, Literature
    and General Information*, 11th edn, New York, 1910, vol. 2, p. 956.

19 A.W. Jose *et al.* (eds), *The Australian Encyclopaedia*, Sydney, 1927,
    vol. 1, p. 15. See also D.J. Mulvaney, 'Walter Baldwin Spencer', in
    Australian Dictionary of Biography, vol. 12, pp. 33–36.

20 ibid., p. 21.

21 ibid., p. 35.

22 O.J.R. Howarth, A.J. Herbertson and G. Taylor, *The World and
    Australasia: Adapted for Use in Australasian Schools*, 3rd edn,
    Oxford, 1922, p. 128. For changes in school text books, see B. Cope,
    'Racism, Popular Culture and Australian Identity in Transition in
    School Textbooks Since 1945', in A. Markus and R. Rasmussen (eds),
    Prejudice in the Public Arena: Racism, Melbourne, 1987, pp. 73–92.

23 See F. Ford, 'Glimpses of Teaching About Australian Aboriginal
    People in Victorian Primary Schools', unpublished paper, Melbourne,
    1990.

24 Foreword to *Sanitarium Children's Abbreviated Australian Encyclo-
    paedia*, revised edn, Cooranbong, n.d. This, the first edition, and the
    Sanitarium booklet *Aboriginal Tribes and Customs*, are in the pos-
    session of the author.

25 For 'Mangrook', see my *Coburg Between Two Creeks*, Melbourne,
    1987, p. 12.

26 N. Peterson, '"Studying Man and Man's Nature": The History of

the Institutionalisation of Aboriginal Anthropology', *Australian Aboriginal Studies*, no. 2, 1990, pp. 5–6, 17.

27 D.J. Mulvaney, '"A Sense of Making History": Australian Aboriginal Studies 1961–1986', *Australian Aboriginal Studies*, no. 2, 1986, p. 5; Mulvaney has estimated that between 1926 and 1961 only 75 Aboriginal projects were funded in Australia (ibid.).

28 T. Wise, *The Self-Made Anthropologist: A Life of A.P. Elkin*, Sydney, 1985, chs 10 & 12.

29 *The Australian Aborigines*, 4th edn, Sydney, 1974, p. 220.

30 On Elkin's view of culture see G. Cowlishaw, 'Aborigines and Anthropologists', *Australian Aboriginal Studies*, no. 1, 1986, pp. 6–9.

31 'Reaction and Interaction: A Food Gathering People and European Settlement in Australia', *American Anthropologist*, vol. 53, no. 2, 1951, pp. 164–86. For another critique of his model, see F. Stevens, *The Politics of Prejudice*, Sydney, 1980, pp. 58–62, 142–43 and index.

32 A.H. Chisholm (ed.), *The Australian Encyclopaedia*, 2nd edn, Sydney, 1958, vol. 1, p. 91.

33 Mulvaney, 'A Sense of Making History', pp. 52–54.

34 *The Prehistory of Australia*, London, 1969, p. 12.

35 M. Sahlins, *Stone Age Economics*, Chicago, 1972.

36 *Australian Encyclopaedia*, 3rd edn, Sydney, 1983, vol. 1, p. ii.

37 *Australia*, Sydney, 1952, p. 25.

38 ibid., p. 29.

39 ibid., p. 97.

40 'The Foundation Years 1788–1821', in G. Greenwood (ed.), *Australia: A Social and Political History*, Sydney, 1955, p. 42.

41 *Australia: The Quiet Continent*, Cambridge, 1962, p. 223.

42 W.E.H. Stanner, *After the Dreaming*, Sydney, 1969, pp. 22–24.

43 *A History of Australia, vol. 1*, Melbourne, 1962, p. 5.

44 *A Short History of Australia*, New York, 1963, pp. 45, 79, 205.

45 'Aborigines and Racism: An Historical Perspective', in F.J. Stevens (ed.), *Racism: The Australian Experience, vol. 2*, Sydney, 1972, p. 9.

46 *The Australian Legend*, Melbourne, 1958, p. 201.

47 *Australia Since the Coming of Man*, p. 7.

48 *Finding Australia: The History of Australia to 1821*, Melbourne, 1987, pp. 412–13.

49 It is gainsaid that Aboriginal history-making has also been very important in this regard, but since Rosemary Hunter's chapter considers this it is unnecessary for me to discuss it.

50 Mulvaney, 'The Australian Aborigines, 1606–1929: Opinion and Fieldwork', *Historical Studies*, vol. 8, no. 30, 1958, pp. 131–51, vol. 8, no. 31, 1958, pp. 297–314.

51 G. Serle, 'Jobs for Historians? The Serle Report', *Australian Historical Association Bulletin*, no. 8, 1974, pp. 4–5; A. Curthoys, 'Into History', in A. Curthoys *et al.* (eds), *Australians from 1939*, Sydney, 1987, pp. 448–49.

52 *The Destruction of Aboriginal Society*, Canberra, 1970, *Outcasts in White Australia* and *The Remote Aborigines*, Canberra, 1971.

53 R. Evans *et al.*, *Exclusion, Exploitation and Extermination: Race Relations in Colonial Queensland*, Sydney, 1975; H. Reynolds (comp.), *Aborigines and Settlers: The Australian Experience 1788–1939*, Melbourne, 1972, 'The Other Side of the Frontier: Early Aboriginal Reactions to Pastoral Settlement in Queensland and Northern New South Wales', *Historical Studies*, vol. 17, no. 66, 1976, pp. 50–63, 'Aboriginal–European Contact History: Problems and Issues', *Journal of Australian Studies*, no. 3, 1978, pp. 52–64, '"Before the Instant of Contact": Some Evidence from Nineteenth-Century Queensland', *Aboriginal History*, vol. 2, pt 1, 1978, pp. 63–69; M.F. Christie, *Aborigines in Colonial Victoria 1835–86*, Sydney, 1979; N. Loos, *Invasion and Resistance: Aboriginal–European Relations on the North Queensland Frontier 1861–1897*, Canberra, 1982; L. Ryan, *Aboriginal Tasmanians*, St Lucia, 1982.

54 *Aboriginal Australians: Black Response to White Dominance*, Sydney, 1982, 2nd edn, Sydney, 1994.

55 *The Other Side of the Frontier: An Interpretation of the Aboriginal Response to the Invasion and Settlement of Australia*, Townsville, 1981, Ringwood, 1982.

56 'Inventing Aborigines', *Aboriginal History*, vol. 11, pt 1, 1987, pp. 14–23.

57 A. McGrath, *'Born in the Cattle': Aborigines in Cattle Country*, Sydney, 1987; M. Fels, *Good Men and True: The Aboriginal Police of the Port Phillip District 1837–1853*, Melbourne, 1988.

58 D.J. Mulvaney and J.P. White, 'How Many People?', in Mulvaney and White (eds), *Australians to 1788*, Sydney, 1987, pp. 115–17.

59 *Economics and the Dreamtime: A Hypothetical History*, Melbourne, 1993, pp. 133–39.

60 B. Gammage, *Narrandera Shire*, Narranderra, 1986; Broome, *Coburg Between Two Creeks*; R. Murray and K. White, *Dharug & Dungaree: The History of Penrith and St Marys to 1860*, North Melbourne, 1988. This followed the early lead of Margaret Kiddle, *Men of Yesterday: A Social History of the Western District of Victoria, 1834–1890*, Melbourne, 1961 and N. Gunson, *The Good Country: Cranbourne Shire*, Melbourne, 1968.

61 R. Broome, 'The Struggle for Australia: Aboriginal–European Warfare 1770–1930', in M. McKernan and M. Browne (eds), *Australia: Two Centuries of War and Peace*, Canberra, 1988, pp. 92–120.

62 *Aboriginal Australians*, p. 6.

63 *The Spectre of Truganini*, Sydney, [1981], pp. 10, 52, 23.

64 *Caledonia Australis: Scottish Highlanders on the Frontier of Australia*, Sydney, 1984, p. 183.

65 'Speech by the Honourable Prime Minister, P. J. Keating MP at the Australian Launch of the International Year for the World's Indigenous People, Redfern, 10 December 1992', *Aboriginal Law Bulletin*, vol. 3, no. 61, 1993, pp. 4–5.

66 'Aborigines and Contemporary Australian Nationalism: Primordiality and the Cultural Politics of Otherness', *Social Analysis*, no. 27, 1990, pp. 59–60.

67 'Mabo v Queensland No. 2', *Australian Law Journal Reports*, vol. 66, 1992, pp. 449, 451 per Deane and Gaudron JJ.

Chapter 5

1 I wish to thank Christine Williamson for discussing with me emerging trends in contact archaeology; Richard Cosgrove, Jim Allen and Greg Lehman for discussions about the politics of Aboriginal archaeology; and Marilyn Truscott and Betty Meehan of the Australian Heritage Commission for information and advice.

2 See the first two issues of *European Archaeologist*. The Ljubljana conference focused on the politics of archaeology in contemporary Europe and considered the implications of the European Convention on the Protection of the Archaeological Heritage, the full text of which appears in *European Archaeologist*, no. 1, 1993, pp. 5–17.

3 Of the many discussions of the general issues now published, the best is P. Kohl, 'Nationalism, Politics, and the Practice of Archaeology in Soviet Transcaucasia', *Journal of European Archaeology*, vol. 1, no. 2, 1993, pp. 181–90. See also F. Baker, 'The Berlin Wall: Production, Preservation and Consumption of a 20th-Century Monument', *Antiquity*, vol. 67, no. 257, 1993, pp. 709–33.

4 'Archaeology and the Contemporary Myths of the Past', *Journal of European Archaeology*, vol. 1, no. 2, 1993, pp. 191–95.

5 Still the best analysis of the influence of Geoffrey of Monmouth's *History of the Kings of Britain* is T. Kendrick, *British Antiquity*, London, 1950.

6 'Is Prehistory Practical?', *Antiquity*, vol. 7, 1933, pp. 410–18, and 'Anthropology and Herr Hitler', *Discovery*, vol. 15, 1934, pp. 65–68.

7 A good general survey of the complicated history of philology in its relationships to the development of nineteenth-century anthropology is G. Stocking, *Victorian Anthropology*, New York, 1987, especially chs 2, 4 & 5. The most accessible of Mueller's texts are *Lectures on the Science of Language* (first series), London, 1861, and *Lectures on the Science of Language* (second series), London, 1864.

8 There is a vast literature on this general topic. One of the best general introductions is A.D. Smith, *The Ethnic Origins of Nations*, Oxford, 1986. Colin Renfrew has recently refocused our attention on the general area with *Archaeology and Language: The Puzzle of Indo-European Origins*, Harmondsworth, 1987.

9 Some of these issues are canvassed in my 'Aboriginal (Pre)History and Australian Archaeology: The Discourse of Australian Prehistoric Archaeology', in B. Attwood and J. Arnold (eds), *Power, Knowledge and Aborigines*, Melbourne, 1992, pp. 1–19; I. McBryde, (ed.), *Who Owns the Past?*, Melbourne, 1985; I. McBryde, 'The Past as Symbol of Identity', *Antiquity*, vol. 66, no. 250, 1992, pp. 260–66; and J. Stone, 'The Ownership of Culture: Reconciling Our Common and Separate Heritages', *Archaeology in Oceania*, vol. 27, no. 3, 1992, pp. 161–67. Statements about Aboriginal viewpoints on ownership

and control are provided in J. Birkhead *et al.*, *Aboriginal Involvement in Parks and Protected Areas*, Canberra, 1992; H. Creamer, 'Aboriginal Perceptions of the Past: The Implications for Cultural Resource Management in Australia' in P. Gathercole and D. Lowenthal (eds), *The Politics of the Past*, London, 1989, pp. 130–40; and I. Davidson, 'Archaeologists and Aborigines', *Australian Journal of Anthropology*, vol. 2, no. 2, 1991, pp. 247–58. Aspects of views held by representatives of indigenous peoples are surveyed by the papers collected in R. Layton (ed.), *Who Needs the Past?: Indigenous Values and Archaeology*, London, 1989, *Conflict in the Archaeology of Living Traditions*, London, 1989; and R. McGuire, 'Archaeology and the First Americans', *American Anthropologist*, vol. 94, no. 4, 1992, pp. 816–36.

10   This is reflected in the draft policy document 'Protecting Aboriginal and Torres Strait Islander Cultural Heritage Places', 1994, which has been produced by the Federal Department of Communications and the Arts (relying on extensive input from the Aboriginal and Torres Strait Islander Commission, the Australian Heritage Commission, and the Australian Institute of Aboriginal and Torres Strait Islander Studies, among others).

11   See J. Allen, 'Radiocarbon Determinations, Luminescence Dating and Australian Archaeology', *Antiquity*, vol. 68, no. 259, 1994, pp. 339–43; R. Roberts *et al.*, 'Beyond the Radiocarbon Barrier in Australian Prehistory', *Antiquity*, vol. 68, no. 260, 1994, pp. 611–16; J. Allen and S. Holdaway, 'The Contamination of Pleistocene Radiocarbon Determinations in Australia', *Antiquity*, in press.

12   Still the most thoroughly analysed example of this kind of regional variation is R. Cosgrove, 'The Illusion of Riches: Issues of Scale, Resolution and Explanation of Pleistocene Human Behaviour', PhD thesis, La Trobe University, 1991. The case is argued differently by J. Allen, 'Notions of the Pleistocene in Greater Australia', R. Jones, 'A Continental Reconnaissance: Some Observations Concerning the Discovery of the Pleistocene Archaeology of Australia', and S. Bowdler, 'Views of the Past in Australian Prehistory', in M. Spriggs *et al.* (eds), *A Community of Culture: The People and Prehistory of the Pacific*, Canberra, 1993, pp. 139–51, 97–122, 123–138. The best general surveys of recent work on the Australian pleistocene can be found in M. Smith *et al.* (eds), *Sahul in Review*, Canberra, 1993, especially M.A. Smith and N.D. Sharp, 'Pleistocene sites in Australia, New Guinea and Island Melanesia: Geographic and Temporal Structure of the Archaeological Record', pp. 37–59.

13   See, for example, my 'The Childhood of William Lanne: Contact Archaeology and Aboriginality in Northwest Tasmania', *Antiquity*, vol. 67, no. 256, 1993, pp. 504–19; J.M. Birmingham, *Wybalenna: The Archaeology of Cultural Accommodation in Nineteenth Century Tasmania*, Sydney, 1992.

14   See, for example, J. Allen, 'Notions of the Pleistocene', and my 'Australian Prehistory', in J. Ross (ed.), *Chronicle of Australia*, Melbourne, 1993, pp. 10–39.

15 See, for example, my 'The Tasmanians and the Constitution of the
    "Dawn of Humanity"', *Antiquity*, vol. 66, no. 252, 1992,
    pp. 730–43, and 'Aboriginal (Pre)history'.
16 Some commentators have explained this focus on antiquity as being
    a central feature of a masculinist discourse about archaeology.
    (This argument was first made by Joan Gero in her 'Socio-Politics of
    Archaeology and the Woman-at-Home Ideology', *American Anti-
    quity*, vol. 50, no. 2, 1985, pp. 342–50; a more developed version
    appears as 'The Social World of Prehistoric Facts: Gender and Power
    in Paleoindian Research', in H. DuCros and L. Smith (eds), *Women
    in Archaeology: A Feminist Critique*, Canberra, 1993, pp. 31–40).
    However, close examination of the research priorities of both men
    and women seems to provide a contrary case to the North American
    example. Indeed the 'classic' division—prehistoric archaeology being
    the preserve of men and historical archaeology being that of
    women—is clearly overdrawn in Australia, with few of either sex
    choosing a career in historical archaeology. Indeed, if one were to
    seek an explanation for the focus on the most ancient passages of
    Australian history (apart from the simple fact that practitioners,
    justifiably, find it a source of consuming fascination) one should not
    look to gender but to race.
17 'Aboriginal (Pre)history', pp. 18–19.
18 See my 'Aboriginal (Pre)history'.
19 There are a number of surveys of heritage legislation in Australia,
    the three most comprehensive being G.K. Ward, 'Archaeology and
    Legislation in Australia', in G. Connah (ed.), *Australian Archaeology:
    A Guide to Techniques*, Canberra, 1983, pp. 18–42; and J. Flood,
    '"Tread Softly for You Tread on My Bones": The Development of
    Cultural Resource Management in Australia', in H. Cleere (ed.),
    Archaeological Heritage Management in the Modern World, London,
    1989, pp. 79–101, 'Cultural Resources Management in Australia:
    The Last Three Decades', in Spriggs *et al.* (eds), *A Community of
    Culture*, pp. 259–65. Much of the current policy in the Australian
    Heritage Commission concerning matters of consultation is an expres-
    sion of recommendations made in W. Jonas, *Consultation with
    Aboriginal People About Aboriginal Heritage*, Canberra, 1991. These
    are currently being revised.
20 It is noteworthy that the profession at large has not been able to
    debate these very significant matters, either in print or public. One
    reason might be the traditional Australian antipathy to self-reflection,
    another could be a fear that justifying the existence of other view-
    points would give rise to charges of being unsympathetic to Aborig-
    inal interests.
21 H. Burke *et al.*, 'Beyond the Looking-Glass: Some Thoughts on
    Sociopolitics and Reflexivity in Australian Archaeology', *Australian
    Archaeology*, no. 38, 1994, pp. 13–22. Mulvaney's most comprehens-
    ive explorations of the cultural context of Australian archaeology are
    his 'The Australian Aborigines 1606–1929: Opinion and Fieldwork',
    Historical Studies Australia and New Zealand vol. 8, no. 30, 1958,

pp. 131–51, vol. 8, no. 31, 1958, pp. 297–314, 'Gum Leaves on the Golden Bough: Australia's Palaeolithic Survivals Discovered', in J.D. Evans and C. Renfrew (eds), *Antiquity and Man*, London, 1981, pp. 52–64, and '"A Sense of Making History": Australian Aboriginal Studies, 1961–1986', *Australian Aboriginal Studies*, no. 2, 1986, pp. 48–56. But see also T. Murray and J.P. White, 'Cambridge in the Bush?', *World Archaeology*, vol. 13, no. 2, 1981, pp. 255–63; J. Golson, 'Old Guards and New Waves: Reflections on Antipodean Archaeology 1954–1975', *Archaeology in Oceania*, vol. 21, no. 1, 1986, pp. 2–12; I. McBryde, 'Australia's Once and Future Archaeology', *Archaeology in Oceania*, vol. 21, no. 1, 1986, pp. 13–28.

Chapter 6

1 See *Australian Financial Review*, 4 June 1993. The research for this paper was greatly facilitated by the newspaper cutting collection of the Australian Institute of Aboriginal and Torres Strait Islander Studies, which encompasses over one thousand articles for the period under review. Grateful acknowledgment is made for access to this collection.
2 T. Rowse, *After Mabo: Interpreting Indigenous Traditions*, Melbourne, 1993, ch. 1.
3 *West Australian*, 19 June 1993.
4 *Age*, 12 June 1993.
5 Victorian Branch, 78th State Annual Conference, 30 June 1993, reproduced in *The Verbatim Report*, vol. 2, no. 7, 1993. Compare I. McLachlan, 'Big Storm Brewing Over Mabo', *Canberra Times*, 1 June 1993.
6 *Herald-Sun*, 28 July 1993.
7 Transcript, Opening Address to the Returned Services League.
8 *Sunday Telegraph*, 6 June 1994.
9 *Australian*, 21 July 1993.
10 *Herald-Sun*, 3 July 1993.
11 *Age*, 26 June 1993.
12 *The Advertiser*, 3 July 1993.
13 *Herald-Sun*, 28 July 1993; Transcript, Opening Address to the Returned Services League.
14 *West Australian*, 8 June 1993; see also *Australian Financial Review*, 3 June 1993.
15 *Canberra Times*, 2 July 1993.
16 *Age*, 7 July 1993; *Herald-Sun*, 8 July 1993.
17 Transcript, Opening Address to the Returned Services League.
18 *Sydney Morning Herald*, 31 July 1993.
19 *Australian*, 23 July 1993; see also *Daily-Telegraph Mirror*, 28 July 1993.
20 *West Australian*, 30 June 1993.
21 See, for example, P. Smark, 'Myths, Malice and Mabo', *Sydney*

Morning Herald, 12 June 1993; *Age*, 2 July 1993; K. Davidson,
   'Mabo: Don't Let the Rednecks Rule', *Age*, 3 July 1993; V. Laurie,
   'The Mabo Monster Unmasked' *Bulletin*, vol. 115, no. 5680, 1993,
   pp. 16–17.
22 2 July 1993.
23 The definition of 'new racism' adopted here is in keeping with Martin
   Barker's analysis in his *The New Racism*, London, 1981. I believe it
   is a misuse of the term 'racism' to apply it to policies of assimilation,
   which may be premised on denigration of the civilisation of the object
   of assimilation, but of necessity denies *racial* (as distinct from cultural) inferiority through the policy of inclusion. The concept of racial
   inferiority is grounded in the impossibility of category change, in the
   permanence of behavioural characteristics; racial inferiors cannot be
   assimilated. Compare the argument of Gillian Cowlishaw in her
   'Mabo Breeds a Sinister New Form of Racism', *Age*, 31 July 1993.
24 Speech dated 4 December 1959, printed as pamphlet, *Australia and
   Asia: The Case for Our Immigration Policy*, Australian Archives,
   Canberra, Series A1838/2, 581/1, part 6.
25 See the excellent article, Glover on Friday, 'Racism: No Bones About
   It', *Sydney Morning Herald*, 2 July 1993.
26 'Clown Princes Lead the Way', *Bulletin*, vol. 115, no. 5876, 1993,
   p. 17; see also *Australian*, 22 June 1993.
27 See my 'Land Rights, Immigration and Multiculturalism', in A.
   Markus and R. Rasmussen (eds), *Prejudice in the Public Arena*,
   Melbourne, 1987, pp. 21–34; R. Libby, *Hawke's Law: The Politics
   of Mining and Aboriginal Land Rights in Australia*, Nedlands, 1989.
   Cf. the findings of an opinion poll, reported in the *West Australian*,
   12 July 1993.
28 *Australian*, 21 July 1993.
29 ibid., 23 July 1993.

Chapter 7

1 I wish to thank John Morton and Gillian Robinson for their helpful
   comments and suggestions on an earlier version of this chapter.
2 I assume, therefore, that the economic and political consequences of
   the High Court's judgment are really quite limited, since while the
   High Court recognised native title it also ruled that this had been
   legitimately extinguished in much of Australia, that compensation
   was not payable for such expropriation, and that Aboriginal claimants have to be able to show that they have maintained a continuing
   relationship to their traditional land, which few can do. Nor did the
   judgment question Australian sovereignty.
3 Cf. H.K. Bhabha (ed.), *Nation and Narration*, London, 1990; E.
   Balibar, 'The Nation Form: History and Ideology', in E. Balibar and
   I. Wallerstein, *Race, Nation and Class: Ambiguous Identities*,
   London, 1991, pp. 86–106.

4   I use 'conservatives' in the same loose sense as Andrew Markus has
    in the preceding chapter.
5   J. Bruner, 'The Narrative Construction of Reality', *Critical Inquiry*,
    vol. 18, no. 2, 1991, p. 8.
6   L. Mink, *On Historical Understanding*, Ithaca, 1987, p. 186.
7   Bruner, 'The Narrative', pp. 5, 7–8.
8   ibid., pp. 7, 18.
9   As Graeme Davison has remarked, perhaps because Australia lacks
    a definite moment of birth and a founding document ('a national
    birthright such as the Treaty of Waitangi, much less a Magna Carta,
    a Declaration of Independence or a Bill of Rights'), it has been
    'obliged to place so much reliance upon the third of the great
    constituent elements of modern nationalism—the idea of common
    lineage, language and relationship with the land' ('Australia: The First
    Postmodern Republic?', unpublished paper, Melbourne, 1994,
    pp. 3–4).
10 My approach here owes much to Johannes Fabian's *Time and the
    Other: How Anthropology Makes its Object*, New York, 1983.
11 See, for example, L. Kramer, 'The Rocky Horror History of
    Australia', *IPA Review*, vol. 38, no. 4, 1985, pp. 183, 185; H.
    Morgan, 'A Day to Remember Realities of History', *Age*, 28 January
    1985, 'The Dangers of Aboriginal Sovereignty', *News Weekly*, 29
    August 1992, p. 11; K. Baker, 'The Bicentenary: Celebration or
    Apology', *IPA Review*, vol. 38, no. 4, 1985, pp. 175–77, 179, 182,
    'The New History', *IPA Review*, vol. 42, no. 3, 1988/89, p. 50; G.
    Henderson, 'Rewriting Our History', *Bulletin*, vol. 115, no. 5855,
    1993, pp. 26–29; G. Blainey, 'Drawing Up a Balance Sheet of Our
    History', *Quadrant*, vol. 37, nos 7–8, 1993, pp. 11, 15; P. Coleman,
    'The Great Australian Death Wish', *Quadrant*, vol. 24, no. 5, 1985,
    pp. 7–8.
12 D.J. Mulvaney, 'Beyond 1788: A Personal Exploration', in B. Att-
    wood (comp.), *Boundaries of the Past*, Melbourne, 1990, p. 10,
    'Discovering Man's Place in Nature', *Proceedings of the Australian
    Academy of the Humanities*, vol. 2, 1971, p. 55, *A Prehistory of
    Australia*, London, 1969, p. 12. As Paul Carter has argued, Austra-
    lian history has conventionally been written as though Australia and
    history was prior to the British colonisers and the historians who
    actually created and create it by their narratives (*The Road to Botany
    Bay: An Essay in Spatial History*, London, 1987).
13 Morgan, 'A Day to Remember', *Opening Address, 78th Annual
    Conference of the Returned Services League, Victorian Branch, 30
    June 1993*, Melbourne, 1993, p. 7; Baker, 'The New History', p. 50.
14 R. Castan, *Australian Catharsis—Coping with Native Title: 1993
    B'nai B'rith Oration*, Melbourne, 1993, pp. 2, 11; V. Brady, *Caught
    in the Draught*, Sydney, 1994, p. 23; *The Australian*, 22 June 1993;
    Sydney Morning Herald, 22 June 1993; *Weekend Australian*, 31
    July–1 August 1993.
15 *Weekend Australian*, 21–22 August 1993.
16 P. Durack, 'The Consequences of the Mabo Case', in P. Durack *et*

al., *Mabo and After*, Perth, 1992, p. 5; my emphases. See also, for
example, Morgan, *Mabo Reconsidered: The Joe and Enid Lyons
Memorial Lecture, 12 October 1992*, Melbourne, 1992, p. 5; C.
Howard, 'The Consequences of the Mabo Case', *IPA Review*, vol.
46, no. 1, 1993, p. 21; J. Stone, 'With the Mabo Six', *Australian
Financial Review*, 22 July 1993.

17 *Opening Address*, p. 3. For a consideration of Morgan and his
long-time speechwriter, Ray Evans, see *Weekend Australian*, 31 July–
1 August 1993.

18 Blainey, 'Pieces of the Mabo Jigsaw', *Age Saturday Extra*, 23 October
1992, 'In God He Trusted', *Age Saturday Extra*, 20 November 1992.

19 See also *Weekend Australian*, 12–13 February 1993; P. P. McGuinness, 'History of Invasion Ignores More Balanced School of Thought',
Australian, 15 June 1994.

20 'The Consequences of the Mabo Case', pp. 21, 22; my emphasis.
Howard also argues that the 'land rights movement . . . is utterly
unhistorical in character' (ibid., p. 22).

21 *Age*, 21 June 1993.

22 Baker, 'The Bicentenary', p. 177; see also Blainey, *Eye for Australia:
Speeches and Essays of Geoffrey Blainey*, Melbourne, 1991, p. 44.

23 *Opening Address*, p. 2; my emphasis.

24 *Age*, 3 May 1984, 18 June 1993; Morgan, *Opening Address*, p. 8,
Mabo Reconsidered, p. 4, 'Religious Traditions, Mining and Land
Rights', in K. Baker (ed.), *The Land Rights Debate: Selected Docu-
ments*, Melbourne, 1985, p. 25; (Hobart) *Mercury*, 18 June 1993.

25 Blainey, *Triumph of the Nomads: A History of Ancient Australia*,
Melbourne, 1975, pp. 103–11; *A Land Half Won*, Melbourne, 1983,
ch. 6; *Age*, 29 May 1982; *Australian*, 10 November 1993.

26 *Opening Address*, p. 8.

27 Fischer, cited Morgan, *Opening Address*, p. 6; *Australian*, 21 June
1993; Howard, 'The Consequences', p. 22. Humphrey McQueen has
aptly described this as the pretence that 'all the misdeeds took place
in some whitefella dreamtime long before most of today's Australians
were born or could vote' (*Weekend Australian*, 17–18 July 1993).

28 *Age*, 25 September 1993; Morgan, 'The Dangers', p. 11; Howard,
'The Consequences', p. 22.

29 'National Damage', *Age*, 1 December 1993.

30 *Age*, 4 & 21 June 1993; Howard, 'The Consequences', p. 22. More
recently, a landowner who fears he will lose leasing rights to nearby
land as a consequence of the *Native Title Act* said: 'I don't think
that you can ever just turn the clock back' (*Age*, 19 October 1994).

31 *Age*, 4 June 1993; Fischer, cited Morgan, *Opening Address*, p. 6.

32 For a discussion of the German *Historikerstreit*, see P. Baldwin (ed.),
*Reworking the Past: Hitler, the Holocaust, and the Historians'
Debate*, Boston, 1990.

33 *Age*, 21 June 1993.

34 F. Nietzsche, Aphorism 68, in his *Beyond Good and Evil* (1886). I
am indebted to my colleague Eleanor Hancock who both drew my
attention to this and provided the translation.

35 As Deborah Bird Rose has argued, colonisation was marked by 'two [critical] moments—death and denial'; violence, 'at one moment understood to be essential, was at a later moment denied or simply lost to memory' (*Hidden Histories: Black Stories from Victoria River Downs, Humbert River and Wave Hill Stations*, Canberra, 1991, pp. 259, 32).

36 Blainey, 'Drawing Up', p. 11.

37 Coleman, 'The Great Australian', p. 7; Henderson, 'Rewriting Our History', p. 29; Morgan, 'A Day to Remember', *Mabo Reconsidered*, p. 2.

38 Baker, 'The Bicentenary, pp. 177, 179, 180, 181, 'The New History', p. 50.

39 Blainey, 'Drawing Up', p. 15, *Eye for Australia*, p. 49; Morgan, 'A Day to Remember', 'The Dangers', p. 13, *Age*, 28 July 1993; Baker, 'The Bicentenary', p. 181, 'The New History', p. 50.

40 *Eye for Australia*, p. 51; my emphasis.

41 'No Puppets of the Past', *Age Saturday Extra*, 13 November 1993. Significantly, Blainey does not attribute this 'silence' to events in the colonial past, and insofar as that historical period is considered he tells a story of accommodation between Aborigines and Europeans, which is compatible with his tales of noble and heroic pioneers.

42 See P. J. Bowler, *The Invention of Progress: The Victorians and the Past*, Oxford, 1989.

43 'Land that Bypassed a Revolution', *Age Saturday Extra*, 21 August 1993, 'Mabo: What Aboriginals Lost', *Age Saturday Extra*, 31 July 1993, 'Drawing Up', p. 15; my emphases. See also *Australian*, 13 May 1993.

44 'Blainey and Aboriginal History', in A. Markus and M. Ricklefs (eds), *Surrender Australia?: Essays in the Study and Uses of History. Geoffrey Blainey and Asian Immigration*, Sydney, 1985, p. 89; Reynolds (comp.), *Dispossession: Black Australians and White Invaders*, Sydney, 1989, pp. 9–11, 19–21.

45 Howard, 'The Consequences', p. 22; *Australian*, 21 June 1993; Morgan, *Opening Address*, p. 8. More recently, one small landholder claimed: 'If you go right through history, the victors have always taken land off the vanquished, that's history' (*Age*, 19 October 1994).

46 *Australian*, 31 June 1993; Blainey, *Eye for Australia*, p. 124.

47 Baker, 'The Bicentenary', p. 181; my emphasis.

48 'Sitting in Judgment on History', *Australian Business Monthly*, vol. 13, no. 10, 1993, p. 44; 'Land that Bypassed'.

49 'Land that Bypassed', 'Fallacies Weaken the Case for a Treaty', in K. Baker (ed.), *A Treaty with the Aborigines?*, Melbourne, 1988, p. 16, 'Drawing Up', p. 14.

50 See *Age*, 17 June 1993, 5 November 1993.

51 *Australian*, 28 October 1993; T. Hewat, *Who Made the Mabo Mess*, Melbourne, 1993, ch. 1.

52 *Age*, 29 May 1982, 3 May 1984, 14 June 1993; Blainey, *Eye for Australia*, p. 125, 'Drawing Up', p. 15; *Australian*, 13 May 1993; *Northern Territory News*, 26 October 1993.

53 This claim is seldom if ever supported by empirical data; it remains, instead, an untested and unquestioned assumption.

54 *Opening Address*, pp. 2, 3; see also 'A Day to Remember'.

55 Morgan, 'The Dangers', p. 13; M. Perron, *Opening Address, Northern Territory Chamber of Commerce and Industry,* 7 *October 1993,* Darwin, 1993, p. 1; *Age,* 25 September 1993; Blainey, 'Pieces of the Mabo Jigsaw'; *Herald-Sun*, cited *IPA Review*, vol. 46, no. 2, 1993, p. 16.

56 The amount of Aboriginal-owned land is also misrepresented diagrammatically in maps; see *Age,* 9 June 1993, *Weekend Australian*, 21–22 August 1993.

57 Durack, 'The Consequences', p. 7; *Age,* 4 November 1993; see also Howard, 'The Consequences', p. 23. Key symbolic spaces were also deemed to be at risk. Two state premiers claimed that Australians' *back*yards—that quintessential private place—were at risk, and the Northern Territory's chief minister alleged that Australians' access to beaches—that treasured public area—was also endangered, *Age,* 10 June, 18 October 1993.

58 *Age,* 24 May, 6 July, 25 September 1993; Blainey, 'Sitting in Judgment', p. 44; T. Sykes, 'Mabo and the Real World', *Australian Business Monthly,* vol. 13, no. 10, 1993, p. 32; see also *Australian Financial Review*, 15 June 1993; Hewat, *Who Made Mabo*, p. 6.

59 As John Morton and Nonie Sharp have remarked, the possibility of the Torres Strait Islands assuming autonomy does not arouse the fears that demands for Aboriginal Sovereignty do, thus underlining the symbolic importance of the outlines of the mainland (Morton to author, personal communication, 21 September 1994; Sharp, 'Native Title in the Reshaping of Australian Identity', *Arena Journal*, no. 3, 1994, p. 131).

60 *Opening Address*, p. 2.

61 F. Devine, 'Tribal Guide Through a Legal Maze', *Australian*, 11 February 1993; Morgan, *Opening Address*, pp. 9, 10; *Age,* 7 July 1993; Howard, 'The Consequences', p. 23; Blainey, 'Land Rights for All', *Age,* 10 November 1993, 'National Damage', *Age,* 1 December 1993, 'Australia: Two Peoples: Two Nations?', *Age Saturday Extra*, 12 June 1993.

62 Blainey, 'Land Rights for All', 'Australia: Two Peoples'; *Age,* 28 July 1993; Morgan,'The Dangers', p. 13. See also Hewat, *Who Made Mabo*, p. 36.

63 Blainey believes that the Northern Territory might 'be the obvious place [for] those seeking to set up an Aboriginal state', and so Australia is further deemed to be at risk because two racial others, Aborigines and Asians, join forces in his fevered imagination. He writes of

> our closeness to the most crowded quarters of the globe . . .
> We stand opposite a nation that has recently become the
> fourth most populous in the world . . . To add to the
> dilemma, the part of Australia that is least populated is very
> close to Indonesia. If Australia were divided into two

> nations, a north and a south . . . that would make it the
> second emptiest land in the world . . . On present indica-
> tions, the Mabo Bill, by multiplying the huge northern area
> already in Aboriginal hands, could further impede the
> increase of population in this empty region so close to Asia.

A decade earlier, Blainey argued that:

> It could just be conceivable . . . that an Aboriginal-domi-
> nated Northern Territory might, during some future
> international emergency, decide to side with, say, Indonesia
> or Papua New Guinea against the rest of Australia.

('How Empty is Our Land?', *Age Saturday Extra*, 27 November 1993; *Age*, 29 May 1982).

64 Blainey, 'No One Has Sole Claim on Racism', *Age*, 17 May 1994; *Australian*, 13 May 1993; Morgan, *Reflections on Coronation Hill: Address to Adam Smith Club, 9 July 1991*, Melbourne, 1991, p. 1, *Opening Address*, p. 10.
65 'The Dangers', p. 13; my emphasis.
66 Hewat, *Who Made Mabo*, pp. 15, 81; R. Brunton, 'A Year to Forget?', *IPA Review*, vol. 46, no. 3, 1993, p. 20; *Age*, 24 September 1993; Blainey, *Eye for Australia*, p. 60, 'Fallacies Weaken', p. 15, Blainey, cited Henderson, 'Time for Blainey to Step Off His Soapbox', *Age*, 23 November 1993.
67 *Eye for Australia*, pp. 125, 124. See also the comments of Senator Peter Walsh, cited Hewat, *Who Made Mabo*, p. 8. Morgan also prescribes modernity as the solution for Aborigines: 'The poverty of the Aborigines . . . arises . . . because of the barriers that we, or they, erect to keep them locked out of modern Australia' (*Age*, 18 February 1988). This solution is not, it should be noted, confined to conservatives (see Tim Rowse's discussion of Charles Rowley's work in his *After Mabo: Interpreting Indigenous Traditions*, Melbourne, 1993, pp. 27–44).
68 *Opening Address*, p. 10.

Chapter 8

1 *Sunday Age*, 21 March 1993.
2 See R. Needham (ed.), *Right and Left: Essays on Dual Symbolic Classification*, Chicago, 1973.
3 Ted Whitten may have accurately predicted Yunupingu's involvement in the Grand Final, but, in an ironic turn of events, he too was to be humbled. In a television programme 'Mr Football' alleged that one of the Aboriginal team that won the Ted Whitten Trophy 'swapped it for a flagon of red', and after an appeal by Koori leader, Alf Bamblett, Whitten apologised: 'Of course I regret it. The trophy was donated by me and it was a joke against myself' (*Victorian Australian Aboriginal and Torres Strait Islander Newsletter*, April 1994, p. 4).

4   *Blackout*, 10 December 1992.
5   *Age*, 25 March 1993.
6   'Birth of a Post-Modern Nation', *Weekend Australian*, 24–25 July 1993.
7   *Blackout*, 10 December 1992.
8   B. Anderson, *Imagined Communities: Reflections on the Origin and Spread of Nationalism*, London, 1983; E. Durkheim, *The Division of Labour in Society* (1893), London, 1984.
9   *Age*, 16 September 1993.
10   *Sunday Age*, 15 May 1994. This, I think, means that we must modify the view that republicanism is in essence 'a flight from femininity and maternal power', whose embodiment is the Queen (M. Lake, 'Sexing the Republic: What Do Women Want?', *Age*, 2 December 1993; see also 'A Republic for Women?', *Arena Magazine*, no. 9, 1994, pp. 32–33). Chilla Bulbeck has suggested that, in the republicanism debate, we should 'retrieve the motherland by claiming . . . that she is everyone's land or a land beyond the relations of possession . . . Like Aborigines, we might argue that the native country owns the children who are sustained by it, and who owe it a duty of conservation and care' ('Republicanism and Post-Nationalism', in W. Hudson and D. Carter (eds), *The Republicanism Debate*, Sydney, 1993, p. 96).
11   *Sunday Age*, 15 May 1994. This may provide the 'wrong' answer to Wendy Brady's rhetorical question: 'Will the President of the next republic be Aboriginal?' Perhaps she is on surer ground when she asks, equally rhetorically: 'Where does the Aboriginal Provisional Government of Australia fit into the debate on the republic?' ('Republicanism: An Aboriginal View', in Hudson and Carter (eds), *Republicanism*, p. 148).
12   *Australian*, 22 December 1994.
13   By 'talked up' I mean to indicate that Aborigines have become more visible, but it is certainly also true that such 'talking up' occurs in a moral sense as well, with academics and others often undertaking advocacy roles. Such roles are not always applauded. See, for example, S.J. Thiele, 'Anti-Intellectualism and the "Aboriginal Problem": Colin Tatz and the "Self-Determination" Approach', *Mankind*, vol. 14, no. 1, 1984, pp. 165–78, and subsequent responses in the journal. For more populist objections, suggesting that 'the greater part of the Aboriginal history of the last 20 years [is] unreliable', see P. P. McGuinness, 'Strict Assay Needed on this Mother Lode', *Australian*, 8 December 1992.
14   See in particular the essays by Andrew Lattas: 'Aborigines and Contemporary Australian Nationalism: Primordiality and the Cultural Politics of Otherness', *Social Analysis*, no. 27, 1990, pp. 50–69; 'Nationalism, Aesthetic Redemption and Aboriginality', *Australian Journal of Anthropology*, vol. 2, no. 3, 1991, pp. 307–24; and 'Primitivism, Nationalism and Individualism in Australian Popular Culture', in B. Attwood and J. Arnold (eds), *Power, Knowledge and Aborigines*, Melbourne, 1992, pp. 45–58.

15   There is certainly suitable inspiration on offer from some Aboriginal
     people. Brady, for example, writes: 'The present debates about Aus-
     tralia as a republic ignore one basic historical fact: that Australia
     was a republic prior to colonisation' ('Republicanism', p. 145).

16   *Sharing the Country*, Melbourne, 1991, p. ix.

17   'Aborigines, Torres Strait Islanders and the Constitution', typescript.

18   Brennan had already sensed the connection when he drew special
     attention to the fact that Michael Nelson Jakamarra stood directly
     beside the Queen when he spoke of reconciliation at the opening of
     the new Parliament House, for which he had designed a prominent
     'Dreamtime' (*tjukurrpa*) mosaic (*Sharing the Country*, p. 1).

19   J. Fiske *et al.*, *Myths of Oz: Reading Australian Popular Culture*,
     Sydney, 1987, pp. 123–30; J. Marcus, 'The Journey Out to the
     Centre: The Appropriation of Ayers Rock', in A. Rutherford (ed.),
     Aboriginal Culture Today, Sydney, 1988, pp. 254–74.

20   The Australian Capital Territory's coat of arms has two swans—one
     white, one black—as shield bearers.

21   *Weekend Australian*, 18–19 December 1993. Australian artist Arthur
     Boyd, 1995 Australian of the Year, recently suggested that the flag
     be redesigned to incorporate the motif of two figures—a black man
     and a white woman—in an embrace. (ABC Television, *7.30 Report*,
     26 January 1995).

22   The representation is not dissimilar to the use of Aboriginal
     Australia's black, red and gold to depict the bedrock of the nation
     on the poster that was used to advertise the conference for which
     this chapter was initially written. Brady claims that the Aboriginal
     flag 'only very occasionally comes into view in the symbols being
     promoted by the various [republican] movements in Australia'
     ('Republicanism', p. 146). This may be true, but there is some
     understandable ambivalence expressed by potential supporters of such
     promotion. Hudson and Carter suggest that while there is an 'exciting
     case to be argued for adopting the Aboriginal flag as part or whole
     of a new Australian flag', this would be 'problematic' and require
     'far more sensitive and informed understanding' of Aboriginality than
     has so far been the case ('Reframing the Issues', in *Republicanism*,
     p. 20). This kind of ambivalence in the nation's collective conscience
     was confirmed during the recent controversy over Cathy Freeman's
     use of the Aboriginal flag in conjunction with the Australian flag
     after winning the 400 and 200 metres races at the 1994 Common-
     wealth Games. Grumbles by Victorian RSL President Bruce Ruxton
     and Liberal MP Bill Taylor aside, Freeman's action drew unequivocal
     praise from prominent politicians on both the left and the right and
     from newspaper editorials (e.g., *Age*, 25 & 26 August 1994), as well
     as from many Aboriginal commentators. For example, ATSIC's
     Charles Perkins gave voice to a common Aboriginal point of view
     when he said 'he believed incorporating Aboriginal colours, or the
     Aboriginal flag in its entirety, was an appropriate way to underpin
     reconciliation' (*Weekend Australian*, 27–28 August 1994). However,
     O'Donoghue and a number of other Aborigines have contended that

'their flag . . . should remain solely representative of indigenous Australians'. According to Reg Blow of the Victorian Aborigines Advancement League, incorporating the Aboriginal flag into a uniform Australian design would be like Aborigines giving up their identity (*Age*, 28 August 1994). This, I think, is precisely what is being required of Aboriginal people at the present time.

23 'Mabo v Queensland No. 2', *Australian Law Journal Reports*, vol. 66, 1992, pp. 451, 449 per Deane and Gaudron JJ.

24 Donald Horne has already argued this ('Multiple Voices', in Hudson and Carter (eds), *Republicanism*, p. 217). As far as I can tell, W.E.H. Stanner was the first to grasp the logic of the case when he wrote: 'All land in Australia is held in consequence of an assumption so large, grand and remote from actuality that it had best be called royal, which is exactly what it was' ('After the Dreaming', in his *White Man Got No Dreaming*, Canberra, 1979, p. 215). However, there is also a sense in which the logic is much older, although here it has a more muted form. As Ian McLean has argued, republican literature in nineteenth-century Australia strongly identified with indigeneity, but, because of the 'transgressive' nature of this identification, 'it could only be sustained by comic form':

> The racist jibes of Australia's republican rags . . . such as the *Bulletin* and the *Boomerang*, are examples of repressed Aboriginalism which unconsciously sought a spiritual identity with aboriginality [*sic*] ('White Aborigines: Cultural Imperatives of Australian Colonialism', *Third Text*, no. 22, Spring 1993, p. 22).

As should become clear later in this chapter, I am sympathetic to the idea that current forms of white Aboriginality constitute a 'return of the repressed'.

25 Graeme Campbell, cited *Australian Magazine*, 11–12 June 1994, p. 32, and Ruxton, cited *Age*, 30 June 1994.

26 I am quoting advertisements by the Northern Territory Tourist Commission and Victoria's Koorie Tourism Unit. Of course, in counter-narratives, the tendency would be to assume that Aboriginality has nothing to offer contemporary Australia—hence well-known comments about the 'stone age' and Aboriginal people's lack of wheels (see Andrew Markus' chapter).

27 A. Harris, *Australia's Too Old to Celebrate Birthdays*, Canberra, 1988.

28 *Age*, 27 January 1994.

29 *Koori Mail*, 4 May 1994.

30 The logic of Australia's birthday in relation to Aboriginality and the republic has been explored by Mudrooroo in his play *The Aboriginal Protesters Confront the Proclamation of the Australian Republic on 26 January 2001 with a Production of 'The Commission' by Heiner Müller*. In a comment on the play, Gerhard Fischer suggests that while current debate largely connects the republic with the Federation Centenary (1 January 2001), the Australia Day date remains much more suitable so long as the declaration of the republic is accompanied

by a treaty and an acknowledgment of Aboriginal sovereignty. This, he suggests, 'would provide the republic with something only the Aboriginal peoples can provide: legitimacy' ('Multiple Voices', p. 229).

31   The ancestral connection between the First Fleet and Aboriginality was made when images depicting each appeared on opposite sides of a special ten dollar note printed to mark the bicentennial year. For comment on the fusion of such identities in the political rhetoric of that year, see P. Gillen, '"Commitment is All": The Aesthetic Foundations of Nationalism', *Social Analysis*, no. 27, 1990, pp. 102–109.

32   Langton also says that 'Morgan raises the possibility for the reader that he or she would thus acquire the genealogical, even biological ticket ("my great-great grandmother was Aboriginal") to enter the world of "primitivism"' ('*Well, I Heard it on the Radio and I Saw it on the Television* . . .': *An Essay for the Australian Film Commission on the Politics and Aesthetics of Filmmaking by and about Aboriginal People and Things*, Sydney, 1993, pp. 29–30).

33   B. Attwood, 'Portrait of an Aboriginal as an Artist: Sally Morgan and the Construction of Aboriginality', *Australian Historical Studies*, vol. 25, no. 99, 1993, pp. 316–17.

34   This qualifies the following assertion by Darlene Johnson: 'Dialogue requires equal subjects engaging in equal exchange. But it is important to remember here that there is historical inequality between blacks and whites: whites neither want to nor can they ever pass as black. In other words, there is nothing intersubjective about passing, it is not negotiable' ('Ab/originality: Playing and Passing Versus Assimilation', *Bulletin of the Olive Pink Society*, vol. 5, no. 2, 1993, p. 22). It is interesting to note that, at a time when whites are beginning to 'pass' as blacks, writers like Mudrooroo claim that Aboriginal passing can be a way of *protecting* one's Aboriginal identity (ibid.).

35   *Reconciling our Differences: A Christian Approach to Recognising Aboriginal Land Rights*, Melbourne, 1992, p. 108. See also John Harris, who interprets Aboriginal interest and leadership in the Church as the ultimate outcome of the Biblical conviction that 'God made of one blood all nations' (*One Blood: 200 Years of Aboriginal Encounter with Christianity*, Sydney, 1990). Harris' book carries a dustjacket bearing a copy of one of Sally Morgan's paintings.

36   Cited A. Hamilton, 'Fear and Desire: Aborigines, Asians and the National Imaginary', *Australian Cultural History*, no. 9, 1990, p. 23. Hamilton's article also has a commentary on the use of Aboriginality in *The Last Wave* and '*Crocodile' Dundee* (pp. 32–33). See also the excellent discussion of Aboriginality in '*Crocodile' Dundee* and related films written by Meaghan Morris in her 'Tooth and Claw: Tales of Survival and *Crocodile Dundee*', *Art and Text*, no. 25, 1987, pp. 55–59.

37   *Age Good Weekend Magazine*, 21 August 1993, pp. 21–35.

38   The R.M. Williams Summer Catalogue for 1993/94 portrayed a

number of images of rural Australia. These included two photographs of a jillaroo in close and lone association with an Aboriginal stockman. A newspaper advertisement also published in 1993 had an interesting gay flavour. The naked torsos of one young white man and one young black man were placed back to back to call attention to the threat to the *Racial Discrimination Act* that loomed large during the Mabo debate. The advertisement was sponsored by the New South Wales Aboriginal Land Council (*Weekend Australian*, 4–5 December 1993).

39 C. Lévi-Strauss, *The Elementary Structures of Kinship*, London, 1969.
40 For example, Queensland and New South Wales recently refused to allow the word 'invasion' to substitute for 'settlement' in the teaching of history in their state schools.
41 P. Wolfe, '"White Man's Flour": Doctrines of Virgin Birth in Evolutionist Ethnogenetics and Australian State-Formation', *History and Anthropology*, vol. 8, no. 4, 1994, pp. 165–206.
42 J. Kovel, *White Racism: A Psychohistory*, New York, 1970.
43 *Freedom Ride*, City Pictures, 1993, directed by R. Perkins.
44 J. Lacan, 'The Signification of the Phallus', in *Écrits: A Selection*, London, 1977, pp. 281–91.
45 *Sunday Age*, 13 June 1993.
46 P. Wolfe, 'Nation and MiscegeNation: Discursive Continuity in the Post-Mabo Era', *Social Analysis*, no. 36, 1994, pp. 93–152; see also J. Beckett, 'Children of Conquest: Miscegenation in Some Colonies of Settlement', manuscript.
47 S. Muecke, 'Margin or Mainstream?', in his *Textual Spaces: Aboriginality and Cultural Studies*, Sydney, 1992, p. 188.
48 Lacan, 'On a Question Preliminary to Any Possible Treatment of Psychosis', in *Écrits: A Selection*, pp. 179–225.
49 'Mabo: Towards Respecting Equality and Difference', in M. Yunupingu *et al.*, *Voices from the Land: 1993 Boyer Lectures*, Sydney, 1994, p. 98.
50 Wolfe, 'Nation and MiscegeNation'.
51 Through Beth and her white husband, *Heartland* builds the critical role of the media into its story. Beth's white husband's role as media personality is a clumsy one when it engages with Aboriginal issues. In the end, however, Beth's secure future at Brooklyn Waters depends on her gaining a job in community radio.
52 Wolfe, 'Nation and MiscegeNation', pp. 126–27.
53 Cited Muecke, 'Appropriation or Post-Colonial Renaissance', in *Textual Spaces*, p. 163.
54 See the discussions by Jeremy Beckett, 'Aboriginality, Citizenship and Nation State', *Social Analysis*, no. 24, 1988, pp. 3–18, 'The Past in the Present; the Present in the Past: Constructing a National Aboriginality', in J.R. Beckett (ed.), *Past and Present: The Construction of Aboriginality*, Canberra, 1988, pp. 191–217, and 'Aboriginality in a Nation State: The Australian Case', in M.C. Howard (ed.),

Ethnicity and Nation-Building in the Pacific, Tokyo, 1989, pp. 118–35.

55 It may, in fact, simultaneously provide instruments of repression and expression. This was illustrated during the Mabo debate when Michael Nelson Jakamarra 'symbolically reclaimed his mosaic that decorates the forecourt of Parliament House', taking 'a hammer and chisel to symbolically cut out the centre stone of his dreaming which he said represented all Australia's indigenous people' (*Age*, 28 September 1993). This shows, of course, that, within the broader context, co-operation with the state is not incompatible with resistance against it. Both are strategic possibilities.

56 R. Rosaldo, *Culture and Truth: The Remaking of Social Analysis*, Boston, 1989, pp. 68–87.

57 In other words, exchange need not be a case of what Sahlins called 'negative reciprocity'. See his 'On the Sociology of Primitive Exchange', in *Stone Age Economics*, London, 1974, pp. 185–275.

58 A. Curthoys and S. Muecke, 'Australia, For Example', in Hudson and Carter (eds), *Republicanism*, p. 199. Keating has stated something very similar: 'Australia has an opportunity to continue to bring the dispossessed out from the shadows . . . Aboriginal and Torres Strait Islander people should be included because they are part of our nation and have unique perspectives to bring to a range of issues, including the debate on the republic, the celebration of the centenary of Federation, and, most importantly, the shaping of Australia's national identity' ('Dispossessed Now Out of the Shadows', *Weekend Australian*, 30–31 July 1994).

59 R. Young, *White Mythologies: Writing Histories and the West*, London, 1990, p. 119.

60 *Weekend Australian*, 1–2 May 1993.

61 ibid., 12–13 February 1994.

62 *Age*, 12 June 1994.

63 ibid., 10 April 1994.

64 At least one academic, Colin Tatz, was churlish enough to say that Collingwood 'will get immense kudos by posing as the good guy condescending to play a bunch of niggers in the north' (ibid., 10 February 1994). Perhaps Tatz would have also been unimpressed by the 'niggers' I spoke to in February 1994 at Yuendumu in the Northern Territory who were making preparations to travel to Darwin to support the Magpies, who happen to play in the same colours as Yuendumu football team. Indeed, Collingwood Football Club supplies Yuendumu with jumpers! I might add that, since this chapter was first written, Collingwood has signed its very first Aboriginal player—from the Northern Territory (ibid., 30 October 1994).

Acknowledgments

Earlier versions of some of the chapters of this book were presented at a conference, Mabo, Aborigines and Australia: A historical revolution?, held under the auspices of The History Institute, Victoria, and funded by the Vice-Chancellor of Monash University, Professor Mal Logan. Gordon Bennett kindly granted permission to reproduce his painting, *Tryptych, 1989, Requiem*, on the cover. Natalee Dalgleish, Donna Finegan and Rosemary Johnston provided secretarial assistance. The authors accepted my editorial advice and requests in good spirit. The book was published with the assistance of the Monash University Publications Committee. I benefited enormously from Gillian Robinson's editorial experience, and her encouragement and support throughout the making of this book.

Bain Attwood

Contributors

Bain Attwood is Senior Lecturer in History at Monash University. He is the author of *The Making of the Aborigines*, co-editor of *Power, Knowledge and Aborigines*, and co-author of *A Life Together, A Life Apart: A History of Relations Between Europeans and Aborigines*. He is currently writing a general study of the relationship between Aborigines, Australia and the discourse of history.

Richard Broome is Reader in History at La Trobe University, and currently the president of The History Institute, Victoria. He has published numerous articles in Australian history and four books, including two commissioned histories and *Aboriginal Australians*, an overview of Aboriginal–European contact history. He is currently working on a history of twentieth-century Aboriginal Victorians.

Rosemary Hunter is Senior Lecturer in Law at the University of Melbourne. She teaches history and philosophy of law and discrimination law, and is the author of *Indirect Discrimination in the Workplace* and articles on discrimination law, and Aborigines and law. She is currently working on a doctorate of Juridical Science at Stanford University.

Andrew Markus is Associate Professor in History at Monash University. He has written extensively in the field of race relations, acted as a consultant for the National Inquiry into Racist Violence and the Fitzgerald Committee on Immigration Policies, and co-edited *Surrender Australia?: Essays in the Study and Use of History. Geoffrey Blainey and Asian Immigration*. His most recent publications are *Governing Savages*, and *Australian Race Relations*

1788–1993. He is currently working on a study of ethnic interaction in the Melbourne suburb of Springvale.

John Morton is Lecturer in Anthropology at La Trobe University. He has conducted fieldwork with Arrernte-speaking groups in Central Australia since 1980 and has assisted the Central Land Council with Aboriginal land claims and sacred site protection. He has published numerous articles, many of which focus on aspects of Aboriginal religion, and has also co-edited Géza Róheim's *Children of the Desert II: Myths and Dreams of the Aborigines of Central Australia*.

Tim Murray is Senior Lecturer in Archaeology at La Trobe University. He is the author of *Remembrance of Things Present: Appeals to Authority in the History and Philosophy of Archaeology*, and numerous articles in local and international scholarly journals, and has undertaken extensive archaeological research in Tasmania.

Henry Reynolds is Australian Research Council Senior Fellow at James Cook University. He is the author of the prize-winning *The Other Side of the Frontier*, as well as *Frontier: Aborigines, Settlers and Land* and *The Law of the Land*. He was a member of the Ministerial Reference Group on Aboriginal Education which reported recently, frequently provides informal advice on land rights claims for lawyers, researchers, and land councils, and has been a respected commentator on Aboriginal history in the media for many years. His most recent book is *The Fate of a Free People*.

Deborah Bird Rose is Senior Research Fellow of the North Australia Research Unit, Australian National University. She has worked on numerous Aboriginal claims to land as senior anthropologist on behalf of the claimants and as consulting anthropologist to the Aboriginal Land Commissioner, as well as assisting Aboriginal people in several contentious disputes. She is the author of the award-winning *Dingo Makes Us Human* and *Hidden Histories*, and writes widely in the fields of anthropology, history, religious studies and Australian studies.

Index

Costello, Peter, 91
counter-culture, xxv, xxviii
Court, Richard, 91, 99
Cowlishaw, Gillian, xiii, 141–2,
  164, 170
Crawford, Max, 63–4, 65, 66
Crowley, F.K., 64
cultural cringe, xxxvii
cultural exchange, 125, 133–4, 181
cultural tourism, xxvi, xxvii, 82,
  123, 146, 178

Dampier, William, 56, 63
Danayarri, Hobbles, 3, 48–9
Davison, Graeme, 171
Dawson, Justice, 11–12, 17–20,
  21, 22–4, 28, 29, 30, 34
Deane, Justice, xxxi, xxxii, xxxiii,
  12, 13–14, 16, 71, 122
decolonisation, xxiv
democracy, Australian, xxxiii,
  xxxviii
Devine, Frank, 114
Dingo, Ernie, 126, 131
Dodson, Patrick, 2
Durack, Peter, 105, 114
Durkheim, Emile, xxv, 61

Edwards, Coral, xix
Eliade, Mircea, xxviii
Elkin, A.P., xvi, 61–2, 64, 164
encyclopaedias, 57–61, 62–3, 71
environmentalists, xxvi, xxviii,
  xxix, 148
essentialism, xxxvi–xxxvii, 73, 75,
  76, 80, 86–7, 96, 153
ethnography, see anthropology
European Association of
  Archaeologists, 73, 74, 75, 166
Evans, Raymond, 68
exploration, viii

Fabian, Johannes, 137, 171
Fels, Marie, 69
Ferguson, Adam, ix
Fischer, Gerhard, 178
Fischer, Tim, 92, 98, 99, 105,
  107, 108, 110, 114, 115
Fison, Lorimer, 58

flag
  Aboriginal, 117–18, 122, 124,
    135, 177–8
  Australian, 94, 106, 117–18,
    121–2, 177–8
  Torres Strait Islander, 117–18
  Union Jack, 121–2
Flood, Josephine, xxvii, 147
football, see Australian Rules
  Football
Foxcroft, E.J.B., 64, 68
Frazer, Sir James, xiii, 61
Freedom Rides, 126
Freeman, Cathy, 147, 177
Freud, Sigmund, xxx, xxxi, 61

Gaudron, Justice, xxxi, xxxii,
  xxxiii, 12, 13–14, 16, 71, 122
Gawler, Governor, 29–30
Gillen, F.J., xxv, 58, 64
Glenelg, Lord, 27–8
globalisation, xxiv
Goodall, Heather, 5
government policies
  assimilation, 62–3, 98, 112, 125
  segregation, 112
  self-determination, 146
Gray, Justice, 39
Greenwood, Gordon, 64–5
Grey, Earl, 31–2, 33
Griffiths, Tom, 145–6, 148
Groom, Ray, 106
Grotius, ix
Gumbert, Marc, 51

Hamilton, Annette, xxiv, xxv, 179
Hancock, Keith, 57
Harris, John, 179
Hartwig, Mervyn, 66
Hasluck, Sir Paul, 64, 68, 151
Hassell, Bill, 91
Hawke, Bob, 127, 149
Hayden, Bill, xxv
Healy, Chris, 2, 3
'Heartland' (television series), 124,
  126–32, 133, 180
Henderson, Gerard, 103
heritage, Aboriginal, xxii, xxxiv,
  77, 81–4, 85, 86, 123

Perron, Marshall, 92, 113–14
Pike, Douglas, 65
place, sense of, viii, 2, 113, 114,
    149, 152–3
Plumb, J.H., vii
possession, legal doctrine, 21–3, 34
primitivism, viii–xiii, xxviii, xxxv,
    55, 56, 57, 60, 71, 92, 116,
    133, 178, 179
primordiality, xxvii–xxviii, xxxv,
    119, 133, 147, 148
'progress', x, xi, xii, xxiii, xxxiii,
    xxxviii, 102, 109, 110, 111,
    113, 116, 136; see also social
    evolutionism
psychoanalysis and the
    unconscious, xxx–xxxi, xxxii,
    178
public history, xv–xviii, xxxviii,
    142; see also history, influence
public opinion, concerning
    Aborigines, xxv, xxxvii, 72, 89,
    99; see also racism
Pufendorf, ix

racial ideas, xii; see also social
    evolutionism
racism, xxxii, xxxvii, 66, 67, 68,
    73, 74, 75, 92, 96–9, 111, 125,
    128–9, 130, 134, 135, 175; see
    also Aborigines, settler
    Australian representations
Radcliffe-Brown, A.R., 44, 61
Reconciliation, xxxi, xxxii, xxxiii,
    xxxv, xxxvi, 84, 92–3, 118,
    119, 120–1, 122, 123, 124,
    125–31, 134, 135, 152, 177
Reece, Bob, 69
Religion, New Age, xxvi,
    xxvii–xxviii
republic and Aborigines, 120,
    176, 177
republicanism, 118–19, 120, 131,
    134, 176, 178
    Aboriginality, 118, 119, 120,
        121, 134, 176, 177, 179, 181
    Mabo, 119–20, 122
Reynolds, Henry, ix, xi, xv,

xvii–xviii, 5, 7, 10, 12, 68, 69,
    110, 138, 141, 142, 155
rights, civil, 62
rights, property, ix, x, xi, xii,
    19–20; see also terra nullius;
    native title
Roach, Archie, 117, 152
Robinson, George Augustus, 30
Rose, Deborah Bird, xxi, 4, 173
Roth, Henry Ling, 58
Rowley, Charles, xvii, 63, 68,
    142, 148, 175
Rowse, Tim, 69, 89, 162, 175
Royal Commission into Aboriginal
    Deaths in Custody, xxii, 11, 150
Rubuntja, Wenten, 127
Russell, Lord, 28
Ryan, Lyndall, 68

sacred sites, 39, 42, 83
Sahlins, Marshall, 63
Said, Edward, xxvii, 140
school texts, 59, 163, 180
Scott, Ernest, 56, 67
Scott, Keith, 95
secret knowledge, 38–9
Selden, John, 21
separation of powers, 13, 16
settlement, doctrine, 6–7, 103,
    104, 105
sexuality
    fears, 125–6
    imagery, 126, 130, 131
    relations, 66, 124–5, 126–7,
        128–9, 130
Sharp, Nonie, 174
Shaw, A.G.L., 64, 66
Smith, Adam, ix
Smith, Bernard, xxix–xxxi, xxxii,
    xxxviii, 70, 137, 148, 149
Smith, William Ramsey, 58–9
social evolutionism, ix, xii, xiii,
    56, 58, 59, 60, 61, 62, 64, 71,
    97–8, 109–10, 136, 163
South Australia Colonising
    Commission, 27–8
sovereignty, Aboriginal, 122, 127,
    131, 132, 179